70 Tips and Tricks for Mastering the CISSP Exam

R. Sarma Danturthi

Apress®

70 Tips and Tricks for Mastering the CISSP Exam

R. Sarma Danturthi
Elizabethtown, KY, USA

ISBN-13 (pbk): 978-1-4842-6224-5   ISBN-13 (electronic): 978-1-4842-6225-2
https://doi.org/10.1007/978-1-4842-6225-2

Managing Director, Apress Media LLC: Welmoed Spahr
Acquisitions Editor: Susan McDermott
Development Editor: Laura Berendson
Coordinating Editor: Rita Fernando

Cover designed by eStudioCalamar

Cover image designed by Freepik (www.freepik.com)

Distributed to the book trade worldwide by Springer Science+Business Media New York, 1 New York Plaza, New York, NY 10004. Phone 1-800-SPRINGER, fax (201) 348-4505, e-mail orders-ny@springer-sbm.com, or visit www.springeronline.com. Apress Media, LLC is a California LLC and the sole member (owner) is Springer Science + Business Media Finance Inc (SSBM Finance Inc). SSBM Finance Inc is a **Delaware** corporation.

For information on translations, please e-mail booktranslations@springernature.com; for reprint, paperback, or audio rights, please e-mail bookpermissions@springernature.com.

Apress titles may be purchased in bulk for academic, corporate, or promotional use. eBook versions and licenses are also available for most titles. For more information, reference our Print and eBook Bulk Sales web page at www.apress.com/bulk-sales.

Any source code or other supplementary material referenced by the author in this book is available to readers on GitHub via the book's product page, located at www.apress.com/9781484262245. For more detailed information, please visit www.apress.com/source-code.

Printed on acid-free paper

Into the divine hands of Swami Sivananda Saraswati and Swami Satyananda Saraswati.

Table of Contents

About the Author

 **R. Sarma Danturthi, PhD, PMP, CISSP,** has a doctoral degree in engineering from the University of Memphis, Memphis, TN and has taught graduate-level courses in engineering, microprocessors, and computer science. He has been in the IT field for several years, and his earlier experience included designing processor-level boards with interfaces and programming with various languages such as C and C++. His current experience includes design, coding, cybersecurity, leading project teams, and project management. He has published several papers in peer-reviewed journals and has written book chapters on software interfaces, modeling, IT security, and simulation. His interests include evolving cybersecurity, cloud computing, intelligent interfaces, and mobile application development. Besides being proficient in various programming languages and databases he has certifications in Java and the Project Management Institute's PMP, CompTIA Sec+, and ISC² CISSP. He can be contacted at danturthi@gmail. com.

About the Technical Reviewer

For the past 33 years, **Trevor L. Chandler** has performed the roles of consultant, network administrator, and educator. Trevor has delivered courses in information technology for both higher education and commercial training organizations. Trevor's primary subject matters include Linux system administration, Cisco networking, cloud computing, C/Python programming, and cybersecurity. Some of the certifications held by Trevor are ISC2's CISSP and CCSP, EC-Council's Certified Ethical Hacker (CEH), CompTIA's CASP+, Cisco's CCNP R&S, Cloud Security Alliance's CCSK, and Red Hat's RHCSA. Trevor believes that attempting certification exams provides, among other things, useful feedback to an exam candidate. He feels that certification exams are one way to vet an individual's knowledge and skills in a particular technical area. His firm belief in technical certifications, along with his lifelong passion for learning, is a strong indicator that he's currently preparing for his next certification exam.

Trevor can be reached on LinkedIn: `www.linkedin.com/in/`
`trevor-chandler-cissp-ccsp-ccsk-ceh-casp-19007915`.

Acknowledgments

Various companies I have worked for have taught me innumerable skill sets, and among these, the US Army and the Department of Defense (DoD) gave me the most opportunities and helped me get both the Sec+ and CISSP certifications, along with the PMP. I can categorically say that after working for at least six different organizations, including public, private, and research institutions, the myriad of ways the DoD thinks about and prepares its software, security, and training is unparalleled. I am forever thankful to the DoD, the US Army, and all the parent associations for providing me with the training, education, boot camps, and certification avenues. I would also like to thank the other organizations I have worked for, for letting me learn the related skill sets, be it .NET, DotNetNuke, or just another programming language, and teaching me their ways of doing things in an order. Also I would like to thank the people in all these organizations, who took me under their wings, for their mentoring, for setting the bars high, and for letting me stand on their shoulders to scale those bars.

I would also like to thank all the staff at APress and Springer from all over the world for their quick response and efficient communication. I have learned a new way to look at my writings when they started editing the book and gave me suggestions to organize the tips and make them more meaniful.

Introduction

If you randomly pick a CISSP boot camp instructor or a person who recently acquired a CISSP certification and ask how tough the CISSP test on a scale of 1 to 10 is, 10 being the highest, the answer is probably a perfect 10, or even a 15. This is not surprising, given the randomness in how the International Information System Security Certification Consortium (ISC)² generates the questions and how often it changes the question set. The real background for these questions is the area it covers with the vast number of domains and related subdomains. Also, as we know, it is nearly impossible to guess where the next cyberattack can come from. ISC² tends to cover the most known issues. This is the main reason why the test is always tough. But remember that it is not impossible to pass. If you know your basics and can think quickly and clearly in a murky situation, it can be easy to pass. On the other hand, you may have 20 or 30 years of experience in networking, software, or any other combination of fields, but if you take it easy and do not prepare in all domains and sub-domains, it is easy to flunk.

The CISSP questions sometimes are lengthy but at other times are surprisingly short, but the questions are almost always thoughtful. To make matters more complicated, of the given four answers, two options seem very close to the answer, but only one stands out. Also, CISSP questions almost always have the wording MOST, BEST, FIRST, etc. Any kind of memorization is a sure way to fail the test if you do not clearly understand the process of doing something in practice—for example, a backup process or a disaster recovery process. Even if you know the process but have never experienced it, it can get really tough to pick the correct answer. At that time, the process of elimination and an educated guess can work out.

After reading dozens of research articles, books, and test preparation materials, and attending a boot camp on CISSP before passing the certification, I noticed how easily one can get confused and yet at the same time how one can think clearly and avoid the distractors and arrive at the correct answer. Having been there and done that, I know it is all easier to say than sitting for the exam and coming out with flying colors.

The CISSP exam is a tough one, an expensive one, and one that takes time. If you either do not have the time to prepare or assume that you know the subject all too well, it is a great recipe for failure. Do not underestimate the test because the questions are coined by experts from various fields who vet each question over two days in a workshop organized by the ISC². This book is a result of my own preparation, notes I made before attempting and passing the CISSP, and the lessons learned.

When I started this book, I had an idea of creating as many tips and tricks I could gather from my own experience. But when I reached 70 tips, I felt they were sufficient for anyone to pass the test since CISSP requires 70 percent of mastery in all domains to pass. The test is also intelligent in that it gets progressively tougher from one level to another in the same domain and from one domain to another. If you are unable to correctly answer a question at a higher level, the test goes a level down, and if you answer it correctly, it goes a level up.

The test can stop at any time after reaching the 100th question. Please remember that passing at or immediately after the 100th question does not make you any smarter than someone who passes on the 120th, 135th, or 150th question. In the end, what you know and can intelligently think and correctly pick as the answer is more important than at what question the test ends and declares you have passed. Also, remember that if the test ends at the 100th question, it does not automatically mean you passed it. The pass or fail paper is given to you after you exit the testing area and collect your results at the front desk. Unfortunately, it is possible to fail by the 100th question if the test determines that your knowledge does not warrant further questioning.

The test "determines" if you can be asked 150 questions or not by taking into consideration what answers you selected for the previous questions. Also note that the CISSP exam does not give you a grade like A, B, or C for passing the test with 100, 130, or 150 questions. It hardly matters at what question you passed or failed. My advice on this number of questions is to ignore where the test stops. Keep going until it stops and do your best with every question. But do know that when you come out of the test, if you failed it, the results are printed on a paper telling you in what areas/domains you need improvement and in what domains you did well. That can serve as a measuring scale if you plan to prepare and attempt the test again.

Importantly, the CISSP test now does not allow going back and reviewing a question once it is answered. It is a "move forward only" test. After you answer a question and move forward, you can never go back and re-check the earlier question. Thus, if you made a mistake, do not dwell on it, but move forward and answer the rest of the questions with zeal. One wrong answer cannot make you fail the test, and one right answer cannot make you pass the test. Most of all, remember that the test is trying to determine—I repeat this word *determine* and not *decide*—if you have the ability to master the concepts. It also means that the test thinks that you have the concepts necessary to become a certificate holder of CISSP.

So, after getting your CISSP certification, will you be able to land a job that offers a $200,000 salary? That depends on how good you are. Certifications and mentioning of the word CISSP on your résumé can help open the interview doors and let you speak with a hiring manger. But in the end it is *you* who have to do the work and excel to be eligible for that $200,000 salary. Like the first line of defense in cybersecurity is *you*, you are the person who can study, gain the knowledge, master the test, get the certification, excel in the field you choose, and command the salary you deserve.

No book, test, or boot camp can guarantee anything, since it is *you* who has to feel comfortable reading the subject, master it, and apply your knowledge to the test to come out with a pass. For example, if you have never seen a smart card or a biometric system, never even read about it, and do not even know it works, then any question on the biometric access system will look like R2D2 robot programming in the *Star Wars* movie. For this reason, all the CISSP domains need to be studied and researched well before the test is attempted. I normally recommend four to six months of preparation time before taking the CISSP test.

While reading this book, it is possible to think that a subdomain included in a domain belongs to another domain. That's because each subdomain can easily fall in any other domain due to the complexity of domain security and how deeply the domain covers the information technology subject. In general, any subdomain can be intertwined with another domain, and there is no strict line dividing one from another. Understanding the process and subject is the key to passing the CISSP exam.

I tried to design the questions in the same mold that the ISC² uses and hope this helps test takers greatly. Thank you for choosing this book, and I wish you Godspeed in your efforts. I welcome your comments to my email address (danturthi@gmail.com).

—*R. Sarma Danturthi, PhD, PMP, CISSP*

How to Use This Book

By buying this book, you have surely made a firm decision to get the excellent industry-standard cybersecurity certification, CISSP. Congratulations for the decision you made because as technology evolves, cybercrime is on the rise too. The CISSP certification exam is the toughest of all existing IT security exams, and that is also the real reason why CISSP certification stands out ahead of others. The CISSP certification subject contains seven domains and various subdomains. Each domain may look like a different topic, but at the core, as you read through the subject, you will be amazed to see that these domains are not physically separate after all, and they mix and mingle easily with each other and with subdomains. It is extremely hard to put a thick separation line among domains.

This book is a culmination of my detailed notes, blunders committed in practice tests, lessons learned after reading and practicing, and attending a boot camp on the CISSP subject. Before you open the book, I assume you have some knowledge of the subject and have grasped the important aspects of each subdomain. This book gives tips on how to pass the CISSP exam because even with 20 years of experience in the IT industry it is extremely hard for professionals to get this CISSP certification without proper preparation for various reasons. The first among these is the vastness of each domain and the subject itself. For example, if you worked as a network engineer in the IT field, you may know everything about bridges, routers, and repeaters including setting up, removing them, and even programming them with ease, but when it comes to CISSP, networking is but just one of the seven domains. Therefore, if you lost touch with software, asset security, or physical security and the control frameworks, you will still fail the CISSP test. The same thing can happen for software developers who find that their field is just one domain on the CISSP test.

This book contains 70 tips to pass the CISSP test and covers all seven domains. Besides giving you important subject-matter tips and things to remember, each tip gives review questions on the related domain/subdomain, analysis of how the question's verbiage can be shortened, how to grasp the exact gist of the question, and how to quickly select the correct answer and ignore the distractors. The book is organized into the seven domains ISC[2] has designed to use on the CISSP test. As most CISSP exam takers have experienced, a single book cannot help you pass the CISSP test. Neither do multiple exam questions because ISC[2] takes extreme care in revising the questions so regularly, it is impossible to find a repeating question or two. Candidates experiencing the same set of questions on a test is extremely rare, even if they take the test on the same day in the same testing center, sitting side by side, with or without following the new COVID-19 social distancing rules. It is a cold truth that *none* of the questions from your practice tests—even if you practiced them in thousands of numbers—will ever appear on the real CISSP test. The test questions that appear on CISSP certification exam are not published on the Internet or sold by anyone in any form. Period.

I recommend using the book one chapter or one domain at a time. Read the subject of a domain, make your own notes, and then read this book's chapter on the same domain. Once you get to the question part, ask yourself what exactly the verbiage in the question is trying to say and what exactly the question is asking. Then in the analysis part, you will find how the unnecessary verbiage can be removed to grasp the details and question. When selecting an answer, remember that the CISSP exam has two distractors that can be easily eliminated, but the problem is with the remaining two options since both look so close to each other that if you think one option is the answer, usually it is the other option that is correct. So, how do you select the correct answer? This is the exact problem my book is going to help you solve. As you read through the book, you will learn how to find the correct solution and why it is the correct solution. Remember that if you falter in a practice question, there is no reason to be depressed. Rather, it is a great opportunity to learn why you made the wrong choice and how you can correct yourself the next time as you move forward. Therefore, I recommend reading this book at least three times cover to cover before you attempt the test.

This book also gives you an idea of the ISC^2 type of questioning with words such as BEST, MOST, WORST, FIRST, etc. Almost 70 percent of the questions on the CISSP test have this kind of word inserted in the question, and as said previously, ISC^2 is looking at you to make the BEST choice out of the given options. It also means there is more than one correct answer in the given choices, but there is only one BEST answer that helps you score on the test.

Even if you are an experienced IT professional, I recommend at least three to four months of solid preparation reading this book multiple times and repeating the questions and practicing the test provided at the end of the book before attempting the CISSP exam. The reasons are that the CISSP testing fee is not cheap, and the test is difficult (but not impossible); oftentimes you will hear people say the test is a killer certification exam. It really is. There is really no point in wasting time, effort, and money if you are not interested in putting in time and effort on this test.

Please remember that the questions can sometimes be very short and sometimes have long verbiage, but each question is not necessarily straightforward. For example, a question can ask something like this: Which layer of the OSI is the equivalent of the TCP/IP's Internet layer? This is a simple one-line question but needs good thinking because it is asking about comparing two layers. This is where my book comes into force: it will help you learn what is given in the question, how to *exactly* decide what is being asked, and how to pick the correct answer without spending too much time on each question.

I wish you Godspeed in your efforts to pass the CISSP test.

CHAPTER 1

Security and Risk Management

In this chapter, you will learn tips on the basics of security, including the governing principles, control frameworks, threats, risks, and legal issues concerning security. Understand these concepts as they apply in day-to-day work of a cybersecurity professional.

Confidentiality, Integrity, and Availability

Tip #1: Remember the security triad "CIA" and the reverse security triad "DDA" and what each letter of the triad stands for

Domain: All domains of CISSP, since every domain deals with security either physically or otherwise. In particular, the Security and Risk Management domain predominantly talks about these triads in every subdomain.

   Subdomain: Every subdomain of CISSP's main domains deals with the CIA and DDA triads because they make up the basic framework on which security is constructed.

   Subject background: The CIA and DDA triads are shown in Figure 1-1. Confidentiality and disclosure are opposite of each other. Likewise, integrity and alteration are. So are availability and destruction.

© R. Sarma Danturthi 2020
R. S. Danturthi, *70 Tips and Tricks for Mastering the CISSP Exam*,
https://doi.org/10.1007/978-1-4842-6225-2_1

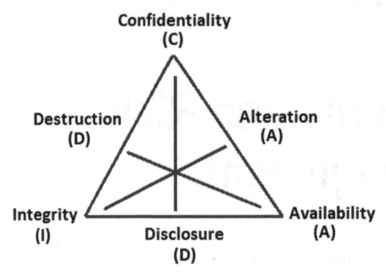

Figure 1-1. *CIA and DDA triads*

Things to Remember

- **Confidentiality (C)** refers to the situation where all information exchange is done at the highest possible confidence to only required people. There can be more than one level of confidence (e.g., open to public, need to know, secret, top secret, etc.). Confidentiality does not just include two people, but deals with whether the giving party and the receiving party trust each other, need to be trusted, and their needs to know the information as well. When confidentiality is not followed, it is considered unauthorized **disclosure (D)**, where data can spill and go to the hands of unwanted criminals or pose risk to the safety of a person or entity.

- By **integrity (I)** we mean that the data is accurate at best and does not change during transmission or after reaching the destination. Parity checks, error checks, and various other methods are used for maintaining the integrity of data. When data transmitted does not reach the destination in a secure manner and shows changes, we call it **altered (A)** data, which is more or less useless.

- **Availability (A)** is the way we provide data to required audience. In general, data is required to be provided on a 24/7/365 basis. Availability of data must conform to integrity and confidentiality as well. When the requested data is not available, we can assume it was either **destroyed (D)** or became stale/corrupted. This can happen naturally when a media where data is stored is destroyed or corrupted or even when we lose a reading medium for the stored data. For example, if we no longer have a video cassette player to play an important video clip stored on a tape, the entire tape can be considered useless though the data on it may still be intact. Some companies and entities also refer to the destruction principle as **denial (D)**.

Example: During the floppy disk evolution era, a credit card company decided to store all its customer data on 5.25" disks. When the technology changed, the company started storing the data on a secure cloud. During a routine cleanup ten years later, one company employee found these floppy disks, but by then there was no technology available to the credit card company to read what was on the disks. Those who knew what was on the disks were no longer working in the company. Unable to read or know the details, the company decided to just discard these disks in the trash. Unfortunately, someone digging in the trash found the disks and with the help of an old disk reader was able to get some older personally identifiable information (PII) credit records to exploit and cause damage to the clients. In disposing of the disks in the trash without proper destruction (D), what factor of the CIA/DDA triad can the credit card company be **BEST** said to have violated?

A) Confidentiality

B) Destruction

C) Identification

D) Availability

Analysis: Note that the verbiage is large, but the main point is that the company just threw away confidential data without destroying the media. If a media is unreadable, it should be physically destroyed or even burnt to avoid losing confidential data. The question basically is asking what factor was violated.

Statement: The statement and question can be trimmed and rewritten as follows:

During the floppy disk evolution era, a credit card company decided to store all its customer data on 5.25" disks. Unable to read these disks with new technologies, the company decided to just discard these disks in the trash.

3

Question: By disposing of the disks in the trash without proper destruction (D), what factor of the CIA/DDA triad can the credit card company be **BEST** said to have violated?

Solution: Obviously, option C is wrong because identification is not a factor of either the CIA or DDA triad. And so is option D because when the company threw out the disks, they made the disks available to anyone for free. In this case, they made the disks available and did not violate that factor. Option B is what the company decided **not** do, but in reality they should have. So it is wrong too. The factor they violated was confidentiality: by throwing away the disks, they chose the risk of disclosing the client base for free to anyone who could read those disks. Simply because the company lacked a medium or method to read the disks does not mean they can simply throw the disks away without proper destruction. Thus, the correct answer is option A.

Note that if the question asks what factor the company "made sure" in the CIA/DDA triads, then the answer is option D since they made the data "available" for free to all. In this situation, the company **violated confidentiality** and **made data available** for all.

Review Questions

Various simple questions or complicated verbiage questions can be made with the simple triad knowledge. The following are some of those questions.

1. What is the opposite of the integrity (I) factor in the CIA/DDA triad?

    A) Confidentiality

    B) Destruction

    C) Disclosure

    D) Alteration

    Answer: Option D

2. What are the three principles of the CIA triad?

    Answer: Confidentiality, integrity, and availability

3. In the case of open source software, what factors are followed by a company when it gives the software away for free with a parity check for correct download to anyone who attempts to download it after accepting the default disclosure agreement?

A) Confidentiality and availability

B) Integrity and disclosure

C) Confidentiality and integrity

D) Availability and disclosure

Answer: Note that the company gives software for free but may not need to guarantee its availability all the time. But when it is available, it gives the data without modifications or alternations and makes sure that the downloaded code is intact. For the code to be intact and reliable, it has to adhere to confidentiality, and when the downloaded program has an error check code, it means the company is making sure you have downloaded the copy without bugs and stands by the integrity of the code. Thus, the correct answer is option C. Though everyone can download the code, note that the code itself is confidential between the company and the person who downloads it. Availability, however, cannot be guaranteed since too many downloaders sometimes may cause the server to crash.

An alternative question can be "What factor can the company NOT guarantee for the downloading public?" Then the answer would be "availability" since the system can crash, or even the open source software company can sell itself and/or go out of business at any time without telling anyone.

4. What degrading factor of the information can cause it to be known by anyone and everyone without proper authorization to see it?

A) Openness

B) Availability

C) Disclosure

D) Integrity

Answer: Option C. Note that the question is asking about the "degrading" factor, which is obviously in the DDA triad rather than in the CIA triad. CIA is for safety.

5. A laptop owned by a particular agency has a program that destroys the entire hard disk data when stolen. What principle is the program following?

    Answer: Destruction

6. What are the factors of the DDA triad (the opposite triad of CIA)?

    A) Delaying, destruction, auditing

    B) Development, destruction, accepting

    C) Destruction, disclosure, altering

    D) Destruction, demeaning, alerting

    Answer: Option C

7. When we make sure data is authentically available, what factor of CIA are we **BEST** conforming to?

    A) Availability

    B) Confidentiality

    C) Integrity

    D) Acceptance

    Answer: Option C. The question is about the authenticity of data (not availability), which can be interpreted that the data is original and is without any modifications.

Security Governance Principles

Tip #2: Remember the various color-coded books and how they define the security levels; also refer to the TCSEC and ITSEC tables and comparisons between both

Domain: Asset Security, Security and Risk Management, Security Engineering.

 Subdomain: Security governance principles; Control frameworks; Confidentiality, Integrity and Availability (CIA); Controls; Control measures; Security evaluation models.

Subject background: Trusted Computer System Evaluation Criteria (TCSEC) was first developed by the Department of Defense (DoD) for stand-alone systems (see Table 1-1). This is no longer in use and has been replaced by the common criteria. Information Technology Security Evaluation Criteria (ITSEC) is a European model and also has been replaced by the common criteria (see Tip #27).

Table 1-1. *Security Levels and Their Meaning*

Level	TCSEC	ITSEC	Meaning/Description
A	A	E6	Fully verified security
B	B1	E3	Labels for access control/labeled security
	B2	E4	Structured protection/covert channels/trusted facility/ configuration management
	B3	E5	Security domains, trusted platform/base to minimize complexity
C	C1	E1	Discretionary protection (user login)
	C2	E2	Controlled access protection (independent login, password auditing, etc.)
D	D	E0	None/minimal security

Notes:

1) B1 < B2 < B3 and C1 < C2. If a system is verified for a level, it is supposed to have been verified for levels below it. **Example:** if a product is verified for B2 level in TCSEC, it means it is verified for D, C1, C2, and B1 levels as well.

2) Level B in TCSEC is also used for Mandatory Access Control (MAC).

3) Level C1 in TCSEC is used for Discretionary Access Control (DAC) and C2 is for Controlled Access Protection.

4) Inside TCSEC levels B and C, security is highest for B1 and C1 and goes up in order as they increase from B1 to B2 to B3 and C1 to C2 (see note 1).

Things to Remember

There are various books named with different colors that are called the Rainbow series. Some of the important books are mentioned here. Please note that the list is not complete. Only the important books are mentioned. The entire list is available at `https://csrc. nist.gov/publications/detail/white-paper/1985/12/26/dod-rainbow-series/final`.

- **Orange book**: This is the book that introduced the TCSEC by the DoD and is for **stand-alone systems**.

- **Red book**: This book was developed in line with TCSEC for networked systems.

- **Brown book**: This book covers understanding trusted facility management.

- **Aqua book**: This book lists the glossary of computer security terms.

- **Green book**: This book contains DoD's guidelines for managing passwords for trusted and managed systems.

TCSEC has emphasis on controlling access to information. But TCSEC does not cover what the users can do with the information, if access is provided. This implies that users who are provided access even after proper vetting can misuse the information.

Example: Per Information Technology Security Evaluation Criteria (ITSEC) guidelines, if a system is verified for level E5, what other levels are it also verified for? Pick the **BEST** answer.

A)   Levels E1, E2, and E6 of Information Technology Security Evaluation Criteria (ITSEC)

B)   Levels D, C, B1, and B2 of Trusted Computer System Evaluation Criteria (TCSEC)

C)   Levels A and B of Trusted Computer System Evaluation Criteria (TCSEC)

D)   Levels E0, E1, and E2 of Information Technology Security Evaluation Criteria (ITSEC)

Analysis: The question is tricky and is comparing levels of ITSEC and TCSEC. From Table 1-1 we can see that E5 in ITSEC corresponds to B3 in TCSEC. Reading the notes in Table 1-1 (note 1), we find that any system that is verified for E5 (equivalent of B3) is verified for levels below it (E0 to E4). Likewise, it is verified for D, C1, C2, B1, and B2, which are all below B3 under the TCSEC. Keeping this in mind, we can check the options and distractors given to pick the correct answer.

Statement: If a system is verified for level E5, what other levels is it also verified for?

E5 is only under ITSEC, and thus the first part of the question is superfluous. If a system is verified for E5, we know it is verified for all other levels below it.

Question: If a system is verified for level E5 under ITSEC, what other levels it is also verified? Pick the **BEST** answer.

Solution: Option A is wrong straightaway since E6 is the fully verified security, which is above E5. Option D is partially correct since verified for E5 means also verified for E0, E1, E2, E3, and E4. Option D does not give E3 or E4. Option B states A and B levels, which means they are A, B1, B2, and B3. Although E5 verifies all levels of B, it does not verify A. This is close to option A (E6 of ITSEC). Thus, option C is wrong. Option B verifies D, verifies C (which is C1 and C2), and also verifies B1 and B2. This means option B verifies all levels below B3 (the same as E5).

Thus, option B is more accurate than option D. In the CISSP certification examination, these kinds of answers given are very close to each other, and the question is also asking the test taker to pick the **BEST** answer. Thus, we conclude that the best answer in this scenario is option B.

Review Questions

Several variations of this subject questions are as follows:

1. Which level of Technology Security Evaluation Criteria (ITSEC) **BEST** matches the Trusted Computer System Evaluation Criteria (TCSEC) level of B2?

    A) E6

    B) D3

    C) E4

    D) E3

    Answer: Option C. Option B is wrong since there is no such level as D3.

2. Discretionary process is provided at what level of Trusted Computer System Evaluation Criteria (TCSEC)?

A) E1

B) C1

C) C2

D) B1

Answer: Option B. Option A is wrong because it is not in TCSEC. Option C is controlled access. Option D is for mandatory access.

3. The Department of Defense (DoD) has defined Trusted Computer System Evaluation Criteria (TCSEC) in the Orange book to **BEST** suit systems that are:

A) Networked together

B) Stand-alone

C) Fully verified for security or access

D) Partially verified for security or access

Answer: Option B

Control Frameworks

Tip #3: Understand control frameworks and their role in implementing the CIA security triad

This tip covers the COBIT, COSO, ISO17799, ITIL, and SOX standards (aka control frameworks) and their details of what and how.

Domain: Security and Risk Management.

Subdomain: Risk, Security of assets, Control frameworks.

Subject background: COBIT and COSO are used for regulatory compliance. ITIL is a standard series of books (designed by the UK government) on IT management topics. Although COSO is a generic model for corporate governance, COBIT only deals with IT part of the COSO. In general, COBIT is a subset of COSO.

The Sarbanes–Oxley (SOX) Act of 2002 is a federal law that establishes sweeping auditing and financial regulation for publicly traded companies. SOX protects shareholders, employees, and the public from accounting errors, either intentional or otherwise and fraudulent practices. SOX adds criminal penalties for certain misconduct.

Things to Remember

- COBIT stands for Control Objectives for Information and Related Technology. It has a set of four generally accepted methods: 1) Plan/Organize, 2) Acquire/Implement, 3) Deliver/Support, and 4) Monitor/Evaluate.

- COBIT is an **operational level** concept that examines the effectiveness of the CIA triad.

- COSO stands for Committee of Sponsoring Organizations of the Treadway Commission. It has an original set of five concepts that were later expanded to eight: 1) Control environment 2) Risk assessment, 3) Control activities, 4) Information and communication, and 5) Monitoring.

- COSO focuses on the **strategic level**. COBIT meets the objectives of COSO from the IT perspective.

- ISO 17799 has risk management as a foundation for each component. Users have a choice of picking up a methodology to accomplish their goals. The ISO 17799 itself does not recommend or point to a particular methodology.

- SOX stands for the Sarbanes–Oxley Act for publicly traded companies. SOX came to life after troubles with companies such as Enron and Worldwide.

- Under the SOX Act one can be imprisoned not more than 20 years and fined.

- ITIL stands for Information Technology Infrastructure Library.

- COBIT and COSO are about security goals and "what should be done." They are recommendations and are not bitter pills that are forced down one's throat.

- ITIL is the standard that explains "how it should be done."

- ITIL has five different steps: 1) Strategy, 2) Design, 3) Transition, 4) Operation, and 5) Continuous improvement.

- ITIL is mapped to COBIT since it is a version of COSO in IT-related areas.

- In ITIL the customers are the internal departments.

Example: A publicly traded company in the United States is known to have a material weakness to keep up with the accounting, and some of the C-level managers are known to have committed fraud that is unknown to their shareholders. The company has advertised that it follows the COBIT, an IT version of a control framework and ITIL standards to the rule book. Due to an independent auditing action being summoned, the company has decided to close its US office and relocate to London, UK where the regulators use a lighter touch with the companies. What act or control framework did the company **MOST** fear from the independent auditing and caused the company to relocate to London?

A) ISO 27005, Risk management framework

B) Sarbanes–Oxley Act of 2002

C) Independent Audit Control Act of 2004

D) Public Company Accounting Oversight Board

Analysis: The words "publicly traded," "committed fraud," and "shareholders" automatically ring the bell that the company fears the Sarbanes–Oxley Act of 2002. The rest of the question is verbiage and can easily be ignored.

Statement: A **publicly traded** company in the United States committed fraud that is unknown to their **shareholders**.

Question: What act did the company **MOST** fear from the independent auditing that caused the company decision to relocate to London?

Solution: The direct answer from the question is option B. Options C and D are close distractors but are incorrect answers. Option A has nothing related to the question. Though the company, per the given verbiage, is said to follow various control frameworks, the question is asking about what *act* the company feared that caused it to move the office to London, UK.

Review Questions

Various possible questions on the control frameworks topic are given here:

1. What do the control framework COSO and COBIT recommend?

   A) When to achieve

   B) What to achieve

   C) How to achieve

   D) Need to achieve

   Answer: Option B

2. How are COSO and COBIT related to each other?

   Answer: COBIT is a subset of COSO. COBIT is only IT-related, whereas COSO is organization-wide.

3. Which of the following frameworks can be **BEST** suited for an operational level?

   A) COBIT

   B) COSO

   C) ISO17799

   D) ITIL

   Answer: Option A. If the question asked for the strategic level, the answer would be COSO.

4. Which are the five steps of ITIL?

   A) Strategy, Design, Operation Testing, and Deployment

   B) Plan, Design, Operate, Transition, and Deferment

   C) Strategy, Design, Transition, Operation, and Continuous improvement

   D) Plan, Design, Operate, Testing, Deployment, and Improvement

   Answer: Option C

5. Which risk management methodology do the frameworks COSO and COBIT recommend for **BEST** results in an organization?

    A) Risk management framework ISO 27005

    B) Users can pick any methodology of their choosing

    C) Enterprise risk management framework (ERMF)

    D) Government Risk Management and Compliance (GRMC)

    Answer: Option B

6. Which of the following was the **BEST** suited primary reason **originally** supported by five private-sector organizations for forming COSO?

    A) To combat fraudulent management projects

    B) To provide hardware and software of high quality

    C) To combat fraudulent financial reporting

    D) To provide best suited human resources control framework

    Answer: Option C

7. What is the full form of COBIT framework?

    Answer: Control Objectives for Information and Related Technology

Legal and Investigation Regulatory Compliance

Tip #4: Learn all details of a legal investigation and its procedures

Coercion, subpoena, search warrant, writ petition, tort, and civil law details are covered under legal and investigation regulatory compliance. These words are complex but need to be learned and remembered correctly.

Domain: Security and Risk Management.

Subdomain: CISSP for legal and investigation regulatory compliance, Information security legal issues, Security governance principles. Also refer to Tip#44.

Subject background: Some of the legal terms are described here in an investigation.

Writ petition: A formal written order issued by an official or judicial jurisdiction (usually court) to perform an action or to stop performing an action.

Coercion: A practice of forcing another party to act by use of threats or force. Coercion is a kind of intimidation via blackmail, torture, extortion, or even sexual assault. This is also known as **duress crime**. The coercion actions force the victim to act in a way contrary to their own interests and can actually involve physical injury.

Search warrant: Usually an authorization issued (usually by judge or magistrate) for searching. A search without warrant might violate individual rights and might end up in court for damages if the act were performed. A warrant is usually issued by court and is directed to a sheriff or a police officer. The warrants can be search warrants, arrest warrants, or execution warrants among various other types such as delivery warrant and possessory warrant.

Subpoena: Often issued by a government agency (court) to compel testimony or production of evidence, which can happen under penalty of perjury.

Civil law: Is any law that is not criminal. A plaintiff sues the defendant to obtain compensation for some wrongdoing. Generic civil law includes divorce, wills, property disputes, contract disputes, etc.

Tort law: A subset and largest area of civil law. In common law jurisdictions, a tort is a civil wrong that causes a loss, harm, or damage resulting in legal liability (car accident damages claims, property encroachments, etc.). Compared to criminal cases, tort lawsuits have a lower burden of proof than "beyond a reasonable doubt." For example, a person can be acquitted in a criminal case for murder but can be still liable for a tort of wrongful death.

Product liability: A product such as a car seat or infant crib may cause death of a child and is liable for both criminal and tort cases. Depending on the jurisdiction, any product can be put into the lawsuit and successfully argued.

Things to Remember

The CISSP examination basically wants the candidate to know the details of laws that govern the IT security. If a system is compromised by a hacker or if data is stolen, what laws apply and how they can be put in practice are some of the details CISSP candidates should be aware of.

Example: A computer company has created a free app for cell phones that provides GPS information of where guns can be purchased and where the gun ranges are located in the United States. The app gives a standard disclaimer to use the app at the user's discretion. A high school student downloads the app to buy a gun online and later uses the gun to kill five students in his school. Under what laws can a plaintiff sue 1) the student who killed the other five students and 2) the computer company that created the app for assisting the shooter via an app?

A) Tort law to the computer company

B) Criminal law to the shooter

C) Criminal law to the shooter and tort law to the computer company

D) Tort law to the shooter and criminal law to the computer company

Analysis: Wrongful death by shooting is considered criminal. Therefore, the first and most applicable law is criminal law to the shooter. The second question of what laws apply to the app's creating company is complicated since the company "may be" responsible for showing the details of gun sales and gun ranges, but at the same time the company can claim that the company included the standard disclaimer and escape from any punishment. The plaintiff, though, can sue the shooter and the company. Note that the question is **not** asking what laws will be applicable and tried. Rather, it is only asking what laws can the plaintiff use to sue. The fine line in the question is, suing does not mean successful litigation and judgment.

Statement: A computer company has created a free app for cell phone that provides GPS information of where guns can be purchased and where the gun ranges are located in the United States. **The app gives a standard disclaimer to use the app at the user's discretion.** A high school student downloads the app to buy a gun online and later uses the gun to kill five students in his school. Under what laws can a plaintiff sue 1) the student who killed the other five students and 2) the computer company that created the app for assisting the shooter via an app?

Question: Under what laws **can a plaintiff sue** 1) the student who killed the other five students and 2) the computer company that created the app for assisting the shooter via an app?

Solution: Options A and B are both partially correct. Option D is a clear eliminator since the shooter can be sued for both criminal and tort, but the computer company cannot be sued for criminal charges because it can successfully argue that the standard disclaimer was set up on the app. Option C therefore looks like a better answer than the other three.

Review Questions

A great variety of questions can be asked, confusing the CISSP exam taker about the laws applicable. Some of them are listed here:

1. What is the name of the paper a sheriff can carry from a court to look through the contents of a cyberattacker's house and all their computers?

    A) Court warrant

    B) Search warrant

    C) Cyber law warrant

    D) Google warrant

    Answer: Option B

2. A sheriff found information of data abuse and submitted it to the court of law. The attacker denies that he abused the data. The judge and the lawyers want to question him in the court of law before the jury. What order should be sent to the attacker to come to court and answer questions?

    Answer: The order sent to attacker is called "subpoena."

3. What practice is also called duress time?

    A) Search warrant

    B) Coercion

    C) Tort law

    D) Lability law

    Answer: Option B

4. What law is also a part of civil law?

    A) Wrongful death law

    B) Writ petition

    C) Tort law

    D) Death due to shooting in war

    Answer: Option C

5. Who issues a writ petition to an attacker—when the attacker is found guilty of stealing data from an IT system—to stop stealing the data and cease attacking operations?

    A) In-charge sheriff of the city who oversees civil law

    B) State government dealing with cybersecurity

    C) Federal government dealing with cybercrimes

    D) The judge from the court where the attacker is tried

    Answer: Option D

6. If you hear from a sheriff who says that the police wants to check your home for some suspect items such as drugs, what should the sheriff carry with him before he enters your private property?

    Answer: The sheriff should have a search warrant.

Vendor, Consultant, and Contractor Security

Tip #5: Master the rules, regulations, and binding documents for dealing with contractors and vendors

Know the terms for SLA, SOP, AUP, NDA, and related terms. These terms are important for understanding the legal issues in information security legal and related issues for an organization.

Domain: Security and Risk Management.

Subdomain: Information security legal issues; Security policies; Standards, procedures and guidelines; Vendor, consultant, and contractor Security.

Subject background: Correct understanding of security and related legal issues protect an organization's assets. Proper document creation allows an organization to have correct version and written instructions on hand when required. Understanding the correct terms is important for a CISSP candidate to avoid risk and manage assets effectively.

Things to Remember

- Service level agreements (SLAs) provide an acceptable level of performance. If a cable company is used as an Internet Service Provider (ISP) Internet provider service (IPS), the SLA states the performance promised such as download speeds, upload speeds, and actions to be taken in case of disruption of service (such as refunding monthly fee, etc.). Note that the SLA does not give any assurance for security of guaranteed service since disruption in service is possible due to a variety of factors that are beyond human control. The SLA also does not guarantee any compliance with any regulations an organization may have in place. The SLA is usually drafted by a legal party from the service provider and is signed by both the service provider and the receiver. The SLA may or may not include prices, refunds, legal battle locations, and the limits of compensation for such legal problems. SLAs are usually very long and cover every aspect of the service.

- Standard operating procedures (SOPs) provide step-by-step instructions for doing a job such as installing software or installing a new laptop with a baseline for a new employee. By definition, procedures are step-by-step instructions. SOPs are created for operating secure IT systems, software, hardware, or any other industrial systems. SOPs provide easy access to a secure system and familiarize an employee to the system easily. In some cases, anything outside SOPs is prohibited by the organization. These prohibitive rules can also be mentioned in SOPs or in standards, policies drafted by the organization. SOPs are usually prepared by technical experts and corrected by a second or third person to allow for accuracy.

- An acceptable use policy (AUP) is a document that instructs and mandates all the employees about their behavior when they work with an organization's assets—either hardware or software and either remotely or on-site. An AUP usually contains stern words and penalties for not following the policy. An example of an AUP can be not using the Internet service to connect to websites that are not used for business. Exceptions to the AUP are few, and AUP applies to all the staff equally. AUPs should be signed on the first day of employment and at regular intervals, such as annually. It should be noted that the AUP can be changed and updated depending on the past experience and behaviors of the employees.

- Nondisclosure agreements (NDAs) protect an organization and prevent an employee from disclosing any information (secret or otherwise) to third parties. An NDA can also be drafted for vendors, contractors, and a wide variety of other parties. Each NDA can have different items and be worded with a different language and terms. Usually an NDA is signed by the employee before starting work or on the first day of work during new employee orientation.

- Note that a single document may not fit every user, and thus an organization may impose one or more of these on a user, vendor, or service provider. And in the case of misuse that may end up in legal battles, all signed documents can be used against the oppressor for damages incurred.

Example: You have a Voice over Internet Protocol (VoIP) phone service by VoP, Inc., at home on the Internet provided by your local cable company. During a thunderstorm, your phone stopped working and did not come back to life for five full days. You can probably get a refund for the service outage. What document do you consult **FIRST** before you file a complaint?

A) No service during outage (NSDO) agreement by VoP, Inc.

B) Standard Operating procedures (SOPs) by VoP, Inc.

C) Acceptable use policy (AUP) by your Internet service provider (ISP).

D) Service level agreement (SLA) by your Internet service provider (ISP).

E) Natural disasters are not qualified for any complaints per government regulations.

Analysis: Identify the two providers first. Find out what document you signed with each. And decide what caused the disruption of service and then who to call.

Statement: You have a Voice over Internet Protocol (VoIP) phone service by VoP, Inc., at home on the Internet provided by your local cable company. During a thunderstorm, your phone stopped working and did not come to life back for five full days. You can get a refund for the service outage.

Question: What document do you consult **FIRST**?

Solution: Basic logic says that as long as the Internet is good, VoIP works fine. During a thunderstorm, the Internet service has experienced disruption and caused the VoIP to go down. Therefore, the option D directly points to the SLA by the cable company that provides Internet. To a lesser extent, the SLA by VoIP may be responsible, but that is not given as one of the five answers. An NSDO (option A) is not a document you sign with either the VoIP or Internet providers. The AUP is signed by an employee when he works for an organization. SOPs are step-by-step instructions to operate a piece of equipment, hardware, or software. Thus, options B and C are wrong. Option E may be applicable if it is mentioned specifically in the SLA, but usually 24/7 service for all 365 days of a year is provided by the cable company, and thus the SLA by the cable company, in option D aligns with the best answer to consult **FIRST** under the given scenario.

Review Questions

Other options include asking questions such as the following:

1. When a new employee is hired, which of the following documents are signed (from SLA, SOP, AUP, and NDA)?

   Answer: The NDA and AUP are applicable to new employees. An SLA is signed when a vendor is hired to provide a service. A SOP is not a signed document.

2. You start a new job with a company, and after two years you leave for another job. How long is the NDA from earlier valid?

   Answer: It depends on what is written and signed in the NDA. Some mention a lifelong ban; some mention a few years.

3. Once you sign an SLA, can it be changed during the contract period?

    Answer: Usually if the service provider anticipates a change, it can be included in the SLA, and thus this option is completely at the discretion of the provider.

4. Your organization is committed to protect the personally identifiable information (PII) of all customers. Employees who deal with PII have to sign what kind of document when they deal with PII?

    Answer: A nondisclosure agreement (NDA) and also acceptable use policy (AUP)

5. What is the **MOST** important reason that an organization asks employees and vendors to sign NDA and SLA documents?

    Answer: To protect proprietary information and information gathered by the organization and per legal requirement

Information Security Legal Issues

Tip #6: Understand the subtle differences among baselines, standards, guidelines, policies, and procedures

These issues include standards, policies, procedures, and guidelines, and baselines since not everything in these are mandatory and "must do."

Domain: Security and Risk Management.

Subdomain: Security policies; Standards, procedures, and guidelines; Legal issues.

Subject background: Standards, policies, procedures, and guidelines and abiding by the legal issues are mandatory for any organization. The legal issues also come from different levels such as city, county, state, and federal regulations. Standards and policies when not properly enforced are completely useless. These are documents that an organization has to live with and enforce to avoid any long-term problems.

Things to Remember

- Standards are documents and obligations on which an organization is built and relies upon. These documents dictate how an organization works and improves day to day. The wording in standards usually has strong words like **must** and **mandatory**. Standards must be enforced strictly. Keyword to remember standards is "**mandatory.**"

- Policies are like standards and have stern wording like **must** and **mandatory**. The difference between policies and standards is that policies can fall into three different categories as advisory, informational, and regulatory (AIR). Advisory policies tell the staff about policies in advance and instruct/warn what should be done and what should not be done. Information policies are for informing the staff of ongoing or upcoming rules, audits, inspections, or the like. Regulatory policies demand that a process or a system conform to the industry related and already set policy (usually a governing body or the federal government). Regulatory policies can mention civil and/or criminal penalties for the entire organization for not following the policies. Examples of regulatory policies include illegal stock trading on Wall Street, not following food packaging labels, etc.

- Guidelines are recommendations given to the users. An example of guideline is to tell the users to create a strong password with various numeric and alphabetic characters. But guidelines are not enforced down anyone's throat unless strictly necessary. This means when a cloud email provider (such as Gmail or Hotmail) says that the password is better protected with 15 characters, a user can still have his password at 8 characters. Guidelines also can be used to define office culture such as the staff is advised to eat lunch in the breakroom. However, a staff member may still eat lunch at his desk ignoring the guideline and cannot be penalized. If this guideline is not working to the satisfaction of the management, usually it will be changed as a policy or standard to make it mandatory and enforce it.

- Procedures are, simply said, step-by-step instructions. Procedures are normally used to install some equipment, software, or hardware or to follow a process. Procedures can be used to evacuate a building systematically after the emergency alarm sounds, to install a baseline operating system for an IT user, or to list the proper steps to follow when an employee is terminated (to avoid legal problems later). Procedures are normally documented and kept with the staff members and used regularly. Procedures exist for each piece of equipment, and each department may have dozens of procedures documented for various operations. More than anything, procedures make life simple for all people since the steps indicated make a system become functional quickly.

- Baselines are a kind of functions and minimal set of rules where an organization tends to stand or bank on. Baselines can dictate what hardware and software is on the new computer for an employee. Note that the baselines differ from one user to another since a low-level employee need not have all privileges that a C-level manage should have. Likewise, the C-level manager need not have development software in the baseline since the manager will not develop software himself. Baselines also help in case of an attack or crash. If an IT system crashes or is attacked with a virus, it can be reverted to the original configuration by using the baseline. These baselines are like recovery disks on a computer with the Windows operating system. At any time the entire system can be recovered to the baseline, but it may sometimes have effect of losing some files. In some circumstances, losing those few files and recovering the machine may be a better option than losing the entire machine. Thus, a baseline dictates the minimum level of requirements.

- All the policies, standards, procedures, and guidelines are documents drafted by the management and are never set in stone. They can and should change as business evolves and prospers and new challenges are faced.

- Importantly, management has the final say in creating these policies, standards, procedures, and guidelines and at its discretion can discontinue some or add a few more at any time.

- Policies, standards, procedures, and guidelines should be regularly viewed as necessities arise or at least annually and updated if required.

Example: After a security breach and a review of the network topology by a regulatory auditor, your organization was found to have passwords that have no length, age, or other restrictions, giving way for rainbow and dictionary attacks. The auditor recommended amending the existing policy and adding longer passwords with special characters and alphanumeric characters. The auditor also recommended using password history. Which organizational document **MUST** you amend **FIRST**?

A) Password length and history guidelines

B) Company's login policy and standard

C) IT department's password complexity policy

D) Organization's acceptable use policy

Analysis: The first thing to note is that there was a breach. So, whatever changes we plan to do must be made mandatory and use strong words to avoid another similar breach. This point indicates that we cannot use guidelines, procedures, and baselines. Whatever changes we make must be for standards and policies. The word "recommend" usually can distract us as changing guidelines. But the question should address what MUST be done.

Statement: After a regulatory audit, the auditor recommended that you amend existing password policy about age, history and length of passwords.

Question: Which organizational document **MUST** you amend?

Solution: Because we need to change policy or standard, option A is not correct. Option B may be partially correct since it uses a login and password, but the login policy does not necessarily dictate what password you should use. Login policy can say something like you cannot log in to another machine in the same department or cannot use machines in another department. The acceptable use policy does not bother about passwords. Rather, it says what you can do or cannot do after gaining access to the IT system. Therefore, options A, B, and D can be eliminated. Option C is the correct answer since the IT department decides how passwords are to be generated or created.

Usually a strong password should have a minimum of two uppercase letters, two lowercase letters, two numbers, and two special characters. Once these rules are met, the length of password must also be made to be at least 15 characters or more. A password also should not sound too familiar even with all these rules followed to the letter. Finally, to keep safety of the IT systems, the password must be changed regularly. Changing the password regularly means setting the password age policy, which can say something like the password should be changed every 90 days or 180 days. Password history dictates that the password used once and earlier should not be re-used. These rules align well with the regulatory auditor's recommendations.

Review Questions

A variation of questions follow here:

1. Which of the following is a good password that **BEST** meets the auditor's recommendation?

    A) CI$$P_examTRICKS_2020

    B) ExamTricksBook100

    C) 3XTrTi_P$$!c2020

    D) MyTricks_$#@!4321

    Answer: Option C would be the **BEST** of the four given answers since the other options can be more or less guessed. Remember that on the CISSP exam you should always pick the best possible answer.

2. After implementing the password policy recommended by the auditor, you found that some users are still not following the policy. What is the **BEST** course of action?

    Answer: Sit with each of the users whose passwords are not conforming to the new password policy and explain why they should follow the new policy. Make it mandatory for users to conform to the policy.

3. How often do you review the new password policy recommended by the auditor?

    Answer: As often as possible or at least once annually

4. A company's password policy is defined as follows:

    i.   Passwords must be a minimum of 12 to a maximum of 25 characters in length.

    ii. Each character in the password must be from the set {A, K, L, O, *, %, #, @} only.

    iii. A letter or symbol given in the previous set can be used more than once.

How many more combinations of passwords are possible at the maximum password length than at the minimum password length?

Answer: A single character in the password can have eight different possibilities (letters/symbols) from the given set. If password length is two, the combinations become 8 * 8. Using three characters, we have 8 * 8 * 8 possible combinations. By the same rule, with 12 characters, we can have 8^{12} password combinations (or for n characters it is 8^n). With 25 characters, the password combinations are 8^{25}. Since the question is asking **how many more** combinations, the answer would be $8^{25} - 8^{12}$. Notice the subtle, confusing, but vast difference between password lengths 25 and 12 and the 8 variations (letters/symbols) for each character of the password mentioned in the question. Number 25 or 12 is the length of password in characters, but 8 is the number of different possible letters/symbols for each character in the password.

Tip #7: CISSP certification holders must adhere to strict rules, principles, and ethics stipulated by the ISC²

Remember the ISC² ethics, because at least one question can appear on these ethics about how to maintain those principles while holding the CISSP certification.

Domain: Security and Risk Management, Asset Management.

Subdomain: Ethics and principles, Membership of ISC², CISSP certification standards.

Subject background: Certification holders have to agree and adhere to the rules of ISC², which are described on the ISC² website. If a complaint is lodged on a certification holder, ISC² can conduct an inquiry and suspend the member. The following rules of PAPA are generally followed and covered on a broad basis.

Note that these are ethics to be followed and are not the laws or bylaws. It means a member has to digest these ethics and follow them in good confidence. Laws and rules can be formulated from ethics but not vice versa. The fine line that separates the ethics, laws, and rules are difficult to define and enforce in all places at all times.

Things to Remember

ISC²'s CISSP ethics can be remembered with the acronym PAPA as follows:

- P – Protect the society, strive for common good, public trust, and confidence and the infrastructure.

- A – Act honorably, honestly, justly, responsibly, and legally.

- P – Provide diligent and competent service to customers and the principals.

- A – Advance and protect the profession.

Example: A company decides to design a website for supplying exotic dancers for a party and takes online payment and collects customer information. When the design is complete, the company hires a CISSP certificate holder to check for security leaks. The certificate holder completes the work and collects his check after giving a green signal to the website. Unknown to the CISSP certificate holder, the company also does other business with the dancers at parties. After a few years, the company is sued in a court of law, and the CISSP certificate holder was included in the law suit alleging that the certificate holder acted dishonorably. What it the **BEST** judgment the judge can give to the certificate holder?

A)   The judge should indicate that the CISSP indeed acted dishonorably.

B)   The CISSP did not act dishonorably but should have known.

C)   The judge should not allow what the CISSP holder has to disclose.

D)   The CISSP acted honorably and has nothing to do with company business model.

Analysis: When looking at the website, it is not the duty of CISSP holder to check what business the company does. Neither is the duty of CISSP to see if the company does any other business behind the veils of the designed website. The CISSP holder in this case checked for security leaks and did not (have to) worry about the business model. The CISSP holder gave the green light depending on what he found for security of the website only. He is not supposed to look behind the scenes and find out what the company does illegally or legally.

Statement: A website for supplying exotic dancers for a party and takes online payment and collects customer information. The certificate holder completes the work and collects his check after giving a green signal to the website. *Unknown to the CISSP certificate holder,* the company also does other business with the dancers at parties. The company is sued in the court of law and the CISSP certificate holder was included in the lawsuit alleging that the certificate holder acted dishonorably. What it the **BEST** judgment the judge can give to the certificate holder?

Question: **Unknown** to the CISSP certificate holder, the company also does other business with the dancers at parties. What it the **BEST** judgment the judge can give to the certificate holder?

Solution: The clear answer will be option D since the CISSP holder acted honorably and checked the website for security leaks for which he was paid. He did not professionally disclose the information he might have known about the website to anyone. He followed the laws and did not violate any rules or regulations.

Review Questions

Various possible questions on this topic can be asked as follows:

1. What ethics factor should a CISSP certificate holder follow about his profession?

    Answer: Advance and protect the profession

2. What should be the aim of a CISSP certification holder's ethics toward the society?

    Answer: Protect the society, strive for common good, public trust, and confidence and the infrastructure.

3. What sort of service a CISSP certificate holder **BEST** provide his clients?

    Answer: Provide diligent and competent service to customers and the principals.

Security Policies, Standards, Procedures, and Guidelines

Tip #8: Master the mathematical calculations and use the calculator provided on-screen

Remember calculations for ARO, SLE, ALE, and EF. Do *not* do mental calculations even for small numbers. Use the writing board supplied and/or the on-screen calculator.

Domain: Security and Risk Management.

Subdomain: Quantitative risk analysis, Calculations required for various values to calculate and predict risk.

Subject background: Asset value (AV) is the value of a resource in monetary funds to replace the asset when damages occur. It is not the value of the asset at the point of time after an initial amount was spent to purchase the asset (like the value of a car after two years of use).

Exposure factor (EF) is the percentage of loss an asset can incur if there were an attack. For example, if floods were to occur, a boat valued at $8,500 parked on the shore may have 30% damage due to high water and tide. Therefore, EF due to flood is 30% on the boat whose asset value (AV) is $8,500.

Single loss expectancy (SLE) is the monetary value if an asset were to have a loss. SLE = EF * AV.

Annualized rate of occurrence (ARO) is a percentage that approximately predicts how often the threat can happen in a 12-month period (one year). If probability of earthquake is 5 times in 10 years, the ARO is 5/10 or 0.5. If flood happens once in 100 years, then ARO is 0.01.

Annual loss expectancy (ALE) is the monetary value of potential loss per year. ALE = SLE * ARO.

ALE tells the company how many monetary funds need to be in reserve as backup, if a threat were to occur in real life.

Total risk is calculated as [threats * vulnerability * asset value].

Uncertainty and confidence level are values that measure how a threat can materialize in real life. For example, if history indicates that a particular area has a 30% chance of earthquake in 10 years, the confidence level is 30% in 10 years, and the uncertainty level is 70% in 10 years.

Risk can <u>never be reduced</u> to zero. It can be reduced to an acceptable level. Whatever risk that remains (acceptable or otherwise) after all measures were taken is known as <u>residual risk</u>.

<u>Residual risk</u> is calculated as total risk * control gap, which is equivalent to [threats * vulnerability * asset value] * control gap. It can also be calculated as total risk minus control measures.

Things to Remember

- CISSP exam center does <u>not</u> allow carrying cell phones or scientific or any small calculators inside the testing room but provides a calculator application right on the screen. Candidates are encouraged to use that calculator for doing mathematical calculations.

- Do <u>not</u> do mental calculations since a small mistake can cost the credit for the question.

- The exam center also provides a scratch board with a pen that one can use for calculations.

- Quantitative analysis always has numbers (monetary values) to show for loss, risk, and other factors.

- Always look closely at what the question is asking despite the verbiage given. A long verbiage does not mean every single quantitative analysis calculation needs to be done.

Example: A web hosting company wants to establish a physical location with proper insurance and backup needs. The insurance company wants to know the details of location and threats involved/anticipated before it can issue a policy to the web hosting company's assets, which may include the servers, workstations, and the physical building. The company estimates from the local history data that the biggest threats to the physical building are a flood that could occur once every other year and an earthquake that could occur once in five years. The web hosting company assets are close to US$3 million all inclusive. It is estimated that floods can damage 30% of the total assets, and earthquakes can damage 50% of the assets. Which of the following is the **BEST** formula to calculate the total annualized rate of occurrence (ARO) if both floods and earthquake occur in the same year?

A) Total annualized rate of occurrence = 50% – 30%

B) Total annualized rate of occurrence = 0.5 + 0.2

C) Total annualized rate of occurrence = 30% + 50%

D) Total annualized rate of occurrence = 2 + 5

Analysis: Despite the given verbiage, the question itself is very simple. It is asking for the total ARO from two events if they were to occur in the same year. The total ARO is the sum of ARO for a flood and ARO for an earthquake. The value of assets given $3 million is superfluous information that is not required to be used.

Statement: A flood can occur once every other year, and an earthquake once in five years. Earthquake damages are worse than the flood damages. Which of the following is the **BEST** formula to calculate the total annualized rate of occurrence if **both** a flood and an earthquake occur in the same year?

Question: Floods occur once every other year, earthquakes once in five years. Calculate the total annualized rate of occurrence if **both** floods and earthquake occur in the same year.

Solution: Flood total annualized rate of occurrence (ARO1) is once in 2 years (or once every other year). ARO1 = ½ = 0.5. The earthquake total annualized rate of occurrence (ARO2) is once in 5 years. ARO2 = 1/5 = 0.2. Total exposure factor if both were to occur is ARO1 + ARO2 = 0.5 + 0.2 = 0.7. Therefore the correct answer is option B. Options A and C are clearly wrong because the 30% and 50% are values for exposure factors (EF) for flood (30%) and earthquakes (50%). option D is wrong since it is adding the year values for flood and earthquake than the AROs.

Review Questions

A variation of the same question given in the previous example can be twisted with language as follows:

If there were an earthquake that also triggered flood damage, how does the company calculate the annualized rate of occurrence for a particular year?

Answer: The question is almost the same; both an earthquake and a flood occurred at the same time, so the ARO becomes a total of ARO due to floods and ARO due to earthquake.

Various possibilities exist for further questions, and some of them are as follows:

1. What is the **BEST** formula to calculate total risk?

    Answer: Total risk = [threats * vulnerability * asset value].

2. What is the uncertainty level if an area has an exposure factor of 45% due to a hailstorm every three years?

    Answer: The uncertainty level is 100 minus the confidence level. Here the confidence level is 45%. Thus, the uncertainty level is 55%.

3. Which of the following is the **BEST** formula for annualized loss expectancy (ALE)?

    A) ALE = ARO * EF * AV

    B) ALE = EF * AV

    C) ALE = EF * ARO

    D) ALE = SLE * AV * ARO

    Answer: Option A is the correct answer. ALE = ARO * SLE = ARO*EF*AV.

4. What is the best formula to calculate residual risk?

    A) Residual risk = risks unaccounted * risk for each asset

    B) Residual risk = total risk – counter measures

    C) Residual risk = risks accounted * counter measures

    D) Residual risk = total risks known – risks unknown

    Answer: Option B.

5. What is the **BEST** way to tackle the residual risks?

    A) Implement additional countermeasures

    B) Implement a full protection proof (FPP) package

    C) Implement no further measures and be ready to absorb the loss, if any

    D) Implement insurance protection for residual risk

Answer: Option C. Residual risk is the risk an organization would deal with if there were an attack and decided not to implement any other countermeasures.

6. An industrial plant situated about 50 miles from a volcano wants to calculate their annual loss expectancy (ALE) with the following data. The volcano has a record of erupting once in every 40 years, and if there is an eruption, the entire plant will be destroyed. The cost of plant is $3 million. What is the ALE?

    Answer: ALE = SLE * ARO = AV * EF * ARO = $3 million * 1 * (1/40) = $75,000. The SLE is the entire plant that will be destroyed, which is the asset value ($3 million) multiplied by the exposure factor, which is 1 (full destruction or 100% loss). The annual rate of occurrence is once in 40 years, or 1/40.

7. If a residential housing area has a chance of getting hit by a tornado twice every 30 years, what is the annual rate of occurrence (ARO)?

    Answer: ARO is how many times it will be hit in a 12-month period. Here, ARO is 2/30, which is 1/15 or 6.67% or 0.067 (once in 15 years).

8. After all countermeasures are implemented, the risk that is still left over is called:

    A) Remaining risk

    B) Resident risk

    C) Irremovable risk

    D) Residual risk

    Answer: Option D. Be careful when you pick an answer to questions such as these. Option B looks very similar to option D, but option B is not the correct answer.

9. When can an organization **<u>COMPLETELY</u>** remove all the risks and make itself 100% threat proof from all threats and vulnerabilities?

    A) When all countermeasures are implemented.

    B) No organization can ever remove all risks and make itself 100% threat proof.

    C) When the risk is totally eliminated and all the control gaps closed.

    D) When the risks are completely addressed and left at tolerable level.

    Answer: Option B

Risk Management Concepts

Tip #9: Remember the correct name of security option that differentiates a human from automated programs

This tip reviews the purpose of CAPTCHA, security with CAPTCHA, and reCAPTCHA.

Domain: Security and Risk Management, Asset Security, Security Engineering.

Subdomain: Access control, Identity management.

Subject background: CAPTCHA stands for "completely automated public Turing test to tell computers and humans apart."

When filling in forms or text boxes on a website, a programmed web bot (a bot is an automated computer program) can do the automatic filling, and the server may not really know if the boxes are filled by a bot or by a human. To clearly distinguish who is filling the boxes or information, a CAPTCHA creates some jumbled text for the user to type manually. Figure 1-2 shows two examples of CAPTCHA.

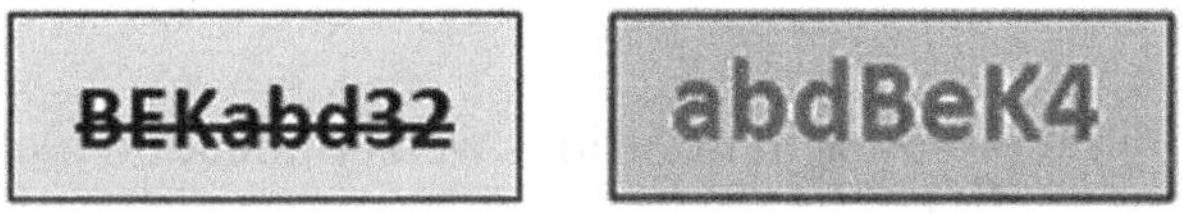

Figure 1-2. CAPTCHA examples

The text inside can sometimes be spoken for people with disabilities, can be in italics, can be twisted sideways, and may even come in many other readable/spoken formats. It also can be specifically asked to be typed back in lowercase or uppercase or case insensitive. If the text is not legible, a button to regenerate a new version of CAPTCHA is usually provided.

CAPTCHA can also come in the form of pictures and graphics where the user is asked to pick pictures with particular patterns. Examples include picking pictures with a store front, pictures with pedestrian crossing, traffic lights, and many more alternatives.

CAPTCHA regeneration and testing for the humans may or may not have an infinite number of attempts to get the user to input it correctly. The logic of the web form can be programmed to limit the number of attempts (like in the case of account information on bank or stock market websites).

The final goal of the CAPTCHA is to determine that a genuine user is trying to enter the data than a bot filling random data to fool the website and attack or gain access.

Things to Remember

- CAPTCHA is not a fix-it-frizzle for every possible problem on the Internet. It is one way of distinguishing humans from bots that may fill up website data. Other ways are two-way authentication via phone, text message, etc.

- CAPTCHA can come in the form of graphics, text, twisted images, voice recognition system, or in any other suitable form.

- Remember the full form of the CAPTCHA acronym. It stands for "Completely Automated Public Turing test to tell Computers and Humans Apart."

- reCAPTCHA is a newer version of CAPTCHA that helps in telling humans and bots apart and also in digitizing books, newspaper articles, etc.

- reCAPTCHA offers a plug-in to various web application platforms such as ASP.NET and PHP and eases implementation.

- As a side note, CAPTCHA or reCAPTCHA are **not** final solutions for every security loophole.

- CAPTCHA can be implemented on Windows applications with suitable programming as well as on website with plugins.

Example: A banking website lets customers log in and pay bills online. The online payments are initiated by a customer who registers on the bank's website and then logs in with the account number and registered password. Since one-step verification has proven to show problems with loose security, the bank wants to implement a two- or three-step authentication to verify and is considering a few options. The bank is considering sending a text message to the customer as a second verification and exploring options for a third verification procedure such as Completely Automated Public Turing test to tell Computers and Humans Apart (CAPTCHA). Which of the following **BEST** fits the bank's verification of authentication methods?

A)   Use of login password with account number and phone text message is sufficient.

B)   Use the login password with account number and an image CAPTCHA is sufficient.

C)   Use login password with account number, CAPTCHA, and phone text message.

D)   Use CAPTCHA and text message but not the account number.

Analysis: It is easy to see that every bank almost always has online payments. Whether or not a bank's website has online payments, the basic operation of authentication is all important in this question. The more factors we implement to authenticate, the better security becomes. Thus, the first factor is the account number and password. But since the first factor can be easily mimicked by key loggers and such programs, we need a CAPTCHA as the second authentication factor. The third and final authentication of verifying via text message comes in handy for better security.

Statement: Removing the verbiage, we can keep the question short, like the following:

The bank wants to implement a two- or three-step authentication to verify customer credentials.

Question: Which of the following **BEST** fits verification of authentication methods?

Solution: The obvious answer is option C since it has the most authentication factors. A three-step authentication is always better than one- or two-step authentication.

Review Questions

A variety of questions can be asked on the same topic of authentication and can be combined with other topics on the CISSP exam. Some of them are as follows:

1. What does the acronym CAPTCHA stand for?

    A) Computer Automated Public Test to tell Computers from Humans Away

    B) Completely Automated Public Turing test to tell Computers and Humans Apart

    C) Computer Automated Public Turing test to tell Computers from Humans Apart

    D) Completely Automatic Public Test to tell Computers and Humans Apart

    Answer: Option B

2. What is the main purpose of a CAPTCHA?

    Answer: To determine that a genuine user is trying to enter the data than a bot filling random data

3. If a website allows people to post comments, it may decide to implement CAPTCHA for authentication. Does CAPTCHA offer foolproof identity verification?

    Answer: CAPTCHA verifies that a human is filling in the blanks and forms on a website, but it cannot guarantee any identity verification. A user's ID has to be verified differently.

4. If a person with a disability cannot read small text displayed by the CAPTCHA, what are other possible CAPTCHA methods?

    Answer: Regenerative voice commands, graphics, pictures, or a combination of these are some of the other options for CAPTCHA.

5. A CAPTCHA-like verification is only designed for web forms and Internet.

    A) True

    B) False

    Answer: Option B. CAPTCHA can be programmed and implemented on a desktop application and is not limited to websites and the Internet only.

Tip #10: Remember various implementation plans and their use in IT security

This tip reviews strategic, tactical, and operational plans that are generally used in the IT industry,

Domain: Security and Risk Management.

Subdomain: Security policy, Software security, Risk Management Concepts, etc.

Subject background: See Table 1-2 for detailed definitions.

Table 1-2. *Various Plans and Their Definitions*

Plan	Type	Duration
Strategic	Stable	Long-term; broad/general goals to achieve
Tactical	Detailed	Short-term; supports strategic plan
Operational	Highly detailed	Regular or daily

Together, these three plans (strategic, tactical, and operational) comprise an organization's "planning horizon."

Things to Remember

- All three plans are stated in the security policy, which specifies how they are carried out.

- Since the security policy addresses the laws and other standards, these plans are laid out automatically to follow those laws and standards.

- Each plan has a different goal.

- the strategic goal is the ultimate/final endpoint of a project.

- Standards, guidelines, etc., help achieve tactical goals, which in turn lead to the strategic long-term goals in the project.

- Operational goals are day-to-day work activities such as maintaining phones, checking logs for errors, finding the cause of crash of a server and fix, or running the antivirus software at a pre-determined time of the day.

- Operational goals are taken care of regularly and need not be day to day.

- In software, website maintenance and such projects need tactical considerations without which the security can be easily compromised due to ever-evolving threats and security holes found by hackers.

- In networking, the control plane is considered as a strategic plane, and a forwarding plane is considered as a tactical plane.

- In the military, "operations" are human endeavors. Forces conduct operations in complex, ever-changing, and uncertain situations. They need continuous and mutual adaptation depending on the situation.

- For strategic and tactical plans, the funding keeps changing due to inflation, change of circumstances, and new developments at various levels.

- The strategic and tactical plans can also be scrapped and/or replaced by new plans.

- Operational plans change too but are implemented regularly.

Example: French defense forces plan to modernize their daily operations and want to implement automatic log checks, ordering automatic deployments depending on a positively identified attack. The entire automation needs to be completed in the next eight months while the current manual log checks continue. The project has been awarded to a contractor who breaks up the eight-month project into four different two-month projects and supplies reports at the end of every two months along with the progress. At the end of four months, the contractor reported that the costs of completing the project are not sustainable and requested to change the deadlines and to be paid more money with a promise to complete the project in 12 months. The French defense authorities at this time decided that the entire project was really feasible and scrapped the entire work and awarded it to another contractor. What plan did the original contractor fail to complete to gain the confidence of the French?

A) Strategic plan

B) Operational plan

C) Tactical plan

D) The defense plan

Analysis: Notice from the verbiage that a long-term project was planned at first, and then it was given as four different two-month projects to be completed. These two-month projects are tactical projects, while the daily operational projects of reading logs manually is not affected. The stipulation was that the operational plans must continue until the strategic and tactical plans were completed. When the initial contractor failed, he failed in completing the tactical projects and turn in the results of these projects.

Statement: French defense forces planning to modernize hired a contractor who breaks up the eight month project to four two month projects. At the end of four months the contractor reported changes to cost and deadlines and requested more money with a promise to complete the project in 12 months. The french defense authorities decided to award the project to another contractor.

Question: What plan did the original contractor fail to complete?

Solution: Simply by reading the verbiage, we find that the contractor failed in completing the tactical plans that are detailed and done over the short term. Without these short-term completions, the strategic long-term plans can never be completed. Thus, the clear answer is option C. Option D is a clear distractor in that there is no such thing as a "defense plan" when a project is taken up or planned. Option B is wrong since operational plans are day-to-day plans or regular interval plans, which have never been the basic idea behind the project.

Review Questions

Some of the possible questions can look like the following:

1. What type of goals does a strategic plan has?

    Answer: Long-term goals

2. What is the planning horizon comprised of?

    Answer: It is comprised of strategic, tactical, and operational plans.

3. In the military, what are the tactical operations?

    Answer: They are human endeavors in an ever-changing complex environment.

4. In doing a website maintenance, what plans are more important for the site to survive?

    A) Strategic plans

    B) Tactical plans

    C) Operational plans

    D) Software maintenance

    Answer: Option B is the correct answer.

5. In computer networking, what planes are considered as strategic and tactical planes?

    Answer: Control and forwarding planes

6. Which of the following can be considered an operational plan?

    A) Traditional telephone network being replaced by an Internet-based protocol

    B) Checking the weekly antivirus reports and the firewall logs

    C) Plan to move the entire physical office to another facility by next year

    D) Constructing a helipad on the rooftop of the building for the C-level executives

Answer: Option B

7. A company has put all the security policies guidelines into place for the tactical plans of all projects the company is currently doing. What do these policies and plans finally plan to achieve and why?

    Answer: All plans and policies guide in reaching the strategic goals. Without achieving each of the tactical goals, it is impossible to achieve the long-term strategic goal.

Tip #11: Remember every step of incident, risk, disaster recovery, etc., is important, but the CISSP certification exam often asks questions about these processes' FIRST/NEXT/LAST steps

Remember the **FIRST** step in each process, such as Incident Response, Audit, Disaster Recovery Planning, Business Impact Analysis, Prevent Data Loss/Leak, Access Control, Threat Modeling, and Data Sensitivity Program.

    Domain: Security Assessment and Testing, Software Development Security, Security and Risk Management

    Subdomain: Prevention and detection tools, Access control, Audit, Incident response, Vulnerabilities, Threat modeling.

    Subject background:

    The disaster recovery process (DRP), business impact analysis, and many other processes that are required for the security of IT systems usually have a list of steps, but CISSP is notorious to ask the exam taker to identify the **FIRST** step, or what comes after another step (as given in Tip #12). Table 1-3 lists some of the processes and the **FIRST** steps involved for each.

Table 1-3. *Disaster Recovery Process Priorities*

Process	FIRST Step/Priority
Incident response	Detection of incident
Audit	Determine goals for audit
Disaster recovery planning	Select team members/assemble or identify team
Business impact analysis	Identify critical systems/conduct risk analysis
Prevent data loss/leak	Conduct data inventory
Access control	Identify assets/define resources
Data sensitivity program	Define classification levels
Threat modeling	Identify vulnerabilities
Disaster/Emergency	Save human lives
Change management	Identify the change required

Note that Table 1-2 is an example only and does not cover everything on the CISSP exam. Memorize all the steps for each process.

Things to Remember

- **Event**: An event can be defined as an "observable change."

- **Alert**: An alert is a flagged event.

- **Incident**: When damage occurs, an incident is said to have taken place.

- The CISSP exam wants to test whether the exam taker is aware of the specific steps. The questions can usually ask what the **FIRST** step of a process is or what comes after another specific step (for example, after identifying a team, what is the NEXT step in disaster recovery planning?). It is important for the exam taker to remember the steps in a clear order.

Example: A company's information technology (IT) team has moved to a new building and is now situated on the 19th floor. The IT project manager was told that the shared server room is located on the 8th floor of the building and works on the mutual goodwill of all companies situated in the building. While visiting the server room, the manager notices that the room is shared by a group of companies, the wiring of the servers is open, the server room doors are accessible to anyone, fire hydrants are located on the other end of the floor far from the server room, and the backups are placed right next to the servers. The manager notes that all these factors in the server room have an impact on the company's business and wants to report them. What is the **FIRST** step the manger should take for his business to not be impacted by the vulnerabilities he noticed in the 8th floor server room?

A) Prepare a list of vulnerabilities and threats and corrective actions

B) Inform the management that mutual goodwill may not work and risk is involved

C) Conduct risk analysis

D) Recommend access control to server room and move the fire hydrants closer

Analysis: Sometimes a lot verbiage can confuse a reader, as in the previous question. If we read through the text, the main aim is to tell the reader that the IT company has moved to a new location and the server room is shared but is unlocked and has lots of problems. The problems listed are both physical and IT related. But before the manager can do anything, what is the **FIRST** step he needs to do?

Usually when a business moves to a new location (assuming that the vulnerabilities were not noticed before moving, but that is not a problem of worry in the question since the statement says the company has "moved"), the first worry is how the location will impact the business. In other words, a business impact analysis (BIA) is conducted as stated in the question. And the exam taker is asked in that BIA what the very **FIRST** step is.

Statement: Removing the unnecessary verbiage, we can read the state as follows:

A company's information technology (IT) team has moved to a new building. The **shared server room** is located on the 8th floor. The room is shared by a group of companies, the wiring of the servers is open, the server room doors are accessible to **anyone**, the fire hydrants are located on the other end of the floor far from the server room, and the backups are placed right next to the servers. The manager wants to report it.

Question: What is the **FIRST** step the manger should take for his **business** not to be **impacted** by the vulnerabilities he noticed in the 8th floor server room?

Solution: Corrective actions will be taken up after the BIA is complete and lists the risks the threats and vulnerabilities pose on the business. Thus, option A is wrong. Informing management that server room sharing may not work is fine, but management can question the project manager what the problems are and how the vulnerabilities he noticed will impact the business. Therefore, option B is wrong too. The very **FIRST** step the project manager has to take is to conduct a risk analysis report and how it impacts the business and then go to management with his report. Option C thus is the correct answer. Recommendations to the server room, access control via some smart card, and all those things will happen after the risk analysis is conducted and shows how the business is impacted. Thus, option D is not the **FIRST** step.

Notice that all four answers come close in the BIA to finding how badly the noticed vulnerabilities affect the business, but not all four are the **FIRST** steps.

For this sort of verbiage, the exam candidate should read the question more than once and filter out what the main gist of the question is before selecting the correct answer.

Review Questions

Other variations of this topic questions can be as follows:

1.   What is the **FIRST** step in a data loss prevention (DLP) process?

    A) Secure backups on-site

    B) Secure backups off-site

    C) Identify the data owners

    D) Conduct data inventory

    Answer: Option D is the correct answer. Unless we first know the inventory where data is stored, used, transmitted, received, or handled in any other way, the rest of the options are useless and do not serve any purpose.

2. In the case of a disaster, what is the **FIRST** priority of the disaster recovery team?

    A) Select team members

    B) Report the disaster

    C) Protect human lives

    D) Salvage from disaster

    Answer: Under any circumstances, the **FIRST** priority of a disaster recovery emergency team is always protecting human lives. Option C is therefore the correct answer.

CHAPTER 2

Asset Security

In this chapter, you will learn tips in these areas: what assets are, the asset security, protecting assets, privacy, memory and data management, data handling as part of asset security, and the public key infrastructure used to protect assets.

Information and Asset Classification

Tip #12: Learning various levels of data classification

Data classification from public (open) to top secret (only a few can access) levels and the classification procedures (first step to the last).

Domain: Asset Security, Security and Risk Management.

Subdomain: Information and asset classification.

Subject background: Classification of information can be for the government and for the private/public-sector companies. Clearly, the private and public sector companies are not governed by the politicians or the government and thus can have their own classification system and need not conform to any single rule. Moreover, the classification system for private industry can be different from one company to the other.

Table 2-1 is one example of private-sector information system classification.

© R. Sarma Danturthi 2020
R. S. Danturthi, *70 Tips and Tricks for Mastering the CISSP Exam*,
https://doi.org/10.1007/978-1-4842-6225-2_2

Table 2-1. Levels of Classification per Private Sector

Type	Description
Sensitive	Strict and limited access to information that needs a high degree of honesty/reliability/job level. Disclosure of this data causes severe damage. Examples: mixing formulas for drinks, patented information.
Confidential	Restrictive information and disclosure may still cause damage.
Private	Private information is generally company-owned data like the patient records or the human resources data that has personally identifiable information (PII). It is mandatory for the company to protect this data.
Proprietary	Proprietary information can be generally given to others on a limited basis but can still cause some problems. Examples: Specifications of a new product, management plans of a new office.
Public	Public information can be freely disclosed. Examples: information used for marketing, demographics of the company, etc.

A government/military classification system is designed by the government to secure the information that relates to the safety of its citizens and the country at large. This system is usually fixed by the government and cannot be changed easily. Most of the government departments have policies in place to stick to the defined classification system. Table 2-2 illustrates the US government's information classification system.

Table 2-2. *Levels of Classification per US Government Regulations*

Type	Description
Top Secret	Strict and very limited access to information that needs a high degree of honesty/reliability/job level. Disclosure of this data causes "exceptionally grave damage."
Secret	Restrictive information and disclosure may still cause "serious damage." This is the second highest classification.
Confidential	Low-level classification for data. Disclosure causes damage but can be disclosed with proper authorization.
Sensitive but Unclassified (SBU)	Some personal information such as medical data. May not cause damage but needs to be kept away from public eyes. Examples: military recruiting numbers, medical PII, etc.
Unclassified	This is not a classification per se but can be said as information that can be provided to anyone without reservation. Examples: passed budget limits for past years, population data, etc.

Things to Remember

- Private or public companies have their own classification schemes to protect data.

- The government/military has a set classification that must be adhered to.

- Always use caution in disseminating information even if the data is at lowest classification level, which is public or unclassified.

- Classification applies to both individuals and the equipment or data.

- Information classification is necessary to protect the assets and the company/government/military or the citizens of the country.

- The **FIRST STEP** in data classification is to decide what/how many classification levels a company must have.

- The **SECOND STEP** of data classification is to decide which asset goes to which classification level and who can access that level.

- Be clear to put assets in one classification level only. There must be no overlap for any information from one level to another.

- When data is being classified, the rules apply to all forms of data— paper, electronic or otherwise (in other words, to all soft or hard copies).

- What data is stored, kept, or destroyed is the decision of the data owner.

Example: A government organization decides to migrate to cloud computing. All the data will be stored **ONLY** on the cloud, and the computers' hard disks will not have any data stored, except some document files that are harmless. The cloud data when disclosed can cause "serious damage" to the country, and its confidentiality is taken care of by the cloud computing provider. Those who operate the computers have Top Secret clearance and do not store any information on the computers' memory. The operators access data on the cloud via a two-step authentication procedure. After the computers are purchased for new cloud computing, to what classification levels should these computers be attached?

A) Top Secret

B) Secret

C) Unclassified

D) Secret but Unclassified

Analysis: From the verbiage, we note that all the data will always be on the cloud. The cloud data and its privacy are taken care of by the cloud provider. The computer operators do not store anything on computer memory. This means if someone hacks into the computer, they cannot access any data since the data is on the cloud and not on the computer itself. Operators access the cloud with two-point authentication, which makes it difficult for hackers to further dig into the cloud. Thus, the computer used to access the cloud is just a mere instrument and will not store anything. Unless someone decides to access the cloud, this computer can be used for even word processing and checking the news on internet.

Statement: Removing the unnecessary verbiage, the statement can be rephrased as follows:

A government organization decides to migrate to cloud computing. All the data will be stored **ONLY** on the cloud. The cloud data when disclosed can cause "serious damage" to the country, and its **confidentiality is taken care of by the cloud computing provider**.

Question: A **government** organization decides to store data **ONLY** on the cloud. The operators access data on the cloud via a two-step authentication procedure. What classification levels should these computers **BEST** belong?

Solution: Option C is the correct answer. Option A is wrong because the Top Secret classification causes grave damage, and it does not fit the statement given. Option B is wrong because the "Secret" data classification, when disclosed, causes "serious damage," but the data is on the cloud and the secrecy is taken care of by cloud provider. The cloud is also accessed separately from the machine. Option D is wrong in that there is no such known classification in the US government.

Review Questions

Many possible questions can be asked in this area. Some of them are listed here:

1. What is the **FIRST** step in data/information classification process?

    A) Decide what data needs classification

    B) Decide who the data owner will be

    C) Define the classification levels required

    D) Define the procedures to classify data

    Answer: Option C

2. Who is the **BEST** person to be in charge of the data and its classification?

    A) The information security officer (ISO)

    B) The data or information owner (DIO)

    C) The chief security office (CSO)

    D) All employees of the information security department

    Answer: Option B

3. Is it possible for an asset to fall into two overriding classification levels?

   Answer: No. Each asset should have only one classification level. If an asset fits two levels, the highest level is usually chosen.

4. How information is usually classified?

   A) On sensitivity

   B) On criticality

   C) Both A and B

   D) Neither A nor B

   Answer: Option C

5. What type of data is the classification level that is attached to data/information?

   A) Unclassified data

   B) Meta data

   C) Secret data

   D) Sensitive data

   Answer: Option B is correct. The data classification level attached to the data/information item is metadata. The other options are classification level definitions.

6. For data classified as "public," what type of auditing is required?

   A) Private and special auditing

   B) Public special auditing

   C) Sensitive but unclassified special auditing

   D) No special auditing required

   Answer: Option D

7. A computer purchased by the government comes with a user manual. If the computer is classified as a Top Secret asset for the data it stores, the user manual must be classified as?

A) Top Secret

B) Secret

C) Confidential

D) Unclassified

Answer: Option D. Simple computer user manuals are always given the unclassified label. Computers may carry digital data with a Top Secret level, but the generic usual manual about how to operate the computer is an unclassified item.

8. A private organization starting to classify its data and information is conducting a meeting in which the data owner proposes to have only three classification levels at **BEST** and would even prefer two classification levels. Is this acceptable?

A) No, data classification must have at least four levels.

B) Yes, private organizations can have their own levels of classification.

C) No, data classification must follow state/federal rules.

D) Yes, but data owner must also consult with other companies.

Answer: Option B

9. A doctor's office stores patients' medical records in digital form only. What classification level is **MOST** appropriate for these records?

Answer: Private data classification fits the medical records.

10. Data classification rules apply to what form of data?

A) Digital data and paper data

B) Digital, paper, video, fax, phone, disks, and all data

C) Only soft and hard copies of data

D) All formats of data except paper data

Answer: Option B. Classification must apply to **EVERY FORM** of data.

Data and System Ownership

Tip #13: Understanding roles in data classification and data management

Differentiate clearly between who classifies data and who implements the business rules, custody, transport, and storage. Other important words are *data warehouse, data mart*, and *data roles* used in day-to-day business.

Domain: Asset Security.

Subdomain: Database security, Data roles, Data ownership, Custodians.

Subject background: Data security is paramount, and each stakeholder associated with data needs to have a different and minimally required permission to protect it while handling. Any data leaks will finally have an adverse reaction on the functioning of an organization since 1) data leaks are difficult to detect, 2) data leaks can be internal or external, and 3) there can be natural disasters and unforeseen circumstances that may cause data leaks. Some NIST documents describe data roles and the duty of each role in protecting the data.

Things to Remember

Data Owner: Usually the boss of the organization is called the data owner. The eventual responsibility of the data remains with the data owner, despite the fact that many stakeholders handle the data. Data owners classify data and decide how to handle it.

Data Custodian: They handle data in the day-to-day operations. Data custodians implement rules that are framed by data owners. They protect, store, back up, and retrieve data in the proper format as required by the rules set by the data owners.

System Owner: System owners are people who own the system that processes the data. System owners have to design and guard the security of a system that handles the data. System owners can be typically the same as data owners but can be different too.

Business Owner: These people own business processes. Processes are conducted on the systems and are guarded by system owners. They can be group project managers below the CEO or another C-level manager.

Data Processor: A data processor is a system or a person who processes the data, per the privileges assigned to them.

Data Controller: This is a person or an entity that controls the data. Anyone who is collecting data and passing it around is a controller. How the controlled data is processed is the job of data processor described earlier. Safe Harbor deals with both the data processor and data controller.

Administrators: These are a group of people who decide what data should go to certain people. In other words, they grant permissions on data to the users. Administrators assign privileges to users.

Users: These are end users who utilize the data to complete a task given to them.

Remember that these roles are given to people depending on their "need to know" and their privilege level, with "least privilege" as the norm. Also, the privileges can be escalated or removed as and when people move around in, join, or leave an organization.

Datamart: This is used for a single application or a single department.

Data warehouse: This houses various applications' data (enterprise-wide depth for data).

Example: During an audit, the auditor found that the data breach happened due to the wrong classification of data on various systems with the users, administrators, controllers, and processors. The custodian has given the auditor all the information about the data classifications used in the organization. Who should the auditor contact to address the problems encountered during the audit about data classification levels?

A)   The data owner or the CEO

B)   The data administrators

C)   The data custodian

D)   The data processors who actually classify and process the data

Analysis: Reading the question, it is easy to see that there are several distractors in the question itself. The names of custodians, administrators, controllers, and processors are put in the question to inform the test taker to divert attention. In fact, once the words "data classification" appear in a question, the test taker should immediately remember that the question is directly linked with a "data owner." It is possible for the question to also ask about other roles of the data, but classification basically is the job of the data owner or the CEO. Remember that the CEO can assign this classification job to another C-level manager (such as a CIO, COO), but the CEO has the ultimate responsibility for breach of data since the CEO remains the owner of the data and decides the classification levels.

Statement: The auditor found the wrong classification of data on various systems. Who should the auditor address the problems encountered during the audit about data classification levels?

Question: Removing the verbiage, we can easily deduce the following cryptic question and quickly find the answer to the question:

Who should the auditor address about data classification levels?

Solution: Data classification is the job of data owner. Whether the data owner is a CEO or another C-level manager, it does not matter. Therefore, the answer is option A.

Data administrators set up passwords, privileges, and controls on the data but do not classify the data. Data custodians follow orders of the data owners and do the daily backup and take care of the day-to-day duties of the data. Data processors only can process data given to them and cannot classify it. Ultimately, it is the CEO who will be held responsible for the data classification and the discrepancies in the audit because the CEO owns the data.

Review Questions

The following questions usually center around a particular role:

1. Who classifies data in an organization? (Or, who is responsible for various classification levels assigned to data in an organization?)

    A) Data custodian

    B) Data owner

    C) System owners

    D) System controller

    Answer: Option B. The data owner assigns classification to data.

2. A new user joining in an organization is given privileges to handle data. Who assigns privileges to the user, and how does the user track the data use?

    A) The administrator gives privileges and tracks users via audit logs.

    B) The data owner gives privileges and asks the custodian to track the user.

    C) The data custodian gives privileges and asks the system owner to track the user.

    D) The data controller gives privileges and asks the data owner to track the user.

    Answer: Option A

3. Who is responsible for the day-to-day storage, backup, and retrieval of data in an organization?

   A) The day-to-day data processor

   B) The retrieve and backup programmer

   C) The data custodian

   D) The data administrator

   Answer: Option C. A data custodian will be the person responsible for the day-to-day handling of data.

4. What is the difference between a data warehouse and data mart?

   A) The data warehouse is for a single application, but the data mart is for several applications.

   B) The data warehouse is for many applications, but the data mart is for a single application.

   C) The data warehouse is the externally funded and provided entity.

   D) The data mart is an internally housed entity.

   Answer: Option B.

Tip #14: Know the rules and regulations that govern the United States, European Union, and overseas data sharing

Remember the details of Safe Harbor and the GDPR.

Domain: Security and Risk Management.

Subdomain: Security, Overseas data sharing, US and EU data sharing regulations and protection, etc., Data and system ownership.

Subject background: Like the United States has data privacy rules, the European Union has its own privacy laws. Simply stated, Safe Harbor is a paradigm or concept on how US-based companies can comply with the EU privacy laws. In other words, Safe Harbor principles state how a non-European entity or company can comply with a European entity about the privacy of data (belonging to EU citizens, companies, etc.). As of May 2018, Safe Harbor has been replaced by the General Data Protection Regulation (GDPR). GDPR is the most important regulation in data protection in the past 20 years.

Things to Remember

- Safe Harbor has a set of seven principles: notice, choice, onward transfer, security, data integrity, access, and enforcement.

- Safe Harbor basically is an agreement between the US Department of Commerce and the European Union to export and handle the PII of European citizens.

- Safe Harbor compliance is a way of building trust.

- EU data protection laws allow the PII of EU citizens to be shared if the receiving country can adequately guarantee the PII data is well-protected.

- Companies or entities must have a mechanism to safeguard the PII of EU citizens when it is transferred to and within the United States.

- GDPR is a regulation and is **NOT** a directive. It is directly binding and applicable and does not provide flexibility for some aspects to be adjusted for anyone.

- In some cases, violators of GDPR can be fined up to 20 million Euros or 4% of the annual worldwide turnover of the preceding financial year.

- Under the GDPR, public authorities and businesses whose core activities consist of processing personal data or PII are required to employ a data protection officer (DPO).

Example: A social engineering website that is getting very popular encourages people to register and stores the username and passwords, along with the location of the person (resident country and the city). Information such as the user's job, tastes in food, and occasionally personal hobbies is also recorded. The site was recently reported to the European Union that the user's PII is not well-protected by the site. The company's legal team argued that the company operated in the United States only and did not break any laws of Safe Harbor or the GDPR since the website did not collect any other personal data than name, city, hobbies, food habits, and interests. If the company is violating any laws and disrupting PII, what measure should it take?

A) Employ Safe Harbor or GDPR directives

B) Implement GDPR regulations and employ a data protection officer (DPO)

C) Employ a data protection officer (DPO) but do not implement Safe Harbor/GDPR

D) Employ Safe Harbor directives but do not hire a data protection officer (DPO)

Analysis: Any company with a website has to know that the website is accessible from all over the world. Any data collected from EU citizens has to follow the Safe Harbor and GDPR regulations. Even if the data collected is only a small amount of PII, the GDPR rules still apply. This is the main reason why a small pop-up keeps appearing on websites telling the users that the website may store cookies that may contain some personal information of the user, such as the computer location, browsing habits, etc.

Statement: The question's verbiage can be shortened as follows:

A social engineering website that stores the **username and passwords**, **location of the person** (resident country and the city), the user's job, tastes in food, and occasionally personal hobbies was recently reported to the EU that the user's **PII is not well-protected** by the site. The company's legal team argued that the company did not break any laws of Safe Harbor or GDPR.

Question: A social engineering website was recently reported to the European Union that the user's **PII is not well-protected.** Is the company violating any laws of PII?

Solution: The simplest answer is yes since any information collected from the user can directly or indirectly lead to the user's other data, which can ultimately pave the way for finding more information about the user. Option A is wrong since the GDPR is not a directive but a regulation. Option C is wrong because employing a DPO alone is not the solution. Option D is wrong for the same reason since both a DPO and data protection are important. Option B, therefore, is the correct answer.

Review Questions

Several variations of the questions are possible and some of them are listed here:

1. What is the full form of the GDPR, which deals with the European Union's data privacy?

A) General Data Privacy Rules

B) General Data Protection Regulation

C) General Data Privacy Regulation

D) General Data Protection Rules

Answer: Option B

2. What is the maximum amount of fine the GDPR can impose?

A) A flat fine of 30 million euros

B) 25 million euros or 5% of the worldwide turnover of the current year

C) 20 million euros or 4% of the worldwide turnover of the preceding year

D) 20 million euros or 5% of the worldwide turnover of the current year

Answer: Option C

3. Corporations and public entities dealing with the processing of personal data are supposed to employ or implement who/what?

A) Data privacy officer

B) Data privacy software and data privacy ownership

C) Data ownership and data privacy

D) Data protection, privacy, and ownership

Answer: Option A

4. The GDPR applies within what geographic area?

Answer: It is a regulation within the European Union.

5. How many principles does the Safe Harbor have?

Answer: It has seven principles: notice, choice, onward transfer, security, data integrity, access, and enforcement.

6. Safe Harbor is an agreement between what two entities?

A) Federation of all US public trading corporations and the European Union

B) US Department of Commerce and the European Union

C) US Consortium of Internet Companies and the entire Europe continent

D) Government of the United States and the European Union

Answer: Option B

7. How does an entity join the Safe Harbor?

Answer: It is a voluntary process but must comply with requirements and publicly declare as such. The entities also self-certify annually to the US Department of Commerce in writing that the entity agrees and complies with the Safe Harbor requirements.

Protecting Privacy

Tip #15: Know the newly introduced privacy laws of the European Union, European Economic Area, and the related GDPR

General Data Protection Regulation (GDPR), is a new regulation aimed at protecting the privacy for all individuals under European Union and European Economic Area (EEA). Failure to follow the regulation can have very adverse effect in the form of fines.

Domain: Asset Security, Security Engineering, and Security Operations.

Subdomain: Protecting privacy, Privacy concerns and limitation of use, Data retention, Handling requirements, Protect data in transit, Resource protection techniques.

Subject background: Data protection and privacy for all individuals in the European Union was implemented via the GDPR in May 2018. The GDPR also addresses exporting data from/to the EU and EEA. It basically states that those who control the personally identifiable information (PII) must implement appropriate technical and organizational measures to implement data protection principles. Business processes should implement pseudonymization and anonymization to protect the PII when and where appropriate.

Data processors must clearly indicate how they data is collected, used, and stored. Subjects can request a copy of the data collected by the businesses. Businesses must report data breaches within 72 hours if the breach had any effect on the PII or privacy. Public authorities and core businesses must employ a data protection officer (DPO).

Things to Remember

- The GDPR is a regulation, **not** a directive. It is directly binding and applicable.

- The GDPR consists of 99 articles grouped into 11 chapters.

- The GDPR applies if the data controller/processor/subject is in the EU and in some cases outside the EU.

- The GDPR does **not** apply to personal/household activity that has no connection to the professional or commercial processing of data.

- The GDPR does **not** also cover deceased persons, scientific or statistical analysis, lawful interception, national security, military, police, or justice departments.

- The right of access (article 15) is a right of the data subject.

- The term "data" includes data provided by the subject and the data observed (such as behavior, physical traits, etc.).

- Data that is adequately anonymized is excluded from the GDPR regulation.

- The GDPR requires that the pseudonymized data and any information used to anonymize or pseudonymize the data should be kept separate from each other.

- Data processors must ensure that PII is not processed unless necessary for a specific process or implementation.

- Data protection under the GDPR is by design and default. This means privacy settings are always set to the highest level by default.

- Data subjects must be informed of their rights on how their data will be used or transferred to a third party if a transfer is required for a business process.

- Data subjects have the right to the following:

  a.   View their PII/access an overview of the PII

  b.   See/request how it is being processed

    c.   Obtain a copy of the stored data

    d.   Erase data under certain circumstances

    e.   Contest the process used by the business

    f.   File a complaint with a data protection authority (DPA)

- Informed consent is used for lawful data processing. Consent must be specific and freely given and with unambiguous words written in plain, simple, and understandable language.

- Data subjects have the right to withdraw consent at any time. This opt-out process must <u>not</u> be harder than the process they originally opted in.

Example: Data protection and privacy for all individuals in the European Union (EU) was implemented via the General Data Protection Regulation (GDPR) in May 2018 that addresses exporting of data from/to the EU and EEA. Under the GDPR, which of the following is one of the rights of the data subject?

A) Sue the European Union (EU) for misuse of subject data

B) File a complaint with the European Economic Area (EEA)

C) Opt in to share data on a particular date and opt out on another date

D) Consent only when the subject provides data to a business for the first time

Analysis: Reading the question, it becomes clear that it is asking about GDPR and the rights of a subject under the GDPR regulations. EU and EEA formulated the rules, but it is businesses that have to take care of implementing the GDPR. So, the first sentence of the question is generally a superfluous statement.

Statement: Data protection and privacy for all individuals in the European Union (EU) addresses exporting of data from/to the EU and EEA.

Question: Under the GDPR, which of the following is one of the rights of data subject?

Solution: Clearly, option C is a better fit than rest of the answers given. The EU and EEA are law makers and political bodies that make the laws. One cannot and do not sue those since these organizations do not handle the data. A subject's data is handled by a business (for example, a credit card company), which has to give option of opt-in and opt-out to a subject. Importantly, opt-in and opt-out are the rights of a subject, and a subject can choose when to opt in and when to opt out at their discretion. Thus, options A and B are wrong. Option D is wrong because consent can be given at any time and taken away at any other time as well, not just at first time. But a subject can always opt in and opt out.

Review Questions

A wide variety of questions can look as follows:

1. Under the GDPR, responsibility and accountability to protect data lies with whom?

   A) Data controller (DC)

   B) Data subject (DS)

   C) Data object (DO)

   D) Data protection agency (DPA)

   Answer: Option A

2. Under the GDPR, businesses have to protect the subject data by:

   A) Business laws of the European Union (EU)

   B) Design and default

   C) Data subject's consent

   D) Signing a service level agreement (SLA) with the subject

   Answer: Option B

3. When implementing the GDPR, what is the **BEST** way for an organization anonymizing or pseudonymizing with an encryption key to store data?

A) Store anonymized/pseudonymized data and the key together in the same location

B) Store anonymized/pseudonymized on-site and the key off-site

C) Keep anonymized/pseudonymized and the key on a single RAID 0 type disk

D) Keep anonymized/pseudonymized on RAID 0 disk, but do not keep the key at all

Answer: Option B

4. What law or ordinance replaced the Safe Harbor law?

A) General Data Provision Rulebooks (GDPR)

B) General Document Protection Reviews (GDPR)

C) General Data Protection Regulation (GDPR)

D) General Document Protection Rules (GDPR)

Answer: Option C

5. The term "data" under the GDPR can be **BEST** referred to as

A) Data provided by the subject and the data collected as observed

B) Data provided by the subject only after proper consent

C) Data consented by the subject and transferred in and out of EU/EEA only

D) Data consented to a business doing business only outside EU/EEA

Answer: Option A

Tip #16: Remember various levels of protection and the ring structure

Remember the protection rings 0, 1, 2, and 3 and where they operate, what they contain, and what they envelope for IT systems that may include mainframe systems or desktop stand-alone systems.

Domain: Security Engineering, Asset Security.

Subdomain: Trusted processes, CPU and IT system security, Protecting privacy.

Subject background: Figure 2-1 gives an idea of protection rings.

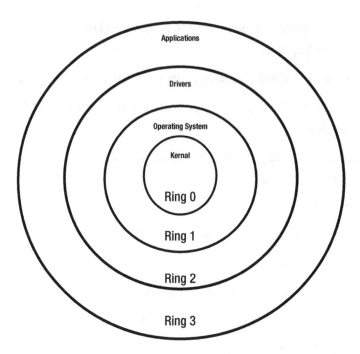

Figure 2-1. *Protection rings*

Things to Remember

The protection rings 0 to 3 and what they contain can be remembered with the acronym KODA as follows:

Ring 0 – Kernel (K): Contains the lowest and safest levels of keepings things protected. This includes kernel or the bare-bones file system that keeps the IT system up and running. But the kernel alone cannot contain everything and needs other items to be built around it for a normal user to work and operate.

Ring 1 – Operating system (O): This level is a step above the kernel where somewhat expert users can operate and do restricted work. Disk formatting, file allocation, and permissions go in this ring and help other users.

Ring 2 – Drivers (D): This level stores the device drivers, like the driver files for various applications, hardware, and how they interact with the operating system. Depending on the operating system, the drivers change as well.

Ring 3 – Applications (A): Databases and applications like Microsoft Word, Excel, etc., go in this level. This level is most accessible to a general user, and there is not much protection offered. This is the area where you let users log in and do generic work like checking email or browsing a website to check the daily news.

For rings 0 to 3, the protection goes from most secure (ring 0) to least secure (ring 3).

Simply because ring 0 is the most secure protection level does not mean everything can be stored at that level.

Example: An IT system being purchased will have a database installed over an operating system, a few devices for network access, and their corresponding drivers for the operating system. The database administrator (DBA) uses a high-level program to access the database at a top level over the operating system and device drivers, but the DBA can also go to the operating system's command-line interface (CLI) and operate the database securely. If the DBA operates at the CLI, what level or protection rings does he access?

A)   Ring 3 – Application level

B)   Ring 2 – Device driver level

C)   Ring 0 – Kernel level

D)   Ring 1 – Operating system level

Analysis: We can easily deduce that the situation in the question refers to a DBA accessing the database at the operating system level.

Statement: A lot of verbiage can be removed from the question since most of it is a description of how the DBA is accessing the database and at what level. It can be read as follows:

The database administrator (DBA) can go to the operating system's command-line interface (CLI) and operate the database securely.

Obviously, the DBA is not accessing the DB at the kernel level or at the device driver level. Thus, options B and C are wrong. The DBA can access the database at ring 3, which is the application level, but note that the question says the DBA is working at the CLI, which falls at the operating system level. So we can easily remove the distractors and come to a conclusion about the correct answer.

Question: If the DBA operates at the command-line interpreter (CLI), what level or protections rings does he access?

Solution: The command-level interpreter (CLI) is the operating system level where a user can access operating system commands over the kernel. This level is not available to all, and if available, it is restricted with limited permissions. Thus, the correct answer is option D.

Review Questions

Various questions can be asked in other formats related to the protection rings. Some of them are listed here:

1. What are the correct protection levels in the order of **MOST** secured to **LEAST** secured?

    A) Ring 0, 1, 2, and 3

    B) Ring 2, 1, and 0

    C) Ring 3, 2, 1, and 0

    D) Rings 0, 1, and 2

    Answer: Option A

2. At which protection ring layer do the **MOST** trusted processes operate?

    A) At the highest-numbered ring level

    B) At the ring level where device drivers work

    C) At the lowest-numbered ring level

    D) At ring levels 3 and 4 only

    Answer: Option C. Option D is a clear distractor since there is no protection ring 4.

3. A network interface card (NIC) is being installed on a computer with the Windows operating system. The NIC comes with a CD that has the driver files. When the NIC is correctly installed, at what protection ring level do the NIC's driver files reside?

    Answer: Driver files always are in ring 2, above the operating system level since the drivers are for that operating system.

4. From an IT system owner's perspective, who should be allowed to operate at protection ring level 0?

    Answer: Only the most trusted people since ring 0 is the most secure level.

5. What is the purpose of layering the IT system into protection levels 0 to 3?

   Answer: Layered protection provides a secure self-defense mechanism of an IT system and the operating system.

6. At what level does a user need the **MOST** privileges for an IT system?

   Answer: At the ring 0 protection level since it is the most secure level

Memory Management

Tip #17: Learn to remember the types of disk storage and their mechanisms

Understand different RAID types and their uses.

   Domain: Security Operations, Software Security, Network Security.

   Subdomain: Memory management, Asset security, Data and system ownership.

   Subject background: Redundant Array or Independent Disks (RAID) is a concept for providing memory sufficiently and without fail for IT systems so that the systems align with the security concept of continuous availability. These RAID disks are designed and provided for an IT system to make sure that the asset (whether it is a database, a running program, or a backup) is available without fail. For RAID, a series of physical disks are provided to make sure that the IT system is available continuously. The disks may be placed in the same physical location or dispersed over an area, but the IT system and the user would not know the difference. For a user, whatever level of RAID is used, it will appear as a single disk. When using RAID, data can be written on a single disk, two disks, or several disks with some data on each disk. The front-end user, though, will never know where the data is exactly stored. The front-end user cannot also decide where the data must be stored. It is not even necessary for the user to know how to optimize the disk storage. In other words, how RAID is designed and maintained is a background process a front end user should never have to worry about.

Things to Remember

- RAID disks are general-purpose simple hard disk drives.

- RAID levels and associated data formats are standardized by the Storage Networking Industry Association (SNIA).

- RAID networks do **NOT** provide recovery of data under catastrophes such as fire, flood etc.

- RAID provides availability but cannot replace the backup process. Backup is a separate process to save the data of the IT systems.

- Parity is a term used for error checks. Parity data is generated for error checks and is added to the original data when transmitting or storing data.

- Striping is a process of splitting data evenly or unevenly. Disks can be split evenly to store data or to make drives.

- Fault tolerance is a quality of the drive/IT system in which the drive or system will continue to operate normally under a failure.

- RAID is generally used where a single point of failure can cause unrecoverable data loss.

- RAID levels can be combined to make them as RAID 10 (1+0) or RAID 60 (6+0), etc.

- The most commonly used RAID level is RAID 5.

- Redundant array of independent tapes (RAIT) uses tapes instead of disks.

- A MAID is a massive array of inactive disks that store large to very large data in the order of several terabytes or more.

- RAID uses general disks (magnetic) and thus can be said to be a direct access storage device (DASD).

Table 2-3 lists the RAID levels and minimum disks required.

Table 2-3. *Levels of RAID*

Level	Details	Minimum Disks
0	Block-level striping without parity or mirroring. If one disk fails, all the data may not be available.	2
1	Mirroring without parity or striping. Data is written independently to two drives. If one fails, the other may be able to provide the required data.	2
2	Bit-level striping with Hamming code parity for error correction. Currently this is no longer used.	3
3	Byte-level striping with dedicated parity. Data is striped, but parity data is held on a separate drive. If the actual data fails, it might be reconstructed with parity.	3
4	Block-level striping with dedicated parity. This is similar to level 3, but parity is now at the block level instead of the byte level.	3
5	Block-level striping with distributed parity. Data is written to several disks, and parity is also written to all disks. It helps to make sure that there is no single point failure since parity data is available on several disks.	3
6	Block-level striping with double distributed parity. This is similar to level 5, but parity data is written TWICE to drives.	4

Figure 2-2 give details of different RAID levels.

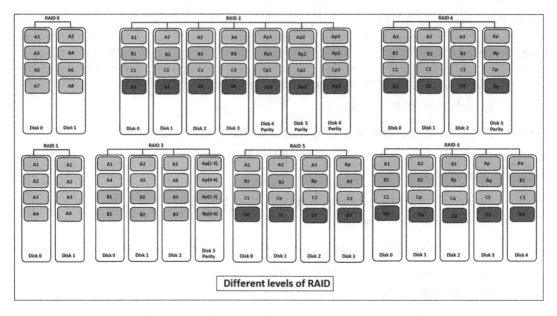

Figure 2-2.   *Different levels of RAID*

Example: An organization wants to develop a fault-tolerant disk drive set up for their data and is considering all levels of redundant array of independent disks (RAID). The chief data manager suggested using RAID 5, but after consideration, RAID 6 was approved. Which of the following options **BEST** describes the additional price the organization has to pay for the RAID 6 over RAID 5, and what advantage will the organization get for selecting RAID 6?

- A) No additional cost to pay and no additional advantage

- B) No additional cost to pay but has a second parity data storage advantage

- C) One additional disk cost to pay and has a second parity data storage advantage

- D) One additional disk cost to pay and no additional advantage

Analysis: Reading the question, it may appear challenging, but in reality it is a simple statement of what the organization has decided to do. The organization has decided to pick RAID 6 as their choice over RAID 5. All we need to know now are the advantages of RAID 6 over RAID 5 and if there is an additional disk cost involved.

Statement: Notice that when we read the verbiage, it becomes clear that none of the first few sentences was required to ask the actual question. All the question asks is the advantage of RAID 6 over RAID 5.

Question: Which of the following options **BEST** describes the additional price the organization has to pay for the RAID 6 over RAID 5, and what advantage will the organization get for selecting RAID 6?

Solution: From Table 2-3, we note that RAID 6 uses parity data twice in two different disks. Thus, to store a second parity, we need an additional disk. Other than the second parity block, RAID 5 and RAID 6 are essentially the same. The advantage of adding a second parity is that if the first parity block data is corrupted or lost, we will still be able to recover data from the second parity block. Option D is obviously wrong since we will not buy an additional disk without getting any advantage from it. Likewise, option A is wrong since RAID 5 and RAID 6 do differ. Option B is slightly tricky since we do not have an additional disk, and it may be possible to create a partition on existing disk for second parity. But the question, like most of the CISSP questions, is asking for the **BEST** answer from the given four choices.

Thus, the correct answer is option C.

Review Questions

Several types of questions can be asked about what level parity can be used in certain situations. Some of them are listed here:

1. What RAID level uses block-level striping with parity data written twice?

   A) RAID 2

   B) RAID 11

   C) RAID 60

   D) RAID 6

   Answer: Option D

2. What is the exact purpose of parity in storing data in RAID level 3?

   Answer: Parity is used for error check.

3. Which of the following RAID levels uses hamming code parity?

    A) RAID level 60

    B) RAID level 6

    C) RAID level 2

    D) RAID level 1

    Answer: Option C

4. Which RAID level uses a minimum of two disks and has no mirroring or parity associated with it?

    A) RAID 10

    B) RAID 11

    C) RAID 1

    D) RAID 0

    Answer: Option D

5. Which of the following **BEST** describes RAID?

    A) Reduced and accomplished independent disks

    B) Redundant array of independent disks

    C) Redundant array of inexpensive disks

    D) Reduced array of inexpensive disks

    Answer: Option B

6. Which successive levels of RAID that improve over the earlier ones have the same type of block-level striping?

    Answer: Level 4, level 5, and level 6. Note that level 0 uses block-level striping, but the successive levels (levels 1, 2) do not.

7. Which is the only level of RAID that uses bit-level striping?

    Answer: Level 2

8. What disks are used for creating a RAID?

    Answer: RAID disks are general-purpose simple hard disk drives.

9. Who decides the standards of RAID levels and associated data formats?

    A) They are standardized by the in-house database manager.

    B) They are standardized by the Storage Networking Industry Association.

    C) They are standardized by storage area networking standards.

    D) They are standardized by hardware and networking vendors.

    Answer: Option B

10. RAID networks do **NOT** provide recovery of data under which circumstances?

    Answer: Catastrophes such as fire, flood, etc.

11. Which part of the CIA security triangle concept/objective does RAID adhere to?

    Answer: The security objective is availability.

12. Which of the following **BEST** describes fault tolerance?

    A) It is a quality of the drive/IT system in which the drive or system will continue to operate normally under a failure.

    B) In the case of corrupted data, fault tolerance provides a clean backup copy.

    C) If data is entered with errors, it corrects data automatically.

    D) If data is saved in two or more disks, fault tolerance can automatically combine data and supply it to the user effortlessly.

    Answer: Option A

13. What is the difference between RAID and RAIT?

    A) RAID uses data, and RAIT uses the timing of the IT systems.

    B) RAID uses databases, and RAIT uses tracks on disk.

    C) RAID uses disks, and RAIT uses tapes.

    D) RAID uses disks, but RAIT is not related to IT systems.

    Answer: Option C

14. Which of the following **BEST** matches the definition of MAID?

A) Massive array of inactive disks

B) Massive array of independent disks

C) Managed array of inactive disks

D) Managed array of independent disks

Answer: Option A

Tip #18: Understand different types of computer memory addressing schemes (machine level)

Different types of memory addressing schemes such as direct, base, indexed, etc., make memory access easy when doing programming at machine level. The addressing schemes allow accessing the memory directly or with an indirect method without knowing the data stored at a location. These addressing schemes are useful at machine level coding and at processor level.

Domain: Security and Risk Management, Asset Security, Security Engineering.

Subdomain: Memory protection, Types of addressing in memory.

Subject background: Machine-level and assembly-level languages use the format of "opcode {operand} {operand}....{operand}" to run instructions. These operands can be registers, memory locations, data, or anything the assembly language can allow. When data is being read from or loaded into the memory, it can be addressed in a variety of ways. These ways are called addressing modes/schemes of the memory.

Things to Remember

Immediate addressing usually has the letter "I" in the opcode. It looks for the data in the operand, as in MVI C 40x. Here the instruction is to "move data immediately into register C." And the data to move into the register C is 40 hexadecimal. Since the data is immediately following the instruction/opcode, this is called immediate addressing.

Let's consider now that the data 40x is in another memory location, say at the "4389 7623" address. This is the address of the memory where our data 40x is stored. To load this data into a register, we use an instruction like "MOV C, "memory address" or in this case "MOV C, [4389 7623]." So the data 40x stored at the location specified [4389 7623] will be moved to register C. Since we are indirectly giving the data location (rather than the data itself), this called **indirect addressing**. Moving data from a location into the register is sometimes called register indirect addressing. If a memory location is used instead of a register, then it is simple indirect addressing.

Offset addressing is where an offset value is added to the existing address. The resulting address is from where data will be obtained. An example is illustrated here:

MVI reg1 "4389 7623" means move the address 4389 7623 into register1.

MV reg2 reg1 34 means add 34 offset to the address in reg1 and move the data from the resulting address into register 2. This means we get data from location "4389 7657" (which is 4389 7623 + 34) into register 2. Also note that in this example the first instruction is immediate addressing and the second instruction is offset addressing. This is sometimes also called **displacement or relative addressing**.

Register direct addressing is when the contents of one register are added/modified/ loaded to another. We do not know the contents of either register, but when we want to add those contents, we use register addressing. An example is ADD B, C. The contents of register C are added to register B.

Indexed addressing happens when an address is specified relative to an address that is in an index register. The index register basically contains the base address, and any offset is added to the index to fetch data from the resulting (index + off set) address. An example instruction looks like this:

MOV Reg1, [Reg2+Reg3]

Reg 2 usually has the fixed base address. Reg 3 has the offset. Thus, by giving the offset value only, we can move the data from the resulting address to register 1. This is useful when arrays are used. Let's assume we have an array with 100 elements and we know the starting address of the array (base address). When we want to move the 79th array element, what we can do is give the instruction as MOV reg1, [reg2+79]. Since reg2 already contains the base address (whatever it is), the data from the resulting address of [base address plus 79 offset] will be moved to register 1.

Auto-increment addressing happens when data is moved/added from one location to another and the second location is incremented "after" the data is moved/added/ modified otherwise. The following example illustrates the process:

MOV reg1, [reg2]+d

The content of register 2 is an address. That address holds some data (say 40x). The data 40x is moved into register 1, and after the move, the contents of the address are incremented by one (default) or a value specified (d). If a value is not specified, the default is 1.

Auto-decrement addressing is similar to auto-increment except that the data is decremented before the data is moved/added/modified otherwise. An example is MOV reg1, [reg2]-d.

Note that both auto-increment and auto-decrement can be used before and after, as follows:

MOV reg1, +[reg2]+d means increment the value **AFTER** moving.

MOV reg1, -[reg2]-d means decrement **BEFORE** moving. Notice that the placement of + or – before or after the operand to decide whether increment or decrement happens before or after.

Note that when we execute an instruction "ADD R1, R2" the movement of data is always from right to the left. It means contents of register R2 are added to contents of register R1. This results in changes to contents of R1. But contents of R2 will remain the same after the instruction is executed.

Example: While addressing an array of 48 memory locations arranged as a 6x8 matrix, a member of the array can be pulled out with the row and column numbers as a two-dimensional member d(i, j) or a single-dimensional member as d(i*j). For example, the d(4, 7) represents the data at the 4th row and 7th column or is represented as d(28) in a one-dimensional array. The base index address of the array is in register 2. If the value of the 32nd array member d(4*8) is required to be loaded into register 1 using offset 32 stored in register 3, what instruction correctly can do this using indexed addressing?

A)   MOV reg1, [reg2+d(32)]

B)   MOV reg1, [reg2+reg3]

C)   MOV reg1, [reg2+32]

D)   MOV reg1, [48+47+32]

Analysis: Note that the verbiage is giving details of where the base address for the index and offset are stored. When all these are stored in registers, there is really no point in using any number or address locations directly. If we can remember that point, we can directly come to a conclusion and pick the correct answer.

Statement: The base index address of the array is in register 2. The value of the 32nd array member d(4*8) is required to be loaded into register 1 using offset 32 stored in register 3.

Question: With the base index address in register 2, if the value of the 32nd array member is required to be loaded into register 1 using offset 32 stored in register 3, what instruction correctly can do this using indexed addressing?

Solution: Note that the correct answer is option B. Options A, C, and D are wrong because they are using a value in the operand, but the verbiage states that the operands and offset are all stored in registers.

Review Questions

Several possible questions can be coined under this category. Some of them are listed here:

1. Register 2 contains the address "4356 9878." If the data in address [4356 9878] is 54, what will the data be after the following instruction is executed under auto-decrement addressing? Assume opcode ADD is used for addition.

   ADD reg1, [reg2]-

   A) 54

   B) 55

   C) 53

   D) 51

   Answer: When no increment or decrement value is specified, the default is 1. Thus, the correct answer is option C.

2. Hexadecimal data "3A4C" is moved to register 1 with the instruction "MOVE register1, 3040." What addressing does the instruction follow?

   Answer: When data is mentioned directly in the instruction, it is immediate addressing.

3. In the register addressing, the instruction "SUB R1, R2" was executed where "SUB" stands for subtract and R1 and R2 are register names. After the instruction execution, what data will the registers R1 and R2 contain? Assume {R1} or {R2} are contents of registers R1 or R2 and data movement is right to left.

   A) R1 contains {R1}, and R2 contains {R1}-{R2}.

   B) R1 contains {R1}-{R2}, and R2 contains {R2}.

   C) R1 contains {R1}, and R2 contains {R2}+{R1}-{R2}.

   D) R1 contains {R1}+{R2}-{R1}, and R2 contains {R2}.

   Answer: Option B

Data Retention

Tip #19: Two options of choosing to stay in or stay out have a very subtle difference

Clearly understand the difference between opt-in and opt-out options.

Domains: Security Engineering and Asset Security.

Subdomains: Data retention, Data security controls, Data handling requirements, Security architectures, Designs, etc.

Subject background: It is a common practice for organizations to collect information from users when the user orders a product either via a website or in person. The data collected can be public or private, and depending on what is collected, the organization is responsible for handling the information collected. Several laws and regulations - either private or public, kick in once data is collected. These include but are not limited to state, federal, and the newly introduced European Union's GDPR. While some organizations collect data before asking the consumers' permission to use it, others collect data and assume they can use it by default unless otherwise the customer objects to its use. Opt-in is a way of a consumer to choose whether they want to allow the organization to use the data collected. In opt-in, an organization cannot use the data collected for any use without the consumer opting in. Opt-out is a way organizations assume the data collected from consumer is free to use unless the customer tells the organization that they no longer want the organization to use their data. In short, opt-in is consumer-driven, whereas opt-out is organization-driven.

Things to Remember

Opt-in and opt-out usually are encountered by the consumers while creating an account on a website or while filling forms at a retail store where the user has to either check a box or uncheck a box. In opt-in, the user has to physically check a box and give consent telling the organization that using his data for uses other than collected is OK. In opt-out, a user may have to 1) uncheck a box that was automatically checked by the company by default (the company assumes the consumer is OK with this), 2) send a personal email to the organization telling them to stop using the consumer's data and stop the marketing blitz of their data and/or stop sending junk emails, or 3) go to the organization's designated website and inform the organization to stop using data or unsubscribe. For opt-out, some organizations make it easy to get out, but others make it difficult by asking several questions, directing the user to a couple of websites and so on.

Example: While registering for a free email account on a website offering limited free email service, a user is required to enter a username; password (twice); personal information such as age, date of birth, and gender; and occasionally the home address of residence in the United States. Before clicking the "Register" button at the bottom of the page, the user notices a checkbox that is automatically checked and disabled, giving permission for the website to use the user data freely for marketing and other purposes. The checked and disabled box is an indication that when getting a free email account the user has to accept the company's terms. What does the checked and disabled box **MOST** appropriately indicate to the user, directly or otherwise?

A)   The user has opted in to other services provided by the website to get the free email account.

B)   The user has opted out of the email service provided by the website to get the free email account.

C)   The user cannot register for the email account because the checkbox is disabled.

D)   The user may opt out later but has to register with the default opt-in to get the free email account.

Analysis: A checked box, whether enabled or disabled, is an indication of automatic opt-in. This means that the user is giving automatic permission for the company to share the information. If the box is disabled, it also means that the company will **NOT** provide email account to the user unless otherwise the opt-in is granted to the organization. That's how the "Register" button is programmed to work. If the user does not want to give the automatic option, for this particular website, there may not be any other way to provide free email service. The option that "may" work later is to call the company or email them to indicate that the user is opting out. That may take several days. In this case, the button indicates that the user must opt-in and may opt-out later in other ways.

Statement: While registering for a free email account, a user is required to enter a username; password (twice); and personal information such as age, date of birth, and gender. Before clicking the "Register" button at the bottom of the page, the user notices a checkbox that is automatically checked and disabled.

Question: What does the checked and disabled box **<u>MOST</u>** appropriately indicate to the user, directly or otherwise?

Solution: The answer is option D. Option A is not correct since the user did not purposefully check the opt-in box. Option B is not correct because the user did not send an email or uncheck a box. Option C is not correct too since one can register for email with the checkbox showing as checked and disabled. Note the wording in the question "MOST appropriately." There could be more than one correct answer, but the test taker has to pick the most accurate answer.

Review Questions

A variation of the question is the following:

1. If the "Register" button is not enabled until the checkbox is checked, what does it mean?

   Answer: In this case, the user is being forced to opt in to give free email access. Since there is no free lunch literally, the user has to opt in by checking the box, which will enable the Register button. This means, though, that the company has forced the user to check the box, and the user understands the risks of sharing their data with the company to get the free email account and access for email.

2. A website selling prescription medicine does not show any checkbox for opt-in or opt-out but shows a lengthy document in PDF in a text box. Before registering the account to order prescription medicine, the user has to read the document and agree to it before clicking the Order button. What kind of permission is the user giving the website?

   Answer: Once the document mentions (anywhere in the myriad of pages displayed in PDF) that the user agrees to the terms, it is an automatic opt-in.

3. After registering for an account on the Internet, David gets daily email about the products the website sells. He also receives weekly emails and annual emails about the stock value of the organization and a report. In every email there is a line that says, "If you do not want any emails from us further, please click here to unsubscribe." David clicks that link and goes to a website and unchecks "unsubscribe me from all emails and reports." What did David do?

Answer: David opted out of the marketing and data sharing of the organization. He is opting out since he physically unchecked the box and has earlier already been on the mailing list. It is his option to stop all the email he has been receiving.

4.   While talking to his pastor at church, Ozzie Ozone learned that he can subscribe to a daily email that gives uplifting thoughts on God and religion. Ozzie signed up for the daily email on the church's website and checked the box that said, "Yes, please send me daily email." What did Ozzie pick?

Answer: Ozzie Ozone picked to opt in since he wanted the email about religion and God in his mailbox daily. If he did not want an email, he should have never ticked the checkbox. In a way, opt-in is the choice of user to join. Likewise, opt-out is his choice of getting out from a list.

Tip #20: Learn to distinguish various types of memories and their use in a computer

Understand different memory types such as SRAM, DRAM, EPROM, EEPROM, Flash HDD, CD-ROM, ROM, and RAM.

Domain: Asset Security, Security Engineering.

Subdomain: Data retention, Types of memory, Backup and restore, Common system components, Security vulnerabilities, Threats.

Subject background: Memory in the computer systems of any IT system can be of two types: volatile memory or permanent memory. Volatile memory is also called random access memory (RAM), which is accessible for read and write and works at high speeds. RAM works as storage for programs to run when the processor needs. Therefore, to run more programs, usually more RAM is necessary. But when the power goes out, all the data in RAM is erased, which is why it gets the name as volatile memory.

ROM or read-only memory is the other type of memory that can hold the data for a long time or permanently. DVDs and CD-ROMs are examples of ROM. They are written once but read many times. But small flash drives or thumb drives that can be written and read many times are also considered partly as ROMs since they can retain data for a longer time without having to refresh with an active power connection.

Things to Remember

- **SRAM**: This is "static" RAM. It is made of digital flip-flops, each of which stores bits of information (true or false/ 1 or 0). Since more circuitry is needed for flip-flops, typically the costs for SRAM are higher as storage increses.

- **DRAM**: This is "dynamic" RAM. It consists of capacitors that store energy. Since the capacitors can "leak" and lose energy, to maintain the memory the DRAM needs power that refreshes it regularly. DRAM is cheaper than SRAM. The refresh process in DRAM is internal to the RAM and the processor.

- **PROM**: This is programmable ROM. Data can be inserted into this kind of chip (or integrated circuit) once by a program and cannot be erased.

- **EPROM**: This is erasable programmable ROM. This kind of memory chip has a window on top through which ultraviolet light can be passed to erase any data. It can also be programmed electrically. Note that exposing an EPROM chip to ultraviolet rays in a closed enclosure (a small unit similar to a microwave) erases the entire memory; there is no facility to erase only a part of the memory. Likewise, programming is done in its entirety to store data, not in parts.

- **EEPROM**: These chips are electrically erasable, programmable memories. They are generally used in IT systems for the firmware that needs updating (cars, desktop computers, microcontroller, keyless systems, smart cards, etc.). The flash drives or the USB thumb drives also come with EEPROM.

- **CD-ROM/DVD/BluRay**: These come both in writable form and in write-once-read-many-times forms. They can store large amount of data and are common to pass around for storage, backup, and restore.

- **HDD**: Hard disk drives (HDDs) are more common in laptop and desktop computers that store the operating system, programs to be installed, and user data. They are cheap and come in gigabytes of memory. A typical 2.5" HDD can hold several gigabytes to terabytes of data.

- **TAPE**: Tape backups and storage are considered sequential memories, since to get some data out of the tape, it has to run to a location sequentially from the current location, either in forward or backward motion. Tapes also can store large amounts of data and are used for backup and restore of the entire IT system infrastructure software.

- SRAM and DRAM also come in a variety of other formats such as video RAM. They can be installed on the motherboard or in an extended slot reserved for memory, also known as memory slots.

- Computer specifications usually list HDD, RAM, and a backup drive such as CD/DVD ROM when marketing a machine. Unless specifically stated, in such advertisements, memory invariably means it is RAM that is required to run the system.

- Programs from hard disk are loaded into RAM to run by the processor, and the data the loaded program uses is also in another part of the hard disk.

Example: A company's data center wants to update all their desktop computers with more memory. There are several options to buy, DRAM, flash, or hard disks. The cost to upgrade the memory is a factor, and the company wants reliable memory for an economical price. What is the **BEST** solution the company can implement across all the desktop and laptop computers?

A)   Implement a large secondary hard disk to avoid any memory problems

B)   Provide cheap and large flash memory sticks to each user as required

C)   Use DRAM to update the memory of desktops and laptops

D)   User SROM for laptops and DRAM for desktops

Analysis: Once the question talks about memory, anything related to hard disk, ROM, or flash is irrelevant since memory means it is RAM that is required to load the programs. Thus, the question is only asking what type of RAM the IT systems can be put with so the total price is economical to the company. Also note that there is no such thing as SROM mentioned in option D.

Statement: A company wants to update all its desktop computers with more memory. **The cost to upgrade the memory is a factor**, and the **company wants reliable memory** for an **economical price**.

Question: The **company wants reliable memory** for an **economical price**; what is the best solution the company can implement across all the desktop and laptop computers?

Solution: The straightaway answer is option C. Option A is wrong since hard disk is not what memory (asked in the question) stands for. Option B is wrong since flash memory is a backup type of device and not main RAM used in desktop or laptop computers. Option D is wrong because there is no such thing as SROM. DRAM is the best and cheapest solution for either desktop or laptop.

Review Questions

Several other questions can be asked such as the following:

1. Which of the following is a write-once-read-many-times memory?

    A) Partition memory (PM)

    B) Read-only always memory (ROAM)

    C) Random access memory

    D) Digital video disk (DVD)

    Answer: Option D

2. Which of the following is the **BEST** write-many-times-read-many-times memory with or without power supply being present?

    A) Read-only memory (ROM)

    B) Erasable programmable read-only memory (EPROM)

    C) Random access memory (RAM)

    D) Compact disk read-only memory (CD-ROM)

    Answer: The **BEST** option is option B. Note that option C can be written to and read from many times, but if power is off, RAM has no data and loses everything. ROM and CD-ROM are typically "write once and read many times" types of memories.

3. Why is flash memory usually flagged for high security?

    Answer: Flash memory sticks and disks are too small (typically the size of a human thumbnail) and can carry very large capacity data. Thus, data theft and loss can be easier compared to other memories. It is always best to encrypt such memory sticks to protect the data.

4. What type of memory is used for BIOS in a Windows operating system computer?

    Answer: EEPROM is the usual version for BIOS. It allows writing updates to BIOS. It can be also flash memory that is not available for the user to modify.

Data Security Controls, Data Protection

Tip #21: Learn the intricacies of mathematical operators used for modulo and division in cryptography

Understand how the modulo (%) and division (/) operators work. These operators are extensively used in cryptography and in ciphers.

Domains: Asset Security, Security Engineering, Communications, and Network Security.

Subdomain: Data security controls, Cryptography.

Subject background: The modulo function is represented by MOD and sometimes also used in math with %. Substitution ciphers and running key ciphers use the modulo operator. Adding a 3 (or any other number) to shift a value and then obtaining the modulo of the resulting value is a common method. For the CISSP certification exam, it is necessary to know how the MOD function works and how cryptography uses the integer division.

Many programming languages use the / operator as an integer division unless the variables used in the division are decimal point variables called decimals or floating-point variables.

The modulo used on two variables X and Y is indicated as X%Y, and integer division used on those is indicated as X/Y.

Things to Remember

The modulo operator is widely used in cryptography for several ciphers. The basic rules of modulo and division are as follows:

- When we say division (/), it is considered as integer division. This means there are no decimal places left over. For example, 12/7 is 1 (remainder 5 is discarded). Other examples are given here:

  - 205/2 = 102

  - 35/4 = 8

  - 93/8 = 11

  - 4/7 = 0

- Modulo gives the remainder of an integer division. For example, 12%7 is 5. Other examples are given here:

  - 28%5 = 3 (divides 5 times with a remainder of 3)

  - 42%7 = 0 (divides 6 times with a remainder of 0)

  - 275%9 = 5 (divides 30 times with a remainder of 5)

  - 3%5 = 3 (cannot divide; the remainder is 3)

Important note   In a modulo value, the remainder is always less than the divisor.

Example: Modulo, integer division, and multiplication functions are indicated as X%Y, X/Y, and X*Y, respectively. Which of the following functions is the **BEST** equivalent of X%Y?

A) X − (X/Y)

B) Y − (X/Y)

C) (X/Y) − (Y/X)

D) X − ((X/Y) * X)

Analysis: If we consider a couple of values for X and Y, we can easily find the solution for this question. The options we can choose for X and Y are X < Y, X > Y when the division is a perfect integer division with zero remainder. When X=Y, the modulo always evaluates obviously to zero.

Case 1: X > Y. Assume X = 13, Y = 3. For these values, the modulo evaluates as 13%3, which has a value of 1.

Option A evaluates as 13 – (13/3) = 13 – 4 = 11. Option B evaluates as 3 – (13/3) = 3 – 4 = -1. Option C evaluates as (13/3) – (3/13) = 4 – 0 = 4. Option D evaluates as 13 – ((13/3)*3). Remember that the inner parentheses, 13/3, is an integer division that evaluates as 4. Thus, we have 13 – (4*3) = 13 – 12 = 1, and option D is correct when X > Y.

Case 2: X < Y. Assume X = 7, Y = 11. For these values, the modulo evaluates as 7%11 = 7.

If we check the options given, option A evaluates to 7 – (7/11) = 7 – 0 = 7; option B evaluates to 11 – (7/11) = 11 – 0 = 11; option C evaluates to (7/11) – (11/7) = 0 – 1 = -1; and option D evaluates to 7 – ((7/11)*7). Since there is integer division inside the parentheses, we get the value as 7 – (0*7) = 7- 0 = 7. Both options A and D are correct answers for this instance.

Case 3: X and Y have a perfect division. Consider X = 125 and Y = 5. X/Y gives us 25, and X%Y evaluates as 0. Checking the options again, option A evaluates as 125 – (125/5) = 125 – 25 = 100. Option B evaluates as 5 – (125/5) = 5 – 25 = -20. Option C evaluates as (125/5) – (5/125) = 25 – 0 = 25. Option D evaluates as 125 – ((125/5) * 5)) = 125 – (25*5) = 125 – 125 = 0. Again, here we conclude that option D is the correct answer.

There are many other options, but these three cases will be sufficient to answer the question.

Statement: Which of the following functions is the **BEST** equivalent of X%Y?

Since we are aware of the symbols %, /, and *, which stand for modulo, integer division, and multiplication, the first sentence is just that – a statement of facts. The second sentence of the question is asking for the **BEST** equivalent of X%Y. In other words, in the absence of a mod function, how can we derive the modular value, if values X and Y are given?

Question: Which of the following functions is the **BEST** equivalent of X%Y?

Solution: Notice that from the analysis section case 2, we found there are two possible solutions, option A and option D. But option A does not work for cases 1 and 3. That's why we always have to choose the **BEST** answer where all cases fit comfortably.

For this reason, the answer is option D. Option D fits correctly for any values, as shown in Table 2-4. Any values for X and Y can be tested, and option D remains true.

Please also note that when there is a double parentheses as in option D, the inner parentheses and the multiplication take precedent first followed by the outer ones. See Table 2-4.

Table 2-4. *Modulo Values Calculated by a Given Function*

X	Y	X – ((X/Y) * Y)	X%Y
18	7	18 – ((18/7) * 7) = 18 – (2*7) = 18-14 = 4	4
13	15	13 – ((13/15)*15) = 13 – (0*15) = 13 – 0 = 13	13
34	17	34 - ((34/17)*17) = 34 – (2*17) = 34 – 34 = 0	0
29	12	29 – ((29/12)*12) = 29 – (2*12) = 29-24 = 5	5
97	97	97 – ((97/97) * 97) = 97 – (1*97) = 97 -97 = 0	0

Review Questions

A variation of question can be asked as follows:

1. Which operator is widely used in cryptography and ciphering and deciphering data?

   A) Multiplication operator ("*")

   B) Modulo operator ("%")

   C) Subtraction operator ("-")

   D) Comparison operator (">" or "<")

   Answer: Option B

2. The Caesar cipher adds a shift of three characters and uses the MOD function. If the ciphered function is stated as C = (P+3) MOD 26, what is the **BEST** possible deciphering function?

   A) P = (C - 26) MOD 3

   B) P = (C + 26) MOD 3

   C) P = (C + 3) MOD 26

   D) P = (C - 3) MOD 26

   Answer: Option D

3.   The value of 39%8 is equivalent to:

A) 8

B) 4

C) 7

D) -1

Answer: Option C

Data Handling Requirements: Markings, Labels, Storage, Destruction

Tip #22: Understanding the methods of physical and virtual destruction of information/data by various methods

Understand data destruction and erasure methods, both physical and virtual either manually or with software/hardware.

Domain: Asset Security, Security and Risk Management.

Subdomain: Data handling requirements, Marking, Labeling and destruction.

Subject background: Deleting files, pictures, or any data from hard disk, may not delete data permanently. Data remanence is a continuous problem on computers, memory chips, hard drives, and even paper copies. Several methods are required for each medium for the data to be completely erased or physically destructed. Data handling such as labeling, marking, storage, and destruction are part of the data life cycle and asset security.

Things to Remember

- Data remanence is the persistent data that remains on a medium after the deletion process.

- It is important to remove data completely when not required because inadvertent disclosure may cause problems.

- Methods to remove data are clearing, purging/sanitizing, overwriting, physical destruction, and degaussing among others.

- The method to adapt to remove data depends on the accessibility of the medium, the type of medium, and the possible consequences of destruction.

- Data destruction must follow the policies and not just destruct anything that is not currently used because data not currently used may be useful in the future.

- The complete removal of data is also known as "elimination of data remanence."

- Many operating systems keep the files in a temporary "holding area" when deleted because accidental deletion can or may require retrieval of the deleted file.

- A permanently deleted file even from the holding area may exist in some part of the disk or media in some cases. Therefore, such devices may need physical destruction or other form of cleaning/purging/sanitization.

- Reformatting, re-paging memory, reimaging, and repartitioning may or may not clear the data completely as well because all these are software-dependent utilities.

- **Clearing**: This is the removal of sensitive data in a way that it cannot be reconstructed with known utilities. But even with clearing, data may be recovered by disassembling and finding bits and pieces of the data.

- **Purging**: Also known as sanitizing, this is the removal of sensitive data so that it can never be reconstructed in anyway, even with physical disassembly.

- **Destruction**: This is the physical destruction. If the physical destruction is not done correctly, the data may still be recoverable. An example is tearing a sensitive document into just four pieces, assuming that nobody can find details. The four (or 8 or 16) pieces can be easily added together to gather the data.

- **Overwriting**: This is a method of repeatedly writing new data over the old tracks so that the old data is completely gone out of the medium. This is purely a software tool and erases data by writing a standard 0 or 1 to all fields/tracks all over the disk or memory device.

- For clearing, the process of overwriting the data, must be **repeated at least seven times** before making sure that the data is completely erased.

- **Encryption** is another process of preventing data theft. The contents of the memory or media are usually encrypted on a file-by-file basis or on an entire disk/media basis. Coupled with self-destructing/erasing methods, encryption is usually implemented by organizations such as the FBI in the case of theft or loss of equipment. After entering the wrong login password a fixed number of times, the device is programmed to self-destruct or encrypt so that the device cannot be used.

- **Degaussing**, as the name suggests, is a form of removing the magnetic field over the medium to erase the data stored on magnetic media. Degaussing needs to be repeated several times before the media is completely free of the old sensitive data. Degaussing will **NOT** work on optical data media such as CD/DVD/Blu-ray disks.

- **Physical destruction**: This includes breaking the media to pieces, altering the tracks with chemicals, pulverizing with a mill, and other such routes.

- Typical hard-wired applications that destroy data on hard disks, tapes, etc., **are ineffective** on solid-state devices (SSDs). Physical destruction is the best way.

Example: A company specialized in storing backup data for other organizations wants to destroy older magnetic tapes, hard disks, and some paper files with the due permission of each organization it represents and after backing up all the data on modern memory devices. The company proposes erasing data by overwriting the media five times, reformatting the hard disks four times, and then giving away the media to local county school systems for reuse. The paper files will be put in the trash for recycling. As a security expert, what do you think is wrong with these procedures?

A) Erasure, reformatting, and rewriting must be seven times.

B) Paper records need to be torn seven times before put in the trash.

C)   Degaussing methods are not used at all.

D)   None of the outlined procedures is really sufficient.

Analysis: Notice that the statement says that the company has several forms of media, such as paper, magnetic, and disks. Paper files put in the trash are not safe since anyone can pull them from the trash and steal the data (dumpster diving). Erasure must be properly done, and clearing data seven times will only work on one media. Since the organization has different media, one method does not fit these media. The options are all talking about one type of destruction or several types that may not suit all media. Note that the media will be given away for reuse. So, the erasing methods must ensure that the media is really, completely and reliably erased.

Statement: A company wants to destroy older magnetic tapes, hard disks, and some paper files. The company proposes to do a process of erasing data by **overwriting the media five times** and reformatting the **hard disks four times**. **The paper files will be put in the trash for recycling.**

Question: A company wants to destroy older magnetic tapes, hard disks, and some paper files. As a security expert, what do you think is wrong with these procedures?

Solution: The obvious answer is option D since none of the other methods given in the distractors of options A, B, and C is sufficient for various media that need to be cleaned up.

Review Questions

Some of the questions on this topic can be as follows:

1.   At a minimum, how many times does the data need to be overwritten for protection?

A) Six times

B) Five times

C) Eight times

D) Seven times

Answer: Option D

2. The **BEST** way to completely erase data on a CD/DVD media is:

   A) Degaussing seven times

   B) Overwriting four times

   C) Physical destruction

   D) Purging with 1s and 0s

   Answer: Option C

3. The **BEST** definition of degaussing a media is:

   A) Rewriting additional data to the existing magnetic media

   B) Removing the data by passing the media through strong magnetic fields

   C) Rewriting magnetic data to other forms of storage

   D) Removing magnetic media for physical destruction

   Answer: Option B

4. Which of the following **BEST** describes the process of purging sensitive data?

   A) Data is overwritten once with 0s and 1s.

   B) Once removed, data cannot be recovered by any method.

   C) Reformatting the storage media for future use.

   D) Reimaging the media with a known baseline image.

   Answer: Option B

5. Which of the following is the **BEST** way to remove sensitive data from any medium?

   A) Physical destruction

   B) Reformat, reimage, and restore

   C) Rewrite data seven times

   D) Degauss and overwrite

   Answer: Option A

6. What is the **BEST** way to clear the data remanence in random access memory (RAM) in an electronic device?

    A) Cool with liquid nitrogen.

    B) Write new data to RAM.

    C) Power down the device.

    D) RAM data clears automatically.

    Answer: Option C

7. The **BEST** way to destroy data on a Blu-ray optical disk is:

    A) Overwrite and reformat data seven times

    B) Submersion in Acetone or other polycarbonate solvent

    C) Submersion in hot water and Clorox for three days

    D) Reimage the CD as a startup disk

    Answer: Option B. It is a chemical process that destroys data.

8. What is the **BEST** definition of data remanence?

    A) Data that remains on the media after deleting/removal

    B) Data that was erased after deleting/removal

    C) Data that remains to be written to the media

    D) Blank data space that is left over on media after writing

    Answer: Option A

9. Why are several methods required to address data remanence?

    Answer: One method is never really sufficient to delete data from a medium in a reliable manner. The **only sure way** to completely remove sensitive data from a medium is by complete physical destruction.

Public Key Infrastructure (PKI)

Tip #23: Securing devices with personal electronic certificates and private and public keys

Learn about Public Key Infrastructure/Certificate Authority (PKI/CA), public and private keys, and certificate publishing.

Domain: Security Engineering, Asset Security.

Subdomain: Cryptography, Key infrastructure, Certificate authority, Public Key Infrastructure (PKI).

Subject background: Public key cryptography deals with public and private keys and how to manage those keys. Asymmetric algorithms that can generate the public and private keys deal with key pairs, do the exchange of keys, and can generate digital signatures. Key pairs can be used with the Advanced Encryption Standard (AES) for authentication, encryption, and electronic signature as well.

Asymmetric algorithms are used to create public and private key pairs. A message that is sent with one key can only be opened with the other key. The same key will not work for both creating/writing and reading. This means if a user creates an email message and encrypts with his private key, other people can only decrypt the message with the user's public key.

Public and private keys are functions of large prime numbers.

Encryption creates cipher text from normal text, and decryption creates a normal text from encrypted text.

Salt is a random number used in the encryption process.

A prime number is defined as a number that has only two factors: 1 and the number itself. Examples are 11, 17, 23, etc.

PKI is a group of formats, programs, data, protocols, associated protocols, etc. PKI is created for a wide range of people to exchange messages, data, and other details.

PKI creates and maintains a level of trust among users who in turn trust the infrastructure.

PKI uses a public key certificate (PKC) and has an X.509 standard for its certificates. PKI can work with different authentication tools among different networks as well.

PKI contains keys, authorities, users, and users' certificates.

A certificate authority (CA) is a trusted third party that allows people to communicate in a secure way. CA issues digital certificates for each user and maintains them.

A private key is known only to the user. But a user's public key is known to all others who communicate with that user.

A CA can be internal or external to an organization. Examples of trusted external CAs are Entrust and VeriSign, which are typically used for credit card processing on the Internet.

The main responsibility of CAs is to <u>create and maintain</u> digital certificates.

When a certificate is revoked or made invalid, it is stored in a certificate revocation list (CRL).

There are several reasons to create an entry in CRL. One is the expiration of certificates, and the others are a user leaving an organization voluntarily and a user's certificate being compromised by a hacking attack.

The Online Certificate Status Protocol (OCSP) is also used instead of CRL.

The registration authority (RA) performs registration duties.

Things to Remember

- Asymmetric algorithms use private and public keys.

- Signature generation and encryption go one way, whereas signature verification and decryption goes the other way in messages (for authentication and security).

- If a message is encrypted with a private key, it can only be decrypted with a public key, or vice versa. The same key will not work for both encryption and decryption. This is also known as a one-way function.

- The work factor is the amount of time and resources that would need to break the encryption method.

- Examples of asymmetric algorithms are RSA, El Gamal, elliptic curve cryptosystem, Diffie-Hellman, and Knapsack among others.

- A session key created from a user's public key has a limited time of life before which it should be used to exchange information.

- The CA issues certificates, and the RA acts as a middleman between the CA and the end user.

- When users need new certificates, the request is sent to the RA, which verifies all the necessary details before the CA can issue a certificate.

- PKI must conform to confidentiality, integrity, and authenticity. It also has the security features of nonrepudiation and access control.

- PKI retains the key history (of users).

- Hashing is a one-way function and provides data integrity only.

- The most challenging job of cryptography is key management.

- A digital signature is created always with a sender's private key, and nobody else has access to this key except the sender.

- In asymmetric algorithm, a message being sent is always encrypted with the receiver's public key, and the receiver will decrypt it with his private key.

Example: An organization has created its own certificate authority (CA), and all the users who communicate over email are issued valid certificates that are used for digital signatures, authentication, and encryption. If a newly joined user David wants to send an email to another user named John, what should David do **FIRST**?

A)   Request a certificate with the certificate authority (CA)

B)   Request a certificate with the registration authority (RA)

C)   Request a certificate with the certificate revocation authority (RCA)

D)   Encrypt email with David's signature and public key

Analysis: Note that the question is asking what a <u>**new**</u> user David should do **FIRST**. When a user joins an organization, his first step is to request for a certificate since the organization has its own CA. Sending email or exchange of information and all that comes much later once the CA issues a certificate.

But how does the new user apply for a certificate? It is through the registration authority that the user confirms his identity and initiates a process for new certificate.

Statement: An organization has created its own certificate authority (CA).

We can easily remove the verbiage used and re-coin the question as follows:

Question: If a <u>**new**</u> user David wants to send an email to another user named John, what should David do **FIRST**?

Solution: Option B is the correct answer. Option A looks tempting, but the CA does not confirm identity or checks. It just issues certificates. To apply for that certificate, David will need the RA. Option C is wrong because the CRA is used for people whose certificates have been invalidated or revoked. Option D is not the **FIRST** thing David needs to do and is thus wrong too.

Review Questions

Some variations of the questions can be as follows:

1. What is the difference between public key cryptography (PKC) and public key infrastructure (PKI)?

   Answer: PKC is the usage of an algorithm. PKI is an infrastructure created to deal with PKC.

2. If David sends an email message with a disclaimer and his digital signature to another user John, the term used for the fact that David cannot claim he did not send the message with disclaimer is known as:

   A) Nondisclaimer

   B) Nonrepudiation

   C) Repudiation

   D) Disclaimer

   Answer: Option B

3. If David wants to send message to John, what key should David use for encrypting the message and for the digital signature?

   Answer: For encryption David uses John's public key, and for the signature David uses his own private key to generate the signature.

4. For which of the following the Online Certification Status Protocol (OCSD) is **BEST** used?

   A) To create new status for a digital certificate

   B) To check for a revoked digital certificate online

   C) To renew the status of an expired digital certificate

   D) To request for a new digital certificate online

   Answer: Option B

5. What is the main purpose of a hash?

   A) To encrypt the message

   B) To provide integrity of the message

   C) To provide a public key to the message

   D) To encrypt and decrypt the message

   Answer: Option B

6. What is the standard for digital certificates?

   A) X.590

   B) X.509

   C) X.950

   D) X.905

   Answer: Option B

7. What is the main purpose of a certificate authority (CA)?

   A) Create certificates via registration service

   B) Create and maintain certificates

   C) Create, maintain, and revoke certificates

   D) Create, maintain, revoke, and register certificates

   Answer: Option B

Intellectual properties and protection

Tip #24: Learning the detailed life spans of intellectual properties such as documents and inventions

Remember the time frames for each of the types of trade documents, intellectual property, etc.

   Domain: Asset security, Security and Risk Management.

   Subdomain: Intellectual properties, Protection of data/trade secrets.

   Subject background: Table 2-5 briefly describes each type of document and how long it is protected.

Table 2-5. *Life Spans of Intellectual Properties*

Type	Length	Details
Trademark	10 years	A symbol, word, slogan, design, color, or logo that identifies the source of a product or service. Can be a product or a service. Examples are iPhone, WhatsApp, etc. Uses SM or TM symbol. Can be renewed indefinitely.
Patent	20 years	Most patents are for businesses as utility patents or design patents. Some can be plant design patents. Improvements of a process also fall as patents. The United States Patent and Trademark Office (US PTO) helps with registration or patents.
Copyright	Lifetime of author + 70 years for people and 95 years for organizations or companies	Print, copy, publish, perform, film or record, etc. Also derivative work like translations, etc. Examples: novels, paintings, films, songs, etc. Uses the © symbol
Trade secret	As long as possible	Trade secrets are usually formulas that mix to make a drink, a medicine, a dose, or anything such. They can be protected for as long as required, and there is no paper registration or document required but can be written down and stored. An example is the drink formula for Coca-Cola or an energy drink.
License	Fixed period mutually agreed between parties and can be usually renewed	These are contracts between one or more parties, called the licensor and licensee(s). the licensees pay a royalty for transfer of intellectual property to the licensor. Licenses help market better products to markets over a wide range of geographic areas.

Things to Remember

- A product or service can have multiple intellectual property rights such as patents, trademarks, copyrights, and so on.

- A service mark (SM) is a typical trademark, but it is for a service rather than a tangible product.

- Royalties are usually based on a percentage of the revenue the licensee generates from the sale of products and pays to the licensor.

- Patents protect the right of original inventor.

- Registering for a trademark is **not** necessary by law but helps the owner of product. Registered trademarks are valid for 10 years and can be renewed and used with the° symbol.

- Patent holders have an obligation to enforce their rights. Failure to enforce rights is considered as patent abandonment.

- There is no fixed number of patents or copyrights or trademarks one can own or a product/service can have.

- Service agreements can also force a user or business to abide the rules of the agreement despite having a trademark or patent. For example, AT&T can enforce a service agreement for two years by selling you an iPhone and service at a lower price than T-Mobile.

Example: After retirement, an international tennis player wants to start a group of businesses. He has a new idea for an energy drink, an idea for a book to write his autobiography, and a new design for a tennis racket. With each of these products, a free new T-shirt exclusively designed by the player will be presented to the buyers. What should the player register for to **BEST** protect his interests in his life and businesses?

A) Patent for tennis racket, copyright for book, trade secret for energy drink

B) License for energy drink, trademark for tennis racket, patent for energy drink

C) Trademark for tennis racket, license for book, trade secret for energy drink

D) Trade secret for energy drink, trademark for tennis racket, patent for book

Analysis: Observe that the player is trying to put more than one business into market and needs several things to be registered. The easiest of these is an autobiography that will be automatically protected under copyright laws. There is no registration required for copyrights. The tennis racket is a tangible product as well, and it needs a patent for the innovative design. The energy drink has a mixture the player alone probably knows and needs a trade secret. It need not be registered but needs to be protected with utmost care. If we know these facts, the question is easy to answer.

Statement: A T-shirt is given freely, and it appears from the question that the player does not want to worry about it since it is being given freely if anyone purchases a racket, book, or the drink. Removing the verbiage we can find the following:

Question: A tennis player has a **new idea** for an energy drink, **an idea for a book** to write his autobiography, and a **new design** for a tennis racket. What should the player register for to protect the **BEST** interests of his businesses?

Solution: Licenses are given for a product after the product is already in the market and when the original inventor wants to expand his marketing territory to larger areas. The license does not apply immediately to a new product. Licenses do not also apply to books. Thus, options B and C are wrong choices. Books also do not carry patents since the writing is considered a type of copyright material. Thus, option D can be easily eliminated. This gives the correct answer as option A.

Review Questions

Several questions can be asked in this area as follows:

1. How long is a copyright valid for a business or an organization?

    A) Lifetime plus 70 years

    B) 95 years

    C) Lifetime plus 100 years

    D) Lifetime

    Answer: Option B. For an individual, copyright is valid for a lifetime plus 70 years, but for a business it is 95 years.

2. The symbol issued by the United States Patent and Trademark Office for a service is:

    A) SMr

    B) SM

    C) SeM

    D) SrM

    Answer: Option B

3. A company wants to protect its intellectual property for a health drink has the **BEST** protection under what?

    A) Trademark

    B) Copyright

    C) License

    D) Trade secret

    Answer: Option D is correct. Trade secrets protect the property better than anything for a health drink.

4. Where should the trade secrets be mandatorily registered?

    A) US Patent Trademark Office

    B) Federal government

    C) State government

    D) No registration required

    Answer: Option D. Trade secrets do not need any mandatory registration.

5. What is the **BEST** term for the money a licensor gets from one or more licensees to transfer intellectual property?

    A) Service fees

    B) License fees

    C) Royalty fees

    D) Product fees

    Answer: Option C

6. An inventor wants to patent his product and give a license to another company to market it in the state of California. How long are the patent and license valid for at **BEST**?

    Answer: A patent is valid for 10 years, and a license is valid for mutually agreeable period.

7. In how many ways can a patent be **BEST** registered?

    A) Service patent, plant patent, and supply patent

    B) Business patent, utility patent, and design patent

    C) Utility patent, trade patent, and product patent

    D) Private patent, public patent, and universal patent

    Answer: Option B

8. A parent, trademark, copyright, or a license of an inventor at **BEST** can protect what?

    A) Intellectual property

    B) Business property

    C) Public and private property

    D) Financial property

    Answer: Option A

9. A publisher translates a book without the original author's permission and releases the book in the translated language in another country. What rights can the original author **BEST** use to protect his literary work?

    Answer: Copyright laws protect the author even for translations and derivatives.

CHAPTER 3

Security Engineering

In this chapter, you will learn tips for security engineering, evaluation models, frameworks, cryptography, digital signatures, and database architecture security, along with the physical security for buildings and facilities.

Security Models, Modes, and Fundamentals

Tip #25: Understand the security models

Remember the security models of Bell–LaPadula, Biba, Clark–Wilson, Brewer–Nash, and other models.

Domain: Security Engineering.

Subdomain: Systems Security, Security modes, Evaluation.

Subject background: The basic aim of security model is to map the goals of the company's security policy to protect the systems. In other words, the models translate the security policy terms to implementable systems specifications for administrators/ programmers.

Note that the security policy itself is not concerned with how the policy rules are implemented.

Things to Remember

Remember that if there is an "i" in the model name, that model stands for integrity (Biba, for example). If the model name does not have "i" (Bell–LaPadula, for example), then it is for confidentiality.

The Bell–LaPadula model has the rule of "no-read up and no write-down." An example is an employee working for a supervisor. The employee cannot read his supervisor's emails or information concerning the supervisor (no read up). The supervisor does not inform the employee about everything occurring at his level (no write down). Note that write up and read down are allowed. It means the employee can

© R. Sarma Danturthi 2020
R. S. Danturthi, *70 Tips and Tricks for Mastering the CISSP Exam*,
https://doi.org/10.1007/978-1-4842-6225-2_3

inform a security breach happening at his level to the supervisor, and the supervisor can read what the employee is doing. This model enforces <u>confidentiality</u>.

Any system that implements **Bell–LaPadula is a multilevel security system**. This is because at each level users require a different clearance, and the system processes data at different classification levels.

Subjects have a clearance level, and the objects have a classification level.

The "simple property" means reading. In Bell–LaPadula, it is no read-up.

The "star property" (* property) means writing. In Bell–LaPadula it is no write down.

The "strong * property" means read and write. In the Bell–LaPadula model, a user can do the "strong * property" at the same security level they are allowed to work. This also means the subject's clearance and object's classification must be equal.

The Biba model is the exact opposite of the Bell–LaPadula model and states the rule as "no read down (simple integrity) and no write up (the * integrity)." Biba deals with the "integrity" of data that is dealt with in an IT system.

In the Biba model, a subject cannot request a service at a higher integrity (the Invocation property).

Bell–LaPadula and Biba are known as <u>information flow</u> models.

The model that combines both Bell–LaPadula and Biba is known as the **Lipner model**.

The Clark–Wilson model also is an integrity model (notice the "i" in "Wilson"). The Clark–Wilson model has a different approach than Biba in that it has different elements: 1) users, 2) transformation procedures, 3) constrained data items, 4) unconstrained data items, and 5) integrity verification procedures.

Clark–Wilson model's main focus is on well-formed transactions (meaning the procedure knows that the data is reliable or can be trusted).

Clark–Wilson separates the data into two different sections: constrained data items and unconstrained data items. Users follow transformation procedures to modify the data. Thus, this model requires separation of duties.

The noninterference model dictates that any changes in actions at a higher level do not interfere with lower-level actions. In other words, this model does not leak information to a lower level.

The Brewer–Nash model deals with a <u>conflict of interest</u> and is used where access controls <u>can change dynamically</u> depending on previous actions. This is also called a <u>Chinese wall</u> model. The subject can write to an object if and only if the subject cannot read another object in any other dataset. It is a kind of separation in an enclosure.

The Graham Denning model addresses the weakness of the Bell–LaPadula and Bibo models. It has eight different primitive protection rights.

The Harrison-Ruzzo-Ullman (HRU) model deals with subjects' access rights and the integrity of those rights. The HRU model is useful in software coding to avoid unforeseen vulnerabilities.

Example: Which of the following models clearly defines a "* integrity property?"

A) Biba model

B) Bell–LaPadula model

C) Graham–Denning conflict model

D) Brewer–Nash Chinese wall model

Analysis: Notice that the question is asking about "* integration." When we say integration model, we know it should an "i" in the wording. There is no such model as given by option C because the Graham–Denning model addresses what is not addressed by Bell–LaPadula and Biba. Also, the Graham Denning model does not talk about separation of duties or data and does not deal with conflict of interest. Thus, our answer is clearly option A. Options B and D can be easily eliminated because both options indicate confidentiality models (no "i").

Statement: Which of the following models clearly defines a <u>strong</u> "* integrity property"?

Question: Which model clearly defines a strong "* integrity property?"

Solution: Option A is a clear solution for this question since it ideals with integrity and has a strong * property.

Review Questions

The CISSP exam really is particular to ask at least two or three questions on these security models, and they need to be remembered for their use. Some of the questions can be as follows:

1. Which model deals with subjects making use of transformation procedures and is an integrity model?

    Answer: Clark–Wilson model.

2. Which model defines separation of duties and enforces data types such as constrained data and unconstrained data be dealt with separately?

    Answer: Clark–Wilson model

3. What is the no read up property defined in the Bell–LaPadula model?

    Answer: Simple property. (Remember, the hint "read" is a simple property and "write" is * (star) property.)

4. Which of the following models deals with confidentiality?

    A)   Biba model

    B)   Clark–Wilson model

    C)   Bell–LaPadula model

    D)   Brewer–Nash mode

    Answer: Option C

5. Which model adjusts access controls dynamically and protects against conflict of interest?

    Answer: Brewer–Nash model

6. This model states that actions done at one level should not be seen or visible to another level, either upper or lower:

    Answer: Noninterference model

7. Which model can combine both integrity and confidentiality and can overcome the drawbacks of individual models dealing separately with integrity and confidentiality?

    Answer: Graham–Denning model

8. Which model offers a multilevel security system that says that subjects at a clearance level have to deal with objects of the same level and not others?

    Answer: Bell–LaPadula model

Tip #26: Know the different operating states a computer's CPU can be found in

Learn the operating states of the CPU such as wait, problem, read and supervisory, etc.

Domain: Security and Risk Management, Asset Security, Security Engineering.

Subdomain: Secure states, Security models, Security modes, and Operating modes in an information system.

Subject background: The central processing unit (CPU) is the heart of an information system and can be programmed in any way one likes. The CPU can work as a multitasking unit, as a single-tasking unit, or as a combination of these. When more than one CPU is used to speed up a process, this can be called a "multiprocessor" environment. Multitasking can be effortlessly accomplished with various programming techniques such as threading.

Ready: The CPU is ready to execute a process given to it. This means the CPU will run the process immediately after the process is attached and will revert to a ready state when the process is completed either successfully or unsuccessfully. In this state, the CPU has all the memory, program, and resources available to execute the process and can start immediately without wait or delays.

Waiting: When the CPU is in the wait state, it is waiting for some action to happen or a resource to become available. For example, if the print process was executed and the printer is busy printing other documents, the CPU will remain in the wait state until it gets the printer ready. Also, this can happen when the DVD drive bay is open for a new DVD to be inserted. When the resource is available, the CPU will get out of the wait state and start executing the process.

Running/busy: The CPU in this state is really executing a process that keeps the CPU busy doing that work. For example, if an infinite loop that has no exit strategy defined is executed, then the process can keep the CPU in running state until something crashes the system. From a running/busy state, the CPU can go back to ready or waiting states depending on what the process does and what it demands. The running state is sometimes called a "problem" state. <u>A problem state is one that is running a problem, **not** causing a problem.</u>

Supervisory: In supervisory state, the CPU must run a process that is executed at a higher level. Whatever the CPU is executing before the supervisory commands are issued are kept in memory as background. After the CPU completes the supervisory process, it can resume the other processes it pushed to the background.

Stopped: When a process does not terminate in the usual way, the CPU is forced to stop it (or when the resource is not available). When the CPU does this action, it is in a stopped state. The stopped state is not permanent since modern CPUs mostly have several processes running, and when the CPU stops a process, it will revert to the next available process to continue executing.

Things to Remember

- The operating states of the CPU are also called process states.

- The security modes (dedicated, system high, compartmental, and multilevel) are different from the security states of the CPU.

- The operating modes (user, privileged, supervisor, and kernel) are also different from the states of the CPU.

- From stopped, running, and supervisory modes, the CPU may go back to "wait" or "ready" states for other processes to resume.

- It is possible to put the CPU in a stopped or waiting mode with a heck of some devil code that can crash the system, but most modern IT systems can probably withstand this kind of code or scripting since "availability" is one of the three themes of the CIA security triad.

- The problem state is also known as the running state since the CPU is solving a problem (rather than being in a problem-causing condition).

- Processes are run in first-come, first-served mode by the CPU unless a supervisory mode process gets into the business.

- When a supervisory state is requested by a process, the current processes that are in queue, running, etc., will be kept in memory (also called a stack) in wait state. When the supervisory process is complete, the CPU will switch back to the queue at a position where it left before starting the supervisory process.

- A supervisory process has the topmost priority to be run by the CPU.

- Processes submitted to the CPU are usually managed by the process scheduler.

Example: An information system's CPU can be programmed to accept processes in a queue or as they occur. Supervisory processes have top priority and should be done first and immediately when a request to start a supervisory process occurs. A CPU has a current queue of processes named A, B, C, and D, with A being the first process followed by B, C, and D. While running process B, a supervisory process named S with higher privileges requests an action from the CPU. When process S is taken up for processing, what does the CPU do with process B, and where does it return after process S is completed?

A) Process B is abandoned, and the CPU goes to process C after process S is completed.

B) Process B is gets temporarily suspended, and the CPU goes to restart the queue from process A after process S is completed.

C) Process B is suspended, and the CPU goes back to process B's suspended point after process S is completed.

D) The entire queue is cleared of any processes, and the CPU goes to the ready state after process S is completed since process S is a top-level priority.

Analysis: Note that there is some verbiage of explanation of process states in the first few sentences. The next one or two sentences explain what is actually in the queue when a supervisory process S is requested. Every IT system has good memory and a queue of processes to run. Whenever a supervisory state is requested, the current queue is kept in memory/the stack, and after completion of process S, the CPU will return the queue to a point where it left before process S was requested. No processes are ever abandoned unless the user/process requests a cancellation.

Statement: A CPU has a current queue of processes named A, B, C, and D, with A being the first process followed by B, C, and D.

Question: While running process B, a supervisory process named S with higher privileges requests an action from the CPU. When process S is taken up for processing, what does the CPU do with process B, and where does it return when process S is completed?

Solution: Clearly, option C is correct answer. Option B comes close to process B suspension but states that the CPU will return to process A, which is wrong. Options A and D are clearly wrong since no process is abandoned by the CPU/process manager and the queue is never cleared automatically by the supervisor process.

Review Questions

Several confusing and straightforward questions can appear on the CISSP exam. Here are some:

1. Which of the following is a valid state of a CPU?

    A) Dedicated

    B) Privileged

    C) Supervisory

    D) Kernel

    Answer: Option C. Option A is a security mode, and options B and C are operating modes.

2. Which CPU state needs a higher set of privileges to run?

    A) Low-security kernel state

    B) High-security wait state

    C) Supervisory state

    D) High-security privileged state

    Answer: Option C

3. A CPU currently in a problem state can return to what state after the process is complete?

    Answer: A CPU can return to the ready state when a problem or running state is completed.

4. For what reason can a CPU be in a wait state?

    A) The CPU is waiting for a resource/process to be ready.

    B) The CPU is in a ready state and waiting for a process.

C) The CPU is in a supervisor state and has nothing in the queue.

D) The process manager has commands to clear the queue.

Answer: Option A

5. What is the difference between a process state and an operating state of an IT system?

A) The process state is when the CPU is in action, and the operating state is when the CPU lies dormant.

B) The process state is when the CPU is dormant, and the operating state is when the CPU is in action.

C) They are both the same.

D) The process state is about the CPU, and the operating state is about the operating system like Windows/Linux/Unix.

Answer: Option C

6. How are processes lined up in a queue processed by the CPU if the CPU uses time sharing?

Answer: Each process is allotted a particular time slot, and the CPU works from one slot to another and completes the processes as first-come, first-served in a round-robin method. In its given slot, a process is worked by the CPU, saved into memory, to be taken up again when the time is available for the same process later.

7. A CPU in a problem state that has no pending processes in its queue can go to which of the following states when it completes the current process?

A) Supervisor state

B) Stopped state

C) Wait State

D) Secure State

Answer: Option B. Option D is wrong because there is no "secure state" for processes.

Security Evaluation Models

Tip #27: Remember the evaluation assurance levels

Remember the evaluation assurance levels and how they are stacked correctly from level 1 to level 7. It is also important to know what each level corresponds to.

Domain: Security Engineering, Security Assessment and Testing.

Subdomain: Security fundamental concepts, Security evaluation models.

Subject background: Common Criteria (CC) is a kind of global criteria to designate a system/product as secure. CC gives ratings for evaluation from 1 to 7, which are given as EAL1 to EAL7. The CC rating does not give a foolproof assurance that the system is completely free of problems and vulnerabilities. Rather, they are some kind of evaluation to say that they were tested, checked, reviewed, or verified. Table 3-1 explains the EAL levels 1 to 7.

Table 3-1. *Evaluation Assurance Levels*

Level	Assurance Level
EAL 1	F: Functionally tested (T)
EAL 2	S: Structurally tested (T)
EAL 3	M: Methodically tested and checked (TC)
EAL 4	M: Methodically tested, designed, and reviewed (TDR)
EAL 5	S: Semiformally tested and designed (TD)
EAL 6	S: Semiformally tested designed and verified (TDV)
EAL 7	F: Formally tested, designed and verified (TDV)

Note: T is Tested, D is Designed, V is Verified, C is Checked.

Things to Remember

- **Structural**: A way to see the program behavior against the code's intent.

- **Functional**: A way to see the program's behavior against the original requirements.

- **Methodical**: A way to go from the design stage until the end using good practices.

- **Semi-formal**: A way that uses direct and rigorous engineering techniques.

- **Formal**: Uses extensive formal analysis (for high-risk cases, high-value assets).

- **Security target (ST)**: The ST is a set of measures a vendor claims to have "provided" to the TOE. These are what are built in to the system.

- **Target of evaluation (TOE)**: A TOE is the system being evaluated. This can be a system, a software package, or anything else.

- **Protection profile (PP)**: A protection profile is what the user "wants" on the TOE. In other words, the PP consists of the given requirements by the user.

Products can be marked as meeting a level such as EAL4, or they can be marked as EAL4+, which indicates the product may meet levels 4 and above. But a product meeting an assurance level is not 100% foolproof. Rather, it is a stamp that says it was tested, checked, designed, and/or verified. It is still possible the product or system can have vulnerabilities that somehow fell through the cracks of the common criteria assurance levels.

Note that the CISSP exam can ask two types of questions. One is to match the left side to the right side by using a drag-and-drop method. These EALs are given in a random order on the left and are asked to be arranged in correct 1 to 7 order on the right. In the second type of question, you need to pick one correct answer out of the given four.

In the first method, remember the order, or FSMMSSF, which is indicated in Table 3-1, and the end values as T, T, TC, TDR, TD, TDV, TDV. This second order follows some kind of alphabetical order starting with T, TC, and TD.

Example: Which of the following **BEST** matches evaluation assurance level 5 (EAL-5) according to the common criteria for a system security?

A)   Methodically checked, tested, verified, and designed

B)   Structurally checked, tested, and designed

C)   Semiformally tested and designed

D)   Semiformally tested, verified, and designed

Analysis: Notice from Table 3-1 given in this tip that there is no EAL that has all four: designed, checked, tested, and verified (TCDV). This alone will disqualify option A. Also notice that none of the EALs has a tested, checked, and designed (TCD) option. Thus, option B is also invalid. Of the remaining options, options C and D, EAL 5 deals with "semiformally" but only tested and designed ways, **not** verified ways. Option D fits well to EAL 6. This is the reason the question asks for the **BEST** possible answer than any answer that is close to EAL-5.

Notice that two answers, options C and D, are very close and distract the reader. Unless one is really well aware of the EAL definitions, it is difficult to pick the correct answer. The same can happen in drag-and-drop questions as well. This is the main reason the CISSP exam taker needs to be familiar with the EALs and their respective ranking.

Statement: Which of the following **BEST** matches evaluation assurance level 5 (EAL-5)?

Question: Which **BEST** matches evaluation assurance level 5 (EAL-5)?

Solution: Option C best matches EAL-5. Option D is actually EAL-6. It is easy to pick the correct answer if you have the levels memorized correctly. But a lot of variations in question can confuse the reader.

Review Questions

Several variations are shown here:

1. EAL-4 of the common criteria is defined as "methodically tested" and what else?

   A) Designed and reviewed

   B) Checked and reviewed

   C) Tested and checked

   D) Checked and designed

   Answer: Option A is correct. EAL-4 is "methodically tested, designed, and reviewed."

2. EALs per common criteria are targeted toward:

   A) Security target (ST)

   B) Target of evaluation (TOE)

C) An assurance guideline

D) Protection profiles

Answer: EALs are given for a system being evaluated. The answer is Option B. Option C does not qualify as an answer.

3. What capabilities of a system does the common criteria (CC) define with various levels of testing and confirmation?

A) Assurance capabilities

B) Security capabilities

C) Threat capabilities

D) Protection capabilities

Answer: Option B. EALs are for checking the security capabilities.

4. The common criteria that defines the seven levels of assurance from EAL-1 to EAL-7 is:

A) An American standard defined by the National Institute of Standards and Technology (NIST)

B) An international standard by the International Standards Organization (ISO)

C) An American standard defined by the National Assurance Institute (NAI)

D) A European standard defined by the General Data Protection Regulation (GDPR)

Answer: Option B. GDPR and NIST have no hand in the EALs. There is no national assurance institute per se.

Database Architectures and Security

Tip #28: Learn the basic principles of database engineering

In this section, you'll learn about database ACID details, what they mean, and how they are applied among various database programs such as Oracle, SQL Server, etc. You'll also learn other database terms of interest that can be featured on the CISSP certification examination.

Domains: Security Engineering, Software Development Security.

Subdomain: Database architectures and security, Database security, Enforcing software security, Software development security fundamentals skillset.

Subject background: Databases are background programs that store data for web pages and front-end applications on Windows or the Internet. Basic modern databases come in two types: relational and object-oriented. Relational databases (RDBs) have tables that are closely related via keys such as primary keys, foreign keys, and candidate keys. Object-oriented databases (OODs) contain programs such as JavaScript inside their tables. RDBs contain only data, but OODs can contain data or programs or anything else a user wants to put in. The most popular relational databases are Oracle, SQL Server, and PostgreSQL, among others. **Note:** RDB tables can be designed to store OOD-type data. Both RDBs and OODs usually have the ACID properties, which are explained next.

Things to Remember

ACID stands for the following:

- **A – Atomicity**: This property of a database dictates that an operation on the database is "all or nothing." This means when an operation to modify/edit/read/write is given to the database, the operation is done in its entirety or it is aborted without doing anything. A partial operation on database is never done.

- **C – Consistency**: This property dictates that when an operation to modify/edit/read/write is given to the database, the DB's state, constraints, and other conditions that are already in place, do not change. The operation completes only what is asked from it and does not work on the original conditions of the DB. In other words, the DB remains consistent and provides accurate data **before and after** the operation is performed.

- **I – Isolation**: When two different operations to modify/edit/read/write are given to the database, one operation does not interfere with the other operation. Each operation works in its own capacity consistently.

- **D – Durability**: The DB can withstand several requests to modify/edit/read/write and will be able to consistently work with all the requests.

- **Primary key**: Each table of an RDB has a primary key that is <u>unique</u>. The primary key maintains <u>entity integrity</u> of an RDB table. For example, a unique ID such as a Social Security number or a customer number can be a primary key.

- **Foreign key**: This is a key that is linked to another table's primary key. The foreign key refers to a primary key in another table and thus maintains the <u>referential integrity</u> of a table in the RDB.

- **Candidate key**: This is a key made up of one or more columns of a table in the RDB. The candidate key can qualify as a unique key in RDB. A table can have <u>multiple candidate keys</u> but only one primary key. All the multiple candidate keys are candidates for a primary key, which is why it's called a "candidate key."

- **Domain**: All values an attribute can take in a table. For example, a string variable defined on a table column can accept strings, numbers, and a wide variety of combination of alphanumeric and special characters.

- **Degree**: This is the number of attributes or columns in a table or relation.

- **Relation**: This is a table, a view, a combination of view and table, or a newly generated view that can pull data from various other tables.

- **Cardinality**: This is usually defined as how one entity relates to another entity. It is given as one to one (1:1), one to many (1:n), or many to many (n:m).

- **One-to-one cardinality (1:1)**: For example, one person has one Social Security number.

- **One-to-many cardinality (1:n)**: For example, one salesperson can have more than one order.

- **Many-to-many cardinality (n:m)**: For example, several courses can be taken by several students.

- **View**: A read-only version of a table or a combination of tables/data objects of a database. A view protects a database from unauthorized modifications by users. Depending on the permissions, several views can be created to cater to individual users. Views are also called virtual tables that are generated on demand from existing tables. Views do not have any physical space in the database itself.

- **Roles**: Roles are given to users depending on their need to know and least privileges. DBs have roles such as administrators and end users. End users have limited access to read and modify, but DB administrators (DBAs) can create and modify databases with more access.

- **Commit**: Committing to the database makes the changes permanent.

- **Rollback**: Rolling back removes any database changes done and restores the database to a condition that it was in, before the operation was executed.

- **Tuple**: This is a single row or a record in an RDB table.

Example: A large online credit card processing system using the SQL Server database on the backend was given a single operation consisting of a set of instructions in the form of a procedure to successively A) access a table named *customers*, B) remove table row data that has customer names like David, and C) update the database. However, after the set of instructions was issued, it was found that steps A and B succeeded, but step C failed, and the database remained unaltered after rolling back the changes done by steps A and B. What property did the database exhibit in rolling back this entire operation containing three instructions?

A)   Isolation property

B)   Consistency property

C)   Atomicity property

D)   Durability property

Analysis: When a set of instructions were issued as a whole, the DB must execute all or nothing. This means if the operation failed halfway through, it should revert the DB to its original state (before operation) since the entire set did not succeed. This is called the atomicity of the DB. Isolation refers to running an operation without interfering with another operation that was issued separately. Durability dictates that the DB withstand my requests. Consistency maintains that the DB remains consistent in its design with the set constraints and restrictions.

Since the DB was issued three different instructions and it failed after the first two, the operation did not complete in full. Thus, the DB found that it had to roll back the partial operations and did it exactly as required.

Statement: A SQL Server database was given a single operation set of instructions to successively a) access a table named *customers*, b) remove table row data that has customer names like David, and c) update the database. It was found that steps A and B succeeded, but step C failed, and the database remained unaltered after rolling back the changes.

Question: A SQL Server database, given a single operation (to successfully access, remove data, and update) remained unaltered. What property did the database exhibit?

Solution: The DB exhibited the atomicity property correctly by rolling back the partial operations. Therefore, the correct answer is option C.

Review Questions

Several variations are possible for DB-related questions. Some of them are shown here:

1.   A table in a relational database has a unique customer number, customer first name, customer last name, customer complaint, customer city, customer state, and customer ZIP code as attributes. What is the degree of the table if it contains 432 rows of data?

     A)   5

     B)   7

     C)   1

     D)   432

Answer: Option B. The number of attributes is known as the degree, which is the same as the number of columns in the table, which is 7.

2. A relation in a relational database has a unique customer number, customer first name, customer last name, customer complaint, customer city, customer state, and customer ZIP code as attributes. How many tuples does this relation have if it contains 432 rows of data?

    A) 7

    B) 432

    C) 1

    D) 425

    Answer: Option B. The tuple number is the same as a row of data.

3. For a database that deals only with accounting, payroll, and reporting, what does the set of properties ACID mean?

    A) Accuracy, correctness, isolation, and duration

    B) Atomicity, consistency, ingenuity, and definiteness

    C) Atomicity, consistency, isolation, and durability

    D) Accounting, correctness, indemnity, and discovery

    Answer: Option C. Whether a DB deals with accounting or any other branch, the ACID definition does not change. The statement that the DB is dealing with accounting is a distractor.

4. Two requests have been sent to a DB administrator (DBA) to create a way for two different users to have read-only access to the same relation but want to see different data. User 1 wants to see data that User 2 doesn't need, and vice versa. What should the DBA create to allow both users to access the data in the relation?

    A) Two different tables from the relation, one for each user

    B) One combined table that pulls data as required from the same relation

C) Two different views of the same table, one for each user

D) One view for both users, with a request for each user not to use other user's data

Answer: Option C. One table data can be viewed by two users without interfering with each other's data easily by creating two different views.

Cryptography: Digital Signatures, Keys, and Cryptanalysis

Tip #29: Know the symmetric algorithms and their intricacies for cryptography

Know the symmetric algorithms, their key sizes, and their block sizes. Pay particular attention to DES, 2DES, and the 3DES key/block actual sizes and effectively used sizes. Also know the number of keys required for the symmetric cryptosystem used with "n" users.

Domain: Security Engineering, Asset Security.

Subdomain: Cryptography, Data security controls, Protecting data at rest or in transit.

Subject background: Cryptography is way a study and practive of various methods to communicate, always assuming that a third person is closely watching the confidential communication between two parties. Cryptography deals with protocols and algorithms that protect the communication with keys, certificates, software methods, protols and so on. Cryptography is synonymous with message encryption based on mathematical and computational sciences. Cryptography deals with confidentiality in the security CIA triad.

Symmetric key cryptography deals with a key that both sender and the reciever use to cipher and decipher the message.

Symmetric key ciphers use block or stream encryption. As their names imply, block encryption uses blocks of data while stream encryption uses streams of data.

Symmetric key is more efficient and is a preferred method of encryption when large amounts of data is encrypted and transmitted.

Things to Remember

- Symmetric algorithms assume that two parties share the key before the process commences or the key is preshared.

- The number of keys required for n users in symmetric cryptography is n*(n-1)/2. This means that for 20 users, the symmetric cryptographic system needs a total of 190 keys.

- A user utilizing the symmetric cryptography trusts the other party in the system and shares the key before both parties communicate with each other.

- The secrecy of the key is maintained by individual parties, and there is no third party involved to keep the keys or the secrecy.

- The symmetric key can be used for communication and disk encryption as well.

- If used in disk encryption, the main problem in the symmetric cryptographic system is how to keep the key secret.

- Symmetric cryptography provides the confidentiality in the CIA triad.

- In symmetric key cryptographys, keys are not freely distributed among users. Keys are exchanged via an out-of-band key exchange method (on courier, via secure email etc., for example).

- Symmetric algorithms (and the cryptography) are very fast.

- Symmetric ciphers are difficult to break if the key is large and maintained confidential.

- Symmetric algorithms can be the stream or block type.

- To remember all the symmetric algorithms, use the acronym 23BRAIDS (see Table 3-2 below).

- Kirchoff's law states that an algorithm can be made public, but the secrecy of the key alone is enough to keep the cryptography safe.

- AES uses the Rijndael algorithm.

- The Data Encryption Standard (DES) uses the Data Encryption Algorithm (DEA), and DES is not the same as DEA.

Table 3-2 shows the symmetric cryptographic standards, bits, and the code word to easily remember them.

Table 3-2. *Symmetric Cryptographic Standards*

Name	Note
2 Fish	128 bit blocks and up to 256 bits key
3DES	Three different keys can be used (minimum of 2 keys used). 48 rounds of computation and 168 bit key size.
Blowfish	32-448 bits of variable length. Operates on 64-bit blocks of text.
RC4, RC5, RC6	RC4 is Stream (128 bit key), RC5, RC5 are block cipers (up to 2048 bits)
AES	Block size of 128 bits with 128 (10 rounds)/192 (12 rounds)/256 (14 rounds) bit keys
IDEA	64 bit blocks; 128 bit key. Can operate in 5 modes of encryption like DES (ECB, CBC, CFB, OFB, CTR).
DES	Works on 64 bit blocks. Effective key used is 56 bits. 8 bits are for parity. 16 rounds of computation
SAFER	Developed by creator of IDEA
CAST	64 bit block size with 40 to 128 bits in 8 bit increments. Succeeded by CAST 256.
SERPENT	128 bit blocks with a keyt of 128/192/256 bits
SKIPJACK	Approved for US federal information processing standard (FIPS). 64-bit blocks and 80-bit key.

Example: Cryptic Data Inc. (CDI) is a third-party provider that supplies cryptographic solutions to various companies. Your company has acquired the software supplied by CDI, which can use either asymmetric or symmetric cryptography with various methods and algorithms. Your company has decided to use the AES algorithm in the software for both communication and data encryption for a total of 23 users. Answer the following question based on this scenario:

What key size and algorithm is **MOST** useful for email communication?

A)   512-bit and the advanced encryption algorithm (AEA)

B)   192-bit and the data encryption algorithm (DEA)

C)   256-bit and the Rijndael algorithm

D)   256-bit and the symmetric cryptographic algorithm (SCA)

Analysis: Removing superfluous information and keeping the important sentences of the question can be done as shown here:

Statement: Cryptic Data Inc. (CDI) is a third-party provider that supplies cryptographic solutions that can be either asymmetric or symmetric. Your company has decided to use the AES algorithm in the software **for both communication and data encryption** for **a total of 23 users.** Answer the following question based on this scenario:

Question: What key size and algorithm is **MOST** useful for email communication?

Solution: Notice that the question is asking about **MOST** useful method. This means we can use more than one method, but which can be the best? Easily we can first eliminate the wrong answers in options A and D since the algorithm names and bits are not symmetric. Option B can be eliminated since DEA operates on 16 bits, and there is no 192 bits.

We are now left with option C. AES uses 128/192/256 bits and is based on the Rijndael algorithm. Thus, we have the answer as C.

Remember to memorize the key sizes and algorithm names.

Review Questions

Several variations of the question give the same statement:

1. How many keys are required for your company when AES symmetric encryption is implemented for 23 users?

   Answer: The formula is $n*(n-1)/2$. In this case, we will need $(23*22)/2$, or 253 keys.

2. If your company decides to switch to asymmetric algorithms, who will handle the certificates and keys?

   Answer: We have to use PKI or a CA with a common trust to handle keys and certificates.

3. If your company decides to switch to asymmetric algorithms, how many keys are required 23 users?

   Answer: Asymmetric algorithms use $2*n$ keys for n users with each user making use of a public key (known to all) and a private key (known only to the user). We will need 46 keys.

4. After trying the AES algorithm, you want to scrap the contract with CDI and decide to use an alternative system that provides the **MOST** security. What do you use?

   A) One-time pad

   B) DES

   C) SAFER

   D) Diffie–Hellman

   Answer: A one-time pad is the most secure since it is considered unbreakable. Option D is not symmetric. DES can be broken and was replaced. SAFER is not better than a one-time pad.

5. Which item **BEST** provides the security in AES cryptography supplied by CDI that you decided to implement?

A) The secrecy of the key

B) The algorithm used in software

C) The secrecy of the software accredited by the management

D) The SLA signed between CDI and your organization

Answer: Symmetric cryptography's security is basically provided by the secrecy of the key. Thus, option A is the correct answer. A close answers is option B, which states the algorithm, but the question is asking about what provides the **BEST** security.

Tip #30: Learn to understand different types of cyberattacks on information or data

In this section, you'll learn about types of attacks such as chosen cipher, chosen plain, known plain text, etc.

Domain: Security Engineering, Software Security.

Subdomain: Cryptography, Ciphers, Keys, Key management, Cryptographic and related attacks.

Subject background:

An **active attack** is said to have occurred when a message of a file is modified. Active attackers also can present themselves as another person/entity with proper permissions. By checking the logs, files, and such other means, it is possible to detect an active attack.

A **passive attack** happens when someone sniffs data or does shoulder surfing. It is hard to find out who sniffs data just by looking or overhearing the conversation, and thus passive attacks are nearly impossible to be detected.

Attack vectors are factors that can be stolen, modified, or newly implemented. In cryptography these vectors can include keys, people, algorithms, and secret data among others.

Known plain-text attack: An attacker knows the plain text and the corresponding cipher text of a few messages. The goal for the attacker now is to find the key so that he can encrypt or decrypt any message or even make his own message and send it. Any known or possible algorithms are all applied to check if the key can be found.

Cipher text-only attack: Several messages are encrypted with the same algorithm/ key. The attacker has the cipher text of all these messages. Somehow the attacker will have to find the key that encrypted these messages. Once that key is found, he can decrypt the messages using the same key. This is easily the common attack since encrypted messages can be sniffed and copied. The hard part is finding the key since the attacker does not have a clue about the encryption process or the key itself. This type of attacking can be easy if the encryption process is not complicated. For example, if each letter in the English language is modified as another character by adding a fixed-length ASCII code, by examining the encrypted characters the attacker might be able to find the key with some trial and error.

Chosen plain-text attack: In this case, an attacker has both plain- and cipher-text messages, and the attacker chooses the plain text of several messages, compares them to encrypted cipher messages, and tries to find the key. Once the key is found, the encryption and decryption processes are all clear to the attacker.

Chosen cipher text attack: This attack is similar to the chosen plain-text attack, but the difference is that the attacker now chooses the cipher text to get the plain text to figure out the key. This kind of attack is the hardest of all attacks.

Adaptive attacks: When the word "adaptive" is added to any of these attacks, it means the attacker is trying these methods and modifying his methods/algorithms to suit the next level of attack. By this trial and error, the attacker can easily break a cryptosystem.

Things to Remember

- Keys are an important part of cryptography, and they should be stored and passed around with utmost security.

- Keys can be short-term or long-term depending on how often they are used.

- Keys should be regularly updated and changed and everyone must follow the organization's rules for setting up keys.

- Unused keys must follow a destruction method approved or in place at the organization.

- Cryptanalysis is the study of breaking an encryption process. It also involves compromising an identification or authentication process.

- Encryption is the process of converting plain text to cipher text (or encrypted message). Encryption is also known as enciphering.

- Decryption is a process of reversing encryption or converting cipher text (encrypted message) back to a plain-text message. Decryption is sometimes called as deciphering.

- Steganography is the process of hiding a message in another message. For example, people who watch a video on TV as a news item may not know that some viewers can depict secret messages from the person speaking on video (such as hand symbols, cues, etc.). Another example is when a person says on video that the users should "take bus 11." While a majority of the people think that bus 11 as the city bus number, a secret code in that message could be to say "use both legs and walk." Steganography is the concealment of information. Another way is to transmit data via pictures wherein the pixels give some hidden data.

- Substitution ciphers use a strict rule like "add 5 or shift 4." The Caesar cipher (which adds three characters to create a code) is a substitution cipher. Under this, "Fox" becomes "ira." F+3 goes to "I," o+3 goes to "r," and since x+3 goes beyond "z," it rolls back to "a." Any other number for the shift can be used instead of 3 as well.

- Both symmetric and asymmetric algorithms can be used in cryptography.

Example: An inside employee of an organization who is notorious for shoulder surfing has found an open port on a network and was able to install a sniffer. Sniffing the data daily, the attacker was able to read all the outgoing encrypted messages on the network. Using some software to decrypt all the encrypted messages, he was able to find the key used in encryption to break the system. In this situation, what is the **BEST** description for the type of attack the attacker carried out?

- A)   Active attack, known cipher text only

- B)   Passive attack, known cipher text only

- C)   Active attack, known plain text only

- D)   Passive attack, known plain text only

Analysis: Note that the first sentence claiming the employee as a notorious shoulder surfer has no bearing on the question. It is a plain distractor because he did not use shoulder surfing to find anything. We know that by installing a sniffer the attacker is a passive attacker. Thus, options A and C are automatically wrong. The wording "sniffing" is an indicator since a sniffer passively checks the data on network.

Statement: An inside employee of an organization was able to install a sniffer to read all the **<u>outgoing encrypted messages</u>** on the network. Using some **software to decrypt all the encrypted messages**, he was able to find the key used in encryption to break the system.

Question: What is the **BEST** description for the type of attack the attacker carried out?

Solution: Obviously, the attack is a passive attack. Once the sniffer found the encrypted messages, the attacker decrypted them to find the original messages and break the system. Thus, a passive attacker using encrypted messages found the plain text. This points us to the solution that the answer is option B.

Review Questions

Several possible questions are detailed here:

1. Under the Caesar cipher using shift 3, what does the message "CISSP-IISSCC" become?

    A)   FLVSS-LVFLVF

    B)   FLVVS-LLVVFF

    C)   FVVSV-LLFLVV

    D)   CIVVS-LVFLVF

    Answer: Option B. Hint: Observing closely, we know that C+3 becomes F, which automatically shows the answer as option B.

2. What is the advantage of an adaptive attack?

    Answer: It helps the attacker to modify the messages, keys, and methods by trial and error to find the message and encrypting process. In other words, the attacker adapts to the situation and refines his attacking methods.

3. Which of the following **BEST** describes steganography?

    A) Hiding messages in another encrypted message

    B) Hiding messages in a plain-text message

    C) Hiding messages in a transmitted picture

    D) Breaking an encrypted message and finding plain text

    Answer: Option C

4. Shoulder surfing is **BEST** described as:

    A) Active attack

    B) Observed plain-text attack

    C) Passive attack

    D) Adaptive password attack

    Answer: Option C

5. Which of the following is the **BEST** description of an attack vector?

    A) The financial or information loss due to the encryption attack

    B) The processor and the computer that run the encrypting software

    C) The trial keys used by the attacker for encryption and decryption

    D) The time taken for a plain-text message to get encrypted by an algorithm

    Answer: Option C

6. What is the **BEST** way to protect a key that is used in encryption?

    Answer: A high level of secrecy both in storage and in transmission

7. Which of the following can be **BEST** called a concealment cipher?

    A) Encrypted cipher text mixed in plain text

    B) Decrypted cipher text mixed in encrypted text

C)   Text inserted in pixels of a JPEG picture

D)   Text encrypted with a proper salt

Answer: Option C

8.   In a known plain-text attack, what is the goal of an attacker?

A)   To find the encrypted text

B)   To decrypt the encrypted text

C)   To find the key of the encryption process

D)   To find the entire algorithm

Answer: Option C

9.   What is cryptanalysis?

Answer: It is the study of breaking an encryption process.

Physical Security

Tip #31: When the CISSP certification exam will stop?

In this section, we'll talk about the number of questions on the CISSP computerized assessment test (CAT) exam and when the exam will close.

Domain: All.

Subdomain: All.

Subject background: The computerized assessment test of the CISSP exam has now reduced the testing time from 6 hours to 3 hours and the questions from 250 to 150.

Things to Remember

- The CAT test can end at 100 questions, or it can go up to a maximum of 150 questions.

- The number of questions you are asked to answer is **not** a reflection of your in-depth knowledge; instead, it calculates the number of correct choices you picked on the exam.

- Some people have passed at a minimum of 100 questions, and other people have failed after answering only 100 questions.

- Technically, the CAT calculates your ability to answer questions in a productive manner and in an increasing level of difficulty.

- Passing the test at 100 questions does not measure one person as having superior knowledge than the person who passed after answering all 150 questions.

- There is no need to feel defeated if the test does not stop after 100 questions and gives you between 100 and 150 questions.

- Remember that there are 25 dummy questions on the exam. The answers you thought were wrong might be right or they might be dummy unscored questions. Do not lose hope until the exam ends.

- The feeling of imminent failure as you go from question to question on the test is pretty common. Do not get bogged down if a question makes you feel bad since you do not know the answer.

- Feeling bogged down can actually spoil the exam since your mood might be affected for the next question.

- Understand that the CISSP test covers a wide variety of topics, but they are not covered at a very technically deep level. A generic rule says that the CISSP test is a mile wide but only a few inches deep. But do not let that statement deter you from learning the subject in a correct manner.

- If you understand what the question is asking, without looking at the answers, you should know the answer first. If you can do that, your success is almost guaranteed.

- At times there is a possibility that you have never read about the question topic or seen such a question (or the answers) on your practice tests. Use the elimination method to remove the unrelated answers and go for an educational guess.

- Remember that two of the four answers can always be eliminated easily, and the best or most closely matching answer is lurking in the remaining two answers.

- Look for keywords that may give a clue to the answer.

Example: The following question is a situation where one has to practically guess (or make an educational guess) to come to the correct answer by using an elimination process.

You work as a security analyst for Unbreakable Cryptography Inc. (UCI) in Palo Alto, California, where there is a high risk of earthquakes. The office you work in is equipped with HVAC systems using natural gas, deluge water sprinkler systems for fire emergencies, and other physical security details. To access the systems, the IT team manager has informed you that they use salts for protecting the passwords.

What is the **BEST** valve system you would recommend in the case of gas-related leaks and fires?

A)   Clapper valve

B)   Delayed valve

C)   Instant release valve

D)   Lock open valve

Here is another question based on the same scenario:

UCI's IT department found that maintaining different salts for each user is tedious and decides to use the same salt for all user passwords. What vulnerability should the IT department now be prepared to face?

A)   Using a single salt or multiple salts does not make any difference.

B)   Shorter hashed values for passwords can be easy to crack.

C)   Single-password cracking can break all passwords.

D)   If a hacker extracts the salt, new rainbow tables can be generated.

Analysis: Removing superfluous information and keeping the important sentences of the question can be done as follows:

Statement: You work as a security analyst for Unbreakable Cryptography Inc. (UCI). The office you work in is equipped with HVAC systems using natural gas; the IT team uses salts for protecting the passwords.

Question: What is the **BEST** valve system you should recommend in the case of **gas-related leaks** and fires?

A)   Clapper valve

B)   Delayed valve

C) Instant release valve

D) Lock open valve

Solution: The first thing you notice in the question is that the valve system is for gas-related fires. The question is **not** asking about how to extinguish the fire. It is asking what value is good for gas-related leaks. Whether UDI is using gas (whether it is natural or otherwise) for heating or cooling is all irrelevant. All we need is to recall what values are good for gas-related fires.

Before attempting to answer, recall the basic step 0 of safety at office: to protect human life. When there is a gas leak, you should allow people to escape safely without getting hurt physically or otherwise. Now continuing the analysis, we can find that option D is a funny answer to distract and can be eliminated. Option C cannot be the answer since if gas is released instantly, people will be harmed breathing that gas. Clapper valves are used for water dispensing in firefighting. This makes the answer option B. But is option B the real answer? It should be because when gas is delayed for a few minutes with a warning light or flashing indication, the delay allows people to escape.

In this question, even if we do not know the correct answer or have never heard of this since we did not see this kind of question in practice tests, we can deduce the correct answer by eliminating the wrong ones and making an educated guess.

For the record, flammable gas-related fires are class B fires in the United States and class C fires in the United Kingdom. They are extinguished best by halon, carbon dioxide, or such.

Question: UCI's IT department decides to use the same salt for all user passwords. What vulnerability should the IT department now be prepared to face?

A) Using a single salt or multiple salts does not make any difference.

B) Shorter hashed values for passwords can be easy to crack.

C) Single-password cracking can break all passwords.

D) If hacker extracts the salt, new rainbow tables can be generated.

Recall that salt is a random value added to the passwords to create a confusing hash. Salt is basically used to make it difficult for the hacker to generate a rainbow table to guess a password. Also, remember that on the CISSP test you should always choose the **BEST** answer whether indicated by the question or not. Oftentimes two options given look very close to perfect answers, but you should always choose the best one. Option

A is not correct obviously. Option B does not sound correct since the statement given or the hashing in itself does not talk about longer or shorter passwords. Option C is not necessarily true since breaking one password does not necessarily break all passwords. But option C is partially true. Option D is the correct choice because if the hacker can somehow extract the salt, he can use the salt to generate new rainbow tables and do an attack. So the **BEST** answer is option D.

Note also that the entire statement in this question talks about gas-related fires, but the question asks about password hashing. Superfluous information can create distractions for the test taker very easily and lead to a wrong answer, confusion, and helplessness. These factors can put you in a bad mood for the next questions. On the other hand, if you are prepared to filter the information, you can easily come to an answer with some effort.

Review Questions

Variation of the question based on same scenario can look like this:

1. The CEO of UDI has informed you that he is worried about barotrauma in the case of a gas leak. What does the word mean?

   Answer: Barotrauma is physical damage to body tissues caused by a difference in pressure between a gas space inside (or in contact with the human body) and the surrounding environment. The pressure difference can cause windows to break. (Tip: "Bar" corresponds to pressure. "Trauma" corresponds to damage.)

2. Before recommending an extinguishing agent, what would you **FIRST** recommend to the CEO to consider in the case of a gas-related fire?

   Answer: Before considering anything, the first step is to consult the local fire department or codes/standards/procedures (state, county, city, local, etc.) to decide what you should do. These codes most probably have a rule book already in place that you can adapt rather than reinventing the wheel.

3. Due to business losses and for fear of incurring more costs, UDI's CEO decides that he doesn't want to install any fire extinguishers in the office. What has the CEO decided?

Answer: The CEO has decided to "accept" the risk. Remember that the risk of fire always remains as long as the HVAC uses gas. The risk cannot be avoided, and there was no mention of buying insurance in the question (and thus no risk transfer). Since the risk cannot be eliminated and not transferred, the CEO has accepted the risk.

4.   Which of the following extinguishers is **BEST** suited for UDI?

Answer: A halogenated agent is best suited for gas-related fires.

5.   What do you advise the IT manager when he informs you of the change to use a single salt for all user passwords?

Answer: You advise him not to use a single salt for passwords since it creates a new vulnerability.

Tip #32: Learn abount physical security and terms related to electricity

Basic problems in the day-to-day interruption of electricity have code names. Memorize the code names and understand what they mean.

Domain: Physical Security, Data Center Security.

Subdomain: Utilities, Electricity, HVAC, Emanation and related areas.

Subject background: Utilities such as electricity provide uninterrupted power to the systems for an organization to function without a major breakdown. But when power is interrupted or does not provide at the needed level, a breakdown can happen. The following are the possible reasons for interruptions in power:

B: Blackout, which is a complete loss of power (from a short duration to long period).

F: Fault, which is a momentary loss of power that can cause spikes and loss in production.

B: Brown out, which is prolonged low voltage. This can be a problem to restart a machine that needs a specific level of voltage and current.

S: Sag, which is momentary low voltage. This may or may not cause a breakdown.

I: In rush, which is an initial rush of power. This can potentially damage circuits and systems.

S: Spike, which is a large high voltage. Spikes are dangerous for systems and can have long-standing side effects on the circuitry.

S: Surge is prolonged high voltage, which can permanently burn/destroy circuits and systems.

These can be remembered easily with the sentence "**B**ob **F**requently **B**uys **S**hoes **I**n **S**hoe **S**tore" from the top to bottom.

Things to Remember

A few other terms to remember are **noise** (unwanted fluctuations), **clean** (good power without noise), and **ground** (common point for the electricity to be grounded, for safety).

Any problems of low voltage or noise, etc., outside the company premises are the responsibilities of the utility company. Internal problems will have to be dealt with by the organization using an uninterrupted power supply (UPS) for clean power.

Low humidity is often a cause of **static electricity**. A high-level static voltage can be a possible cause for permanent damage to circuits, even if it is for short duration.

Example: During a trip from Milwaukee, Wisconsin, to Orlando, Florida, with a stop at Cincinnati, Ohio, there was an announcement by the pilot that your flight from Cincinnati to Orlando has to turn back to Cincinnati due to a blackout at Orlando airport. What was the pilot trying to convey to you with the word "blackout"?

A) Orlando airport's power was on low voltage.

B) Orlando airport's power was on momentary high voltage.

C) The pilot cannot fly the plane to Orlando due to a hurricane.

D) Orlando airport's power was completely lost.

Analysis: Reading the question again and ignoring the verbiage, we find that the question basically is asking what a blackout is (that happened at the Orlando airport). Other than the key word "blackout," there is not much in the verbiage to worry for the question.

If we remember the basic definitions given the subject background section, the solution presents itself quickly. Also, we can note that when the power is completely off, every device goes off and without electricity, and darkness reins; thus, it's all black.

Statement: There was an announcement by the pilot that your flight from Cincinnati to Orlando has to turn back to Cincinnati due to a **blackout** at the Orlando airport.

Question: What was the pilot trying to convey to you with the word "blackout"?

Solution: A blackout is a complete loss of power. The answer, therefore, is option D. Option C is not connected with any of the electricity problems. Options A and B say that there is some voltage, and the power is not completely knocked off.

Review Questions

Variations of questions look as follows:

1. In an office that has low humidity, what is a potential problem that can damage circuitry?

   Answer: Static electricity can be a potential problem in low-humidity conditions.

2. When supplying clean power, a utility company wants avoid noise. What is noise in this context?

   Answer: Noise is the variations/fluctuations in power (and should be avoided).

3. What is the purpose of an uninterruptible power supply (UPS)?

   Answer: UPS provides power when the primary power source is lost and provides protection against power surges.

4. When you arrive at home from work, you find that the microwave and cooking range are showing a flashing display of the wrong time and your phone has a message from the utility company that there was a fault in the power supply around noon. What is the fault in the power supply?

   Answer: Momentary loss of power. A fault can shut off all devices and restart them when the power is back on.

Tip #33: Learn about various classes of of fires, causes, and suppressing agents

In this section, we'll talk about common fires, classes they are made into (both US and UK classes), and the agent used to stop those fires depending the cause and source of fire.

Domain: Security Operations, Security Engineering.

Subdomain: Physical security, Water flooding, Fires, Storage security, Common causes, Site and facility security.

Subject background: Table 3-3 gives you an idea of classes of fires, source, how to fix them, and what agents are used to fix them.

Table 3-3. *Classification of Fires, Their Causes, and Suppressing Methods*

Class (UK)	Class (US)	Type	Cause	Suppress Agents or Methods
A	A	Common combustibles	Wood, paper, textiles, trash, etc.	Water, foam
B	B	Flammable liquids	Petroleum products, coolants, etc.	Halon, CO2, foam, dry powders, etc.
C	B	Flammable gas	Gas	Inert gases, chemical agents Halon, FM-200
E	C	Electrical fires	HVAC, wiring, etc.	Halon, CO2, dry powders
D	D	Combustible metals	Sodium, magnesium, potassium, etc.	Dry powders
F	K	Kitchen fires	Cooking oils, sprays, animal fats	Wet chemicals (for example, Potassium acetate)

The classes of fire are different in the United States and United Kingdom. Note that electrical fires in the United States are classified as class C, but in the United Kingdom they are class E. Likewise, kitchen fires in the United States are class K, but in the United Kingdom they are F.

Things to Remember

Fires are natural or environmental threats. Others in the same threat group are floods, tornadoes, hurricanes, storms, dangerous temperatures like heat/cold waves, etc.

Fire needs fuel, oxygen, and heat/temperature to burn.

Human life is the first thing to be saved or worried about in the case of fires.

Water lowers temperature and heat.

Soda acid removes fuel from the fire.

Carbon dioxide removes oxygen.

Fire detection can be done both via heat-activated and smoke-activated devices.

Halon (or related product) disrupts chemical reaction. Due to environmental concerns (ozone layer damage), Halon is no longer used. An acceptable substitute is FM-200.

Wet pipe used in buildings has a continuous water supply to the valve. The valve opens when a temperature-controlled device sends an alarm. The problem with this type of pipe is that if there is an alarm (real or false), there can be a lot of damage due to water dispensing.

Dry pipe does not contain water at all times. The alarm actually releases water from the tank to the pipes. Dry pipes are somewhat safer in the case of false alarms. Dry pipes are better suited for colder climates where water can freeze in the pipes due to low temperatures.

Pre-action is similar to dry pipe, but water is not immediately released. A thermal fuse on the sprinkler has to melt before water is released. The time it takes for the fuse to melt allows people to escape and may be able to help save some equipment.

Deluge, as its name indicates, releases a large amount of water quickly. They are more suitable for large chemical laboratories and where fires happen and spread quickly. Deluge systems are usually not suitable for data processing centers or computer equipment.

Example: A new data center constructed in the United States has plenum space for wiring and pre-action water pipes for fire suppression, and yet there was a fire caused by combustible metals that caused some damage to the backup tapes in the data center. After seeing the fires, another employee poured water on the fires, but the fires could not be put out. What kind of fire suppressant should have been used to put out these fires?

A)   Foam

B)   Carbo dioxide

C)   Halon

D)   Dry powders

Analysis: Notice from the question that the fire was caused by combustible metals despite whatever care was taken by the data center. Any existing ready-to-use fire extinguishing equipment of classes A, B, C, and K will not work. An employee pouring water is useless in case of fires caused by metals.

Also notice that the options listed Halon as a distractor since Halon is no longer used due to fears of the ozone environment. Carbon dioxide will not help, and neither does foam, which is used for common combustibles and flammable liquids.

Statement: A new US data center has a fire caused by combustible metals. An employee poured water on the fires, but the fires could not be put out.

Question: What kind of fire suppressant should have been used to put out the fires caused by **combustible metals**?

Solution: A simple and straightforward solution is to refer to Table 3-3 and recall that the fires caused by combustible metals are class D. Class D fires in the United States can be put out easily with dry powders. Option D is the correct answer.

Review Questions

The following are some of the questions on this topic:

1. Flammable liquids and gases are classified as what class of fires in the United States?

    Answer: Class B

2. What is the **BEST** suppression agent used for class B and class C fires in the United States?

    A)   FM-200

    B)   FN-200

    C)   FA-200

    D)   Water

    Answer: Option A. Option D is for class A fires. Options B and C are invalid and confusing.

3. What factors does a fire need to start and continue to expand?

    Answer: Oxygen, heat/temperature, and fuel

4. Which of the following can remove fuel from an existing fire?

    A)   Temperature

    B)   Carbon dioxide

    C)   Soda acid

    D)   Water/foam

    Answer: Option C

5. In the United Kingdom, fire caused by a flammable liquid is class B, and fire caused by a flammable gas is class C. How are these classified in the United States?

    A)   Flammable liquid is class L, and flammable gas is class G.

    B)   Both are classified as class C.

C)   Both are classified as class B.

D)   Flammable liquid is class B, and flammable gas is class D.

Answer: Option C

Tip #34: Learning about building/facility's physical security, piggybacking, and tailgating

Remember why physical security is important and how to avoid piggybacking. Know the differences between piggybacking and tailgating. Know why to use a mantrap, fail secure, and fail safe configurations.

Domain: Security Engineering.

Subdomain: Physical Security, Personal security, Building/room security.

Subject background: **Piggybacking** is a term used for someone who uses other people's credentials to enter a building, a facility, or a controlled room like a computer server room. It means an individual closely follows another individual (**with** the latter's permission or approval) and sneaks inside a facility.

Tailgating is a term used for entering a controlled facility along another individual **without** the latter's approval or permission. This term is similar to one car tailgating another on the highway.

Things to Remember

Doorways are usually secured with fail-safe or fail-secure mechanisms in a controlled facility.

A **fail-safe** setup for a system means that if there is a disruption of power, the system will open the doors for people to escape and be safe. In this case, doors will be unlocked. In other words, since the safety of humans is of the utmost important, fail safe means in the case of a power failure, people can safely escape, and the doors will be unlocked.

A **fail-secure** system will keep the doors locked in the case of a power failure. If there are no people working inside a room or if the people do not use the fail-secure doors in the case of a power failure, then a fail-secure door system is the best option to use.

The best protection against tailgating or piggybacking is to use a **mantrap** consisting of two doors with two controls, either human or biometric, or some type of card/ID reading mechanism. A mantrap works in a way to keep the unauthorized person locked in between the two doors if the identity provided cannot be verified correctly.

Turnstiles can be used at the building entrance to track who is entering the building, and they can be locked if the proper identity is not provided.

Example: A company employee using a smart card to enter the building facility brings with him a visitor who goes inside the building without informing the security personnel. Later it was found that many thumb drives were missing from the building, and an investigation found through the closed circuit video cameras reconfirmed the theft by the visitor. What kind of entry **BEST** describes how the visitor got in?

A) The visitor entered the building when the building security failed.

B) The visitor tailgated an employee entering with a valid identification.

C) The visitor piggybacked an employee entering with valid identification.

D) The visitor entered with the help of security guards.

Analysis: The statement in the question says that the visitor was brought in by an employee. This implies that the intruder came in with the permission of the employee. Thus, it is a case of piggybacking. Tailgating indicates that the visitor never needed the permission of an employee. The information about stolen thumb drives and the investigation to find the intruder's actions through video cameras are all distractors.

Statement: A company employee using a smart card to enter the building facility brings a visitor with him who goes inside the building without informing the security personnel.

Question: A company employee brings a visitor with him. What kind of entry **BEST** describes how the visitor got in?

Solution: Since the visitor was brought in willingly by an employee, this is called piggybacking. The answer is option C. Options A and D are obviously wrong. Since the intruder entered with the permission of an employee, it is not tailgating, and thus option B is wrong too.

Review Questions

Possible questions on this topic will look as follows:

1. What is the difference between tailgating and piggybacking?

    Answer: Tailgating does not need any permission, but piggybacking needs permission.

2. What is the **BEST** method to prevent piggybacking?

   Answer: Mantraps, turnstiles, or physical security guards are the best methods.

3. Why are fail-safe door systems considered the **BEST** alternatives?

   Answer: They allow the personnel to safely escape in case of power failure.

4. If the personnel working inside a building do not use it's entrance door to escape in case of a fire, what kind of doorway can this entrance door be **BEST** designed as?

   Answer: If the door is not used for personnel to escape, it can be best designed as a fail-secure door, which locks in the case of a power failure.

Tip #35: Physical security and crime prevention through environmental design (CPTED)

Understand security through environmental design principles. Look at the roads, trees, lights, and paths to the buildings and surrounding crime in the area. Also, understand the camera's pan and zoom aspects attached to the building to track activity. Crime prevention through environmental Design (CPTED) deals with the physical environment.

Domain: Security Operations, Security Engineering.

Subdomain: Physical security, Environmental security, Building security, Other physical issues.

Subject background: CPTED deals with the physical environment and can reduce how human behavior can affect security. It deals with what should be installed, what should be recorded, and how long the records are kept, and it gives an understanding of who is entering the building, etc. Buildings and their approach roads, trees around the building, and lights that illuminate the area all fall under the CPTED.

Things to Remember

The main idea of CPTED is that a modified and secure physical environment can affect human behavior and reduce crime. For example, posting a strong warning sign such as "Private area, trespassers will be prosecuted to the fullest extent of law" can affect curious onlookers trying to enter a secure building. CPTED can be memorized as Captain Ed.

Since information and data are the most important assets an organization can have, the data center is always recommended to be set up at the center of the building.

Fences, locks, warning signs, smart card (or the like) access at entrance, and cameras to record the surrounding activities all fall under the CPTED.

CPTED recommends a careful design depending on the activity that goes inside a building. A bank building may have a different design than one office housing a mail delivery facility or a pharmaceutical company manufacturing unit.

CPTED can be done in two ways: target hardening and access control. **Target hardening** is the physical way of securing a building or facility. This includes type of wall or construction material to withstand fires, lighting, alarms, fire-resistant material, water sprinklers, locks, glass doors for viewing where required, type of glass used, ceiling height, and so on. **Access control** limits entry to one or more areas of the building. Access is granted to people depending on their job function and security clearance.

Organizations should comply with state and local fire codes and protection policies, building codes, and other regulations. The Occupational Safety and Health Administration (OSHA) and the Environmental Protection Agency (EPA) requirements need to be complied with where required and deemed necessary.

A physical security and protection program is important because poor physical security practices can lead to a flurry of lawsuits, criminal complaints, and unsafe environments.

Under any circumstances, the highest priority of the CPTED is the protection of human life first.

Example: A data storage company planning to store data as escrow on tapes, thumb drives, DVDs, and other media wants to construct a building that can store data for hundreds of software companies. When selecting a site, constructing approach roads to the building, and designing a secure environment of the building, per crime prevention through environmental design (CPTED), what is the **MOST** important aspect or component of CPTED?

A)   Access control of the building and surroundings

B)   Environmental control of the facility and the building

C)   Target hardening of the facility and the building

D)   Live surveillance of the entire building and facility

Analysis: Reading the question, we can easily recognize that except the last sentence, everything else is pure verbiage to confuse the test-taking candidate. Whether the company is planning to maintain a data center or whatever, the question here is, what is the most important component of CPTED? Access controls and environmental controls are important and so is live surveillance, but those are not the most important aspects.

Statement: Removing the verbiage, we can look at the question like this:

A data storage company planning to store data as escrow on tapes, thumb drives, DVDs, and other media wants to construct a building that can store data.

Question: What is the **MOST** important aspect or component of CPTED?

Solution: Option C is the best answer for the most important aspect. Whether the building has surveillance outside/inside or not, one has to always do the target hardening. The target in the question is the data center and the building that houses the center.

Review Questions

Various other questions on CPTED can be as follows:

1. What is the space between the ceiling of a current floor and its immediate upper floor used for wiring called?

    A) Floor space

    B) Plural space

    C) Plenum space

    D) Attic space

    Answer: Option C. The plenum space is used for wiring and other items. The plenum space protects the environment from toxic chemicals or such in the case of fire or accident.

2. What are the **FIRST** rules to follow for fire safety per CPTED if a building construction is planned in Salt Lake City in the state of Utah?

    A) State regulations and building codes of Utah

    B) County and state regulations of Salt Lake City, Utah

    C) Local fire codes where building is planned in Utah

    D) Federal regulations of building codes that apply to all US states

    Answer: Option C

3. What does CPTED reduce when followed correctly?

   A) Security loopholes

   B) Environmental breakdown

   C) Crime in the surroundings

   D) Loss in the physical assets

   Answer: Option C

4. The big iron blocks placed in front to avoid vehicles coming in direct contact with the building are called:

   A) Bollards

   B) Vehicle blockers

   C) Safety blocks

   D) Entry points

   Answer: Option A

5. Signs on display boards and lighting are **BEST** classified as:

   Answer: Deterrents because they give a warning

6. Locks, keys, and smart cards are used for:

   Answer: Access control mechanisms

7. Walls, doors, and windows are what type of barriers?

   Answer: Physical barriers

8. To reduce/prevent crime a company wants to follow CPTED. What is the full form of CPTED

   A) Comprehensive protocol to eliminate disasters

   B) Criminal protection to an extended duration

   C) Crime prevention through environmental design

   D) Complete protection to employee on demand

   Answer: Option B

Tip #36: Types of access cards used for physical entry and information/data access on an IT system

Learn different aspects of access cards, methods, and their types that are used for physical security (CAC/transponder, etc.) and information access.

Domain: Security and Risk Management, Security Engineering.

Subdomain: Physical security, Due diligence, Asset security, Access to systems.

Subject background: There are dozens of methods by which a person's access to a building or an IT system can be controlled. Most common are common access cards (CACs), transponders, physical IDs that are manually checked, biometric sensors, and a combination of these. Depending on the assets in the building, the building, and the access required, more than one method can be incorporated into the access methods.

Simple ID: This is an identity card issued by the employer to access and identify the employee. This card may not have any security features and just serves as an identity only. An ID card of this type may not contain any PII of the employee other than a photo.

CAC: A common access card is useful for many functions. It can be used to access the door locks where permitted, entrance doors, and computer login access, and it may work alone by itself or may work with a second authentication factor such as a PIN or password. CAC contains a gold chip like the credit cards and can be programmed to do a variety of functions. CAC also contains all or some of the PII of the employee, which can be exploited if the employee were to lose the CAC by misplacing or by theft.

Transponder: A transponder card communicates with the access locks wirelessly and allows or rejects a person to enter a facility. These can be used at toll gates or access gates where the facility's antenna reads the transponder code and allows or rejects access. These are touchless access controls, and there is no need to pull the actual card out and scan it in a reader every time one needs access.

Manual access: This is for facilities that do not have high security equipment, do not have funds to employ high-level scanning, or do not need high-level access. Anyone can be designated as a checker who can randomly check the IDs or just do the headcount. This kind of checking is dependent on a third person who can accurately report fake IDs but is prone to human errors

Biometric access: This falls into several different types, including facial recognition, fingerprint scanner, iris/pupil scan, hand scan, and double biometric scan (two persons are required to open). These are all high-level security systems where several steps are required to access the facility. Usually these facilities contain highly sensitive data. Government organizations such as the CIA and FBI may opt for this sort of access controls.

Double door/mantrap: These are generally required to limit access via piggybacking when one person tries to enter behind another. In double door technology, one door should be closed before the next can be opened. Mantraps help identify fake people entering the facility and trapping them into a location where they can be easily caught.

Revolving/rotating doors: These work best when only one person is allowed to enter the facility at one time via the revolving door. The door allows only one person to move in, while the second person is waiting until the first one enters with proper authentication. In the case of an authentication failure, the door is locked automatically.

Things to Remember

- A single security feature may not fit the exact situation, and oftentimes a company has to use more than one method to filter the IDs and fake entrants.

- In biometric scanning, a 100% match is considered a fake entry since nothing can match 100% in real world.

- CACs and transponders may contain RFID chips that store PII information and thus are prone to other security attacks if the CAC is lost/stolen.

- CACs and intelligent cards can be used for more than one function such as login access to computers, door access, secret file access, and so on. They can also be programmed to do more than one function at regular intervals to suit the changing circumstances.

- Transponders can be used for gate access in gated communities, in aviation, on highways for EZ passes, and many others. They emit one kind of signal and receive a different kind of signal.

- Physical and manual checking of each ID of a person is prone to error and is dependent on expert recognition of people by another designated person. Human error and judgment can cause problems in this method of authentication process.

- A simple ID may be useful only for small organizations that have fewer than 10 or 15 employees where the ID card serves only as an identification of a person.

Example: A company that stores personal data for other organizations wants to implement two types of identities for its employees. The C-level managers must access the building quickly, and the regular employees need two-factor authentication. The regular employees also must be able to use the same authentication factors they use for physical access for logging into their IT systems. Which of the following is **MOST** suitable for the company to implement with lower costs and the **BEST** possible protection?

A) Biometric system for C-level staff and manual door check for employees

B) Transponder for C-level staff and common access card with a PIN for employees

C) Biometric scan for employees and common access card for C-level employees

D) Simple ID with a PIN for employees and common access card for C-level staff

Analysis: Notice that the question wants to implement two different access methods. One is for C-level managers who need to go in quickly. This means they have less time to stand in a line to scan a card or enter a PIN. So, the best option for them is to have some sort of wireless scan that automatically scans their cards and allows them to go in. The second form is for employees who have time to stand in a line and scan their own card. And that card must be two-step authentication. It means they scan the card and may also put in a PIN or some password to get into the building. The first factor is "what you have," which is the CAC or some ID card. The second form is "what you know," which is the PIN. With this two-factor authentication, one can access the building and can go in. Once inside, the IT system can accept the same form of authentication. The ID card can be inserted into the card reader attached to the IT system and verified with the PIN to give access to the IT system. That way, the CAC with a PIN serves as a two-factor authentication system and works both for building access and for IT system access. Note that the two factors here are "what you have" and "what you know," not building access and IT access. Ironically, both building access and IT system access may need to be input with two factors before access can be granted.

Note that the last sentence is asking you to choose a lower-cost implementation. Biometric systems are all high-cost systems. Thus, we can take a hint and safely avoid the option that says biometric system.

Statement: A company wants to implement two types of identities for its employees. The **C-level managers must access the building quickly**, and the **normal employees need two-factor authentication**. Which of the following is **MOST** suitable for the company to implement?

Question: A company wants to implement two types of identities for its employees: **C-level managers must access the building quickly**, and the **normal employees need two factor authentication**. Which of the following is **MOST** suitable for the company to implement?

Solution: Examining the given options, options A and C can be easily noted as wrong answers since they have a biometric system that is normally expensive. Option D says a simple ID and PIN for employees as two-factor authentication, and this part can be implemented. But does a CAC work for C-level employees? CACs usually have a chip that needs to be scanned in an electronic unit, which means the C-level employees need to stand in line if required and insert the card in a reader, which takes time and is not easy. The requirement in the question is that "a C-level employee must access the building quickly." Thus, option D is partially correct. Examining the remaining option, which is option B, we find that a transponder for C-level employees will work well to minimize waiting time. A transponder is like the EZPass on the highway. One does not have to stop to scan the card. And the CAC with a PIN is a two-factor authentication for regular employees will work too. Thus, the correct answer is option B.

Note that 90% of the CISSP questions are coined this way: two clear distractors that can be eliminated and the remaining two that are close to the answer. But the candidate is tested to pick the better of the two to arrive at the correct answer. This is another reason why almost all questions of the CISSP have the wording **MOST**, **BEST**, **CLOSEST**, etc.

With the same verbiage, a variation of the question can be as follows:

Question: What two factors are the **BEST** suited for regular employees with lower costs and the **BEST** possible protection?

A) What you know and where you are

B) What you are and what you have

C) What you have and what you know

D) What you have ad what you are

Answer: In the case, the answer can avoid the "what you are," which is a biometric system. Thus, options B and D can be removed. Option A is wrong because where you are is a hard factor to consider, though some GPSs can be involved to find that factor. If such a system is involved, the cost will increase, and thus option A is clearly wrong. The correct answer is option C, which can be used with a CAC: the card you have and the related PIN you know.

It is easy to get confused with the wording "what you" repeated two times in each option distractor and in all four options given, but if we clearly know our answer, it is easy to eliminate the distractors and pick the correct answer. The logic to pick correct answer here is to know what the question is asking clearly (two factors) and what constraints (lower costs) we have to pick that answer.

Review Questions

Several possible questions can be asked, mixing one area of domain and another on the CISSP exam. Some of them are listed here:

1. What are the main reasons to use a transponder in building access?

   Answer: Speed, ease of access, and invisible security. On a highway, an EZPass offers an easy payment option for a toll gate entrance as well.

2. What is the full form of the acronym CAC that is used for various security functions?

   A) Critical access card

   B) Creditable access card

   C) Common access card

   D) Clandestine access card

   Answer: Option C

3. A company that has a biometric recognition system has recorded a 100% match to a person's fingerprint. How accurate is the access system?

   A) Absolutely accurate since it matches 100%.

   B) It has failed the match since no access system can match 100%.

    C)   It is near 90% accurate but adjusted to 100% by software.

    D)   Reliably accurate but needs another access method.

Answer: Option B

4. Why is a mantrap important?

Answer: It prevents piggybacking and helps filter out fake people entering a facility.

5. In which way should revolving doors work?

    A)   Only allow people from inside to leave to outside

    B)   Only allow one person from outside to enter inside

    C)   Open only to outside for people to leave the building

    D)   Open both sides for people to enter and leave

Answer: Option B. Options A, C, and D are obviously wrong since people who leave a facility do not generally pose a threat to the facility. Those who enter the facility need to be screened well.

6. What are the three basic considerations for multifactor authentication?

    A)   Who you are, what you know, where you are

    B)   What you know, where you are, what you do

    C)   What you are, where you know, what you have

    D)   What you have, what you know, what you are

Answer: Option D. Remember the three factors as KHA (know, have, and are). What you are is a biometric identification such as fingerprint or pupil scan. What you know is the PIN or some password/passphrase. What you have is the physical card in your possession.

7. What is an RFID chip used for in a common access card (CAC)?

    A)   It is used to store a PIN.

    B)   It can be programmed to store a variety of data.

C) It is used to identify the owner of the card and the organization issuing the card.

D) It transmits radio frequencies to the card reader.

Answer: Option B. Options A and D are close distractors, but option B is more correct.

8. Why is a simple identification card with a photo ID not suitable for secure building access?

Answer: A simple ID with a photo ID needs to be verified by another human being and is prone to human errors and mistakes.

9. An office facility needs two people scanning their palm prints on a biometric system to open the secure door. The two palm print scan system can **BEST** be called:

A) Double biometric system (DBS)

B) Two-factor identification (TFI)

C) Complex biometric scan (CBS)

D) Double scan door system (DSDS)

Answer: Option A. Options C and D look close but are wrong. In two-factor identification, both factors must come from the same person.

CHAPTER 4

Communications and Network Security

In this chapter, you will learn about the intricacies of computer communication on networks, network architecture, TCP/IP and OSI models, IP addresses and their types, attacks on networks, access controls, assessment testing, and authentication details.

Secure Network Architecture: IP, Non-IP Protocols

Tip #37: Master the intricacies of the TCP/IP and OSI models and layers

Master the intricacies of the OSI layers and what each layer corresponds to and how the TCP/IP layers correspondingly match those in the OSI model. You must remember the protocols for each layer.

Domain: Communication and Network Security.

Subdomain: Networks, Protocols, Routing, Wire and wireless transmissions, Network architecture, IP, IPSec, TCP, and all hardware and network connected areas (even remotely).

Subject background: See Table 4-1 for full details of the OSI model and the corresponding TCP/ITP model and the layers. Going from layer 7 down to layer 1 is how data is transmitted and from layer 1 to layer 7 is how the data is received by the user. Also note that each layer that serves or is served by a protocol is not necessarily a physical layer.

© R. Sarma Danturthi 2020
R. S. Danturthi, *70 Tips and Tricks for Mastering the CISSP Exam*,
https://doi.org/10.1007/978-1-4842-6225-2_4

Things to Remember

- The OSI model can be recalled with an acronym—from top to bottom—"**P**lease **D**o **N**ot **T**hrow the **S**ausage **P**izza **A**way." Similarly, TCP/IP can be remembered with the letters "NITA."

- The lowest-level layer in both the TCP/IP and OSI models always deals with bits and cables.

- Nonrepudiation is related to users and means that a user cannot deny that they sent an email after sending it. This is accomplished with digital signatures and email encryptions. Therefore, the kinds of standards that are related to the users always fall at the highest level, or level 7 in OSI (level 4 in TCP/IP), which is the Application layer.

- It is important to remember the protocol data units for each layer. From high level to low level, the units are broken down as Data ➤ Segment (Datagram) ➤ Packet ➤ Frame ➤ Bits.

- CISSP questions can vary widely and may look off-topic when referencing the OSI or TCP/IP model by including something like "If hexadecimal format is only allowed to be used to transmit data, what layer of the OSI model does deal with hexadecimal data?" The question may seem odd and out of place, but if we examine it in depth, the solution will become very simple. (See the following analysis.)

Example: Which layer of the OSI model deals with binary data being sent on RJ45 wires?

A)   Application layer

B)   Network layer

C)   Transport layer

D)   Physical layer

Analysis: The Application layer deals with the end user and can therefore be ruled out as the answer. The Network and Transport layers deal with protocols that send and receive data or dialog management work. Therefore, options A to C are wrong.

The Physical layer, or layer 1, at the bottom deals with cables and bits. An RJ45 cable is another name for an Ethernet cable. Therefore, option D is the correct answer.

Statement: Since the question is straightforward, there is no ambiguity, and the only confusing part is the mention of RJ45. If we remember that RJ45 is another name for Ethernet cable, we can quickly conclude that the question is about the "cables and bits" layer. In the OSI model, this is the Physical layer, or layer 1, and in TCP/IP it is the Network or Link layer.

Question: Which layer of the OSI model deals with **binary data** being sent on RJ45 **wires**?

Solution: We can notice that the question is about "bits and cables," from the bold and underlined words. Since the question is asking about the OSI model, the answer is the Physical layer of the OSI model.

Review Questions

A typical question can be asked as follows:

Which layer of the **TCP/IP model** deals with **binary data** being sent on RJ45 **wires**?

Answer: In the TCP/IP model, layer 1 is the Network or Link Layer.

Variations can be as follows:

- Which layers in the OSI model combine to form the TCP/IP model's Link layer?

  A)   Application and Data Link layers

  B)   Network, Transport, and Application layers

  C)   Physical and Data Link layers

  D)   Data and Network layers

  Answer: The obvious answer can be found from Table 4-1. Option C is the correct answer.

- Which other layer of the OSI model combines the Session and Application layers to form the TCP/IP model's Application layer?

  A) Data Link layer

  B) Transport layer

  C) Presentation layer

  D) Physical layer

  Answer: The TCP/IP model's Application layer consists of the Session, Presentation, and Application layers from the OSI model. The question already supplied two of these three layers. So, the answer is option C.

Here is a slightly more confusing question:

- Which OSI layer encapsulates network data packets into frames and synchronizes them?

  A) Data Link layer

  B) Transport layer

  C) Internet layer

  D) Network layer

  Answer: Understand that the question is asking in which layer the packets are converted to frames. This conversion (or encapsulation) happens in the Data Link layer of OSI (or the Network layer of TCP/IP). Have a clear understanding of what data encapsulation is. Encapsulation is a form of packing the data from the top layer to the bottom layer (as data is sent).

Also understand that the question is asking about the layers of OSI. The Network layer in OSI has data as packets, not frames. So, the words "network" and "packets" are very bad distractors. However, if the question is worded as "Which OSI layer encapsulates data packets and synchronizes them?" then the answer is option D, the Network layer (the Internet layer for TCP/IP).

Note that the same question can become very intriguing if it is worded as "Which layer of TCP/IP" instead of "Which OSI layer."

Likewise, some confusion can be inserted into the question by wording it differently. Here's an example:

- Which TCP/IP layer deals with communication management and dialog management?

  A)   Session layer

  B)   Transport layer

  C)   Application layer

  D)   Presentation layer

  Answer: A quick look at the TCP/IP layers reveals it does **not** have Session and Presentation layers. So, options A and D can be easily removed. The Transport layer deals with transporting data, not with communication or dialog management. Thus, the answer is option C, the Application layer, which is a combination of the Session, Presentation, and Application layers of OSI.

Note that the same question can be worded as "Which OSI layer deals with communication management and dialog management?" with same the four answer options. Then the answer will be option A, the Session layer.

- Fiber optics belong to what layer of the OSI model?

  A)   Physical layer

  B)   Data layer

  C)   Transport layer

  D)   Presentation layer

  Answer: Cables and bits belong the lowest layer, known as the Physical layer. The answer is option A.

Table 4-1. *OSI Model vs. TCP/IP Model, the Protocols and the Protocol Data Units for Each Layer*

OSI vs. TCP/IP Models					
		Protocol Data Unit	**Function**	**TCP/IP Model**	**Protocol(s)**
Host layers	7	Application	Data	High-level APIs, including resource sharing, remote file access for end user. Nonrepudiation.	Application	HTTP, FTP, TFTP, SNMP, Gopher
	6	Presentation		Translation of data between a networking service and an application, including character encoding, data compression, and **encryption/decryption**.		HTML, JPG, GIFF, TIFF
	5	Session		Managing **communication sessions**, i.e., continuous exchange of information in the form of multiple back-and-forth transmissions between two nodes, dialog management.		NFS, Radius, SQL, PAP, RPC
	4	Transport	Segment, Datagram	Reliable **transmission of data** segments between points on a network, including segmentation, acknowledgment, and multiplexing.	Transport	TCP, UDP, SSL, SSH, SSH-2, SYN

(continued)

Table 4-1. (*continued*)

OSI vs. TCP/IP Models						
			Protocol Data Unit	**Function**	**TCP/IP Model**	**Protocol(s)**
Media layers	3	Network	Packet	Structuring and managing a multinode **network, including addressing, routing**, and traffic control.	Internet	IP, IPSEC, X.25, BGP
	2	Data link	Frame	Reliable **transmission of data** frames between two nodes connected by a physical layer. This layer is further divided to the Logical Link Control (LLC) and Media Access Control (MAC) sublayers.	Network or Link	MAC, ARP, RARP
	1	Physical	Symbol	Transmission and reception of **raw bit** (cables and bits).		ISDN, ATM, USB

Tip #38: Learn about private and public IP addresses used on the Internet

It is really important to remember what IP addresses are publicly visible and what addresses are not.

Domain: Communication and Network Security.

Subdomain: Network devices, Network architecture, Secure design.

Subject background:

Private IP addresses are designated as follows:

- 10.0.0.0 to 10.255.255.255 (24 bits)[8-bit mask]

- 172.16.0.0 to 172.31.255.255 (20 bits) [12-bit mask]

- 192.168.0.0 to 192.168.255.255 (16 bits) [16-bit mask]

Things to Remember

Notice from the private IP addresses shown that their initial value for corresponding bits is 0 and ends with 255 (FF in hexadecimal), which is 8 bits in computer terminology. If 16 bits are used, then the values are 0.0 and 255.255 (FF FF) in two groups of octets.

For 24 bits, three groups of octets go from 0.0.0 to 255.255.255. This is for IP addresses starting with 10.

For 20 bits, the values go from 16.0.0 to 31.255.255. This is for IP addresses starting with 172.

Exam questions can be simple and straightforward or can be as confusing as possible asking for an IP address to be identified or the bits that work for each of the IP address groups.

Example: A corporation designing a development environment for their internal use wants to allocate a group of IP addresses to machines that the programmer can remotely connect. Which group of the following **BEST** suits the IP addresses the company can use without worrying about hacker attempts, attacks, and the related incidents?

A)   10.147.200.255 to 11.255.255.255

B)   193.168.0.0 to 193.168.0.255

C)   172.18.0.0 to 172.18.255.0

D)   147.16.0.0 to 147.255.255.255

Analysis: Looking carefully into the question, we find that the corporation is looking to reserve a group of IP address **for internal use**, which gives the hint that they should not be accessible for public and should be private.

Important   Read the numbers in options carefully and slowly. Otherwise, it is easy to pick a distractor as an answer.

Statement: A corporation designing a development environment for their internal use wants to allocate a group of IP addresses.

Question: For a corporation designing a development environment for its **internal use**, which group **BEST** suits the IP addresses?

Solution: Option A starts with a private IP octet of 10 but ends with a public IP octet of 11. Therefore, it is a wrong group. Option B starts with an octet of 193 and ends with 193, which is a public IP address. Starting with an octet of 192 is private, but as a distractor, this option starts with a close number: 193. Option D is all public IP addresses and is invalid for private addresses. Therefore, we come to option C, which matches correctly the private IP addresses.

Review Questions

Here are few more questions on the same topic:

1. When installing a new wireless router and adjusting new passwords and other settings, a user types an IP address as 10.24.167.234 to access the WiFi settings. But the user is worried that the settings might be stolen from this Internet website and wants to be careful protecting the website. How can the user protect the website's IP from hackers?

    Answer: The IP address is a private address and is not accessible to the public. Therefore, it is safe. The best thing the user can do is to protect the WiFi router via settings (using a difficult to guess password, disabling broadcast, firewall settings, etc.).

2. In a dentist's office, a patient can see his full-mouth X-ray on a giant screen. When not in use, the same screen displays an IP address of 192.168.10.34 as a screensaver text. The patient fears that the IP address is exposing his dental/medical/personal information records on the Internet and asks the dental office about it. What is the **BEST** answer from the options given that can put the patient fears to rest?

A) The dental office has taken enough care to protect patient privacy.

B) The IP address displayed is not accessible to anyone from the Internet.

C) The IP address used by dental office was very well vetted by a security professional.

D) Patient dental and medical records alone cannot expose patient identity.

Answer: Option B

3. Identify a public website from these options.

A) 10.2.255.234

B) 10.17.23.321

C) 192.168.54.254

D) 171.30.78.65

Answer: Option D. Note that the question can ask for identifying a private IP as well instead of a public IP from a given list of IPs. Read slowly and pay close attention.

Tip #39: Understand IPv6 address, its blocks, validating, finding an invalid IPv6 address

Understand IPv6 address blocks and validating, and know how to find an invalid IPv6 from a given set of IP addresses.

Domain: Communications and Network Security.

Subdomain: Secure network architecture design, IP, Non-IP protocols, Segmentation.

Subject background: IPv4 was the original addressing for the Internet. IPv4 had 32 bits and can cater to only 2^{32} addresses (about 4.3 billion). Network growth around the world warranted for more addresses giving way to IPv6, which as 128 bits; 128 bits translates to about 2^{128} addresses (340 followed by 36 zeros). Also, with IPv6 Internet control message protocol (ICMP) functions identically like it does with IPv4. The main reason for the IPv4 addresses to run out was allocation of private IP addresses and the NAT—network address translation. To allocate more devices to Internet now and in the near future IPv6 evolved over IPv4.

Things to Remember

- An IPv6 address contains eight groups of hextets (16 bits) as shown in an example here below:

4098:4D7B:CA10:ABCD:3876:FEAD:12EA:CE54

40 and 98 are octets, and 4098 is a hextet since each number in the octet or hextet is a hexadecimal number (0 to F) that consists of 4 binary digits (bits). Thus, 16 octets or 8 hextets in the IPv6 address makes it 128 bits long.

- The notation of IPv6 is not case sensitive. 4D7B can be written as 4d7B, 4d7b, or 4D7b.

- Two colon symbols can be substituted for one or more zero fields. For example, 4098:4D7B:0000:0000:0000:0000:12EA:CE54 can be written as 4098:4D7B::12EA:CE54 (zero compression).

- Leading zeros of the address can be suppressed. This means 4098::12EA:007B can be written as 4098::12EA:7B (zero suppression).

- Network addresses can be grouped with a "/." For example, a network address written as 4098:7B:2EA::/48 has a range addresses starting from 4098:007B:02EA:0000: 0000: 0000: 0000: 0000 and ending at 4098:007B:02EA:FFFF: FFFF: FFFF: FFFF: FFFF.

- The routing preferences of the interface address can be combined too. For example, 4098:4D7B::EA connected to the subnet 4098:4D7B::/64 can be written as 4098:4D7B::EA/64.

- The management of IPv6 addresses is delegated to Internet Assigned Numbers Authority (IANA).

Example: An Internet hosting company developing Xbox games wants to migrate from IPv4 addressing to IPv6 addressing and wants to manually select an IPv6 address. The lead programmer suggested that the company select an IPv6 address to show the letters X, B, O, X since the company is doing Xbox games. But the network person thinks that this kind of approach is weird and may not work. Which of the following is the **MOST** valid IPv6 address the Xbox gaming company can select manually?

A)   4098:4D7B::12EA:::CE54

B)   4098:4D7B:X:BO::X000:12EA:CE54

C)   4098:4D7B:0000:0000:XBOX:0000:12EA:CE54

D)   4098:4D7b::12eA:ec54

Analysis: Before going any further, the first point to note is that the X character is not a hexadecimal character and does not even fit in any IPv6 addresses. Hexadecimal characters are only from 0 to 9 and from A to F. IPv6 addresses allow for zero compression, and thus option A may look tempting, but on close examination we will find it is invalid. Whether a company makes Xbox games or not is really a distractor in the question. The question also has a helpful hint on what may not work. The question can be reworded as follows:

Statement: An Internet hosting company wants to manually select an IPv6 address.

Question: Which of the following is the **MOST** valid IPv6 address?

Solution: Options B and C are obviously wrong since they do not have valid hexadecimal characters. Option A is wrong since it has a colon (:) appearing three times for zero compression, which is invalid. Thus, the **BEST** answer is option D.

Review Questions

Several variations in questions on the subject of IPv6 addressing are possible. Some of them are addressed here:

1.   Removing the leading zero hexadecimal numbers in the hextet in the IPv6 addressing is called:

     A)   Zero suppression

     B)   Zero comprehension

     C)   Zero compression

     D)   Zero shortening

     Answer: Option A

2.   Which of the following is the **BEST** reason on why IPv6 replaces IPv4?

     A)   To accommodate different types of businesses.

     B)   To meet the growing demands of cybersecurity.

C)   IPv6 can accommodate more IP addresses than IPv4.

D)   It is a natural process of version upgrade from 4 to 6.

Answer: Option C

3.   Who is delegated to the mangement of the IPv6 address allocation process?

A)   Global Internet Controlling Authority (GICA)

B)   The United States Federal Government (USFG)

C)   Internet Assigned Numbers Authority (IANA)

D)   Internet Assigned Architecture Board (IAAB)

Answer: Option C

4.   IPv6 addressing is also known as:

Answer: Next-generation (ng) addressing or IPng

5.   How many hextets are in a valid IPv6 address, suppressed or otherwise?

Answer: Every IPv6 has 8 hextets or (8*16) = 128 bits.

6.   Who maintains the list of assigned IP numbers for both IPv4 and IPv6?

A)   Global Internet Evaluation Authority (GIEA)

B)   Internet Assigned Numbers Authority (IANA)

C)   The US-European Internet Authority (TUIA)

D)   Internet Architecture Federation and Board (IAFB)

Answer: Option B

Secure Network Components: Access Control, Transmission, Communication Hardware

Tip #40: Remember port numbers and what they are used for

Memorize different port numbers used for different services.

Domain: Security Engineering, Communications and Network Security

Subdomain: Secure network components, Network communications, Network architecture.

Subject background: Three types of ports are known in general.

- **Well-known ports**: These have port numbers of 0 to 1023. These numbers are standard for any device and are thus called "well known." These are also the "stardard ports," for any device.

- **Registered ports**: These are numbered from 1024 to 49151. These ports can be registered with the Internet Corporation for Assigned Names and Numbers (ICANN) for a specific use.

- **Dynamic ports**: These have numbers from 49152 to 65535. These can be programmed or assigned as needed. Once assigned, these ports can also be removed after the purpose for which a port was assigned a number is over.

Things to Remember

Memorize Table 4-2.

Table 4-2. *Port Numbers and Their Purpose*

Port Number	Purpose
20/21	File Transfer Protocol (FTP). All data transfer is in plain text.
22	Secure Shell (SSH).
23	Telnet.
25	Simple Mail Transfer Protocol (SMTP).
69	Trivial FTP (TFTP).

(continued)

Table 4-2. (*continued*)

Port Number	Purpose
80	Hypertext Transfer Protocol (HTTP).
88	Kerberos Authentication System.
161/162	Simple Network Management Protocol (SNMP).
443	Secure HTTP (HTTPS).
636	Lightweight Directory Access Protocol (LDAP).
1080	SOCKS.

Example: A new Internet company designed a website to sell various rocket parts online for users who can build their own battery-powered rockets at home for fun. The website allows payment via credit cards, bank accounts, and online pay pal accounts. What is the **BEST** port number the Internet company can choose for its website to securely process its customers' personally identifiable information (PII)?

A)   69

B)   434

C)   443

D)   80

Analysis: It is clear that the website designed is processing PII, which can contain name, shipping address, credit card data, etc. For this data to be secure, the currently known methods are to use a secure HTTP protocol, which is HTTPS. The rest of the statement has distracting data that can be safely ignored.

Statement: Removing the superfluous data, we can easily make the question as follows:

A new Internet company designed a website that allows payment via credit cards, bank accounts, and online pay pal accounts.

Question: What is the **BEST** port number to securely process their customers' personally identifiable information (PII)?

Solution: Option C is correct since HTTPS uses port 443. Port 69 is for Trivial FTP, and 80 is for plain HTTP that offers no security. The other options are distractors.

Review Questions

Other variations of questions are as follows:

1. Which of the following can be **BEST** considered as a dynamic port?

   A) 67234

   B) 65560

   C) 49155

   D) 35655

   Answer: Option C. The dynamic ports range is 49152 to 65535.

2. If a programmer in an organization wants to register port 48765 for a particular purpose, who should be contacted to register the port?

   Answer: Internet Corporation for Assigned Names and Numbers (ICANN)

3. Which of the following statements **BEST** describes the difference between standard ports and registered ports?

   A) Registered ports are the same across all devices, whereas standard ports are not.

   B) Standard ports are the same across all devices, whereas registered ports are not.

   C) Any port can be programmed to act either as a standard or as a registered port.

   D) Ports 1024 to 49152 are registered. Ports 0 to 1023 are standard.

   Answer: Option B

Tip #41: Remember the common computer network nomenclature

Know the meaning of each device such as bridge, switch, router, hub, repeater, attenuator, and other computer networking hardware and their basic functions. It is important to note what happens when a port is left open and how an attacker can exploit an unattended open port.

Domain: Communication and Network Security.

Subdomain: Media, Network components, Communication hardware, Wireless transmission and routing, VPN, VLAN, Secure communication channels.

Subject background:

- **Network card**: A network card is required for a computer or information system unit to communicate with external units. They can be wired or wireless. Network adapters have a unique MAC address. The Data Link protocol of the card allows the system to detect other devices. The speed of the network card is usually in gigabits but can support slower speeds like 10 or 20 Mbps (megabits per second). The network interface card (NIC) is slotted in computer system units as a daughter board.

- **Hub**: A hub splits one connection into multiple computers. Hubs are akin to a distribution center. Hubs **do not filter** any information. They just forward the information they receive. Hubs are old-school and are no longer used due to security concerns.

- **Switch**: A switch is an advanced hub. Switches distinguish the MAC address sent to them and send the information only the MAC address specified. This means a switch is a kind of MAC filter that selectively forwards information to only the MAC specified and not to all addresses.

- **Router**: Routers are like traffic controllers between networks. Routers are more like intelligent switches that know how to route the information they receive. If a particular known route is broken or not reachable, routers can figure out an alternative route to send information. In short, routers work to transmit information like a switch does but between two or more independent LANs. Routing does not combine the networks.

- **Gateway**: A gateway is a network hardware component that allows information exchange among discrete networks. Gateways can work in any layer of the OSI model. A gateway can contain protocol translators, protocol converters, signal converters, and many other networking hardware as deemed necessary.

- **Repeater**: This is a re-transmitter that can boost a signal. Repeaters can be used for radio signals, cell phone signals, and a variety of other electronic signals.

- **Attenuation**: This term refers to the loss or weakening of a signal. Attenuation is a natural process of losing signal strength as it moves from one location to another over a long distance.

- **Bridge**: A bridge combines two separate networks and makes them work as a single network. The bridge can be wired or wireless depending on how the networks are linked.

- **Modem**: The full form of MoDeM is "modulator and demodulator." It is used to communicate from one system to another via DSL or a high-speed cable or phone line.

- **Cable**: These are simple wires that connect the networks or devices in a single network. There are many varieties of cables to transmit data. Some examples of cables are twisted pair, coaxial, and fiber optic. Ethernet cables are generally used cables for computer systems.

- **Port**: If a network address is like a street address, a port number is the apartment, house or suite address. Ports usually have a number to determine the process (for example, 80 for HTTP and 443 for HTTPS) they can handle. Open and unsecured ports are often easily detected and exploited by hackers.

Things to Remember

- A bridge connects two networks and makes them function as a single network.

- A router functions to send/receive data from more than one network, but the networks themselves remain independent. A router can therefore be an IP filter.

- Attenuation usually refers to loss of signal.

- Hub is old-school and is obsolete.

- A network proxy (a word often used for a network proxy server) is a kind of gateway that hides the information and/or network address. They help in the encapsulation of the distributed systems.

- A **network protocol** is a formal standard with rules, recommendations, and regulations to conduct secured and managed data transfer across networks. Examples are Internet Protocol (IP), Transmission Control Protocol (TCP), and File Transfer Protocol (FTP).

Example: A company employing a large group of people is stationed in a remote location where cell phone signals are weak, due to lack of phone towers. Which of the following devices **BEST** serves the company to boost the cell phone signals?

A) Attenuator

B) Switch

C) Repeater

D) Bridge

Analysis: A simple reading of the question gives the information that the company wants to **boost** the signal. Attenuation does not boost a signal. Switches and bridges are used for computer networks and are not necessary required for phone signals.

Statement: A company's cell phone signals are weak.

Question: Which of the following devices **BEST** serves the company to boost the cell phone signals?

Solution: The obvious correct answer is option C, a repeater.

Review Questions

The following are some of the other questions on this topic:

1. A router can **BEST** act as a:

    A) MAC filter

    B) IP filter

    C) Hub

    D) Bridge

    Answer: Option B

2. Which cable can transmit the signal the **FASTEST**?

    A)   Ethernet cable

    B)   Thick-net cable

    C)   Fiber-optic cable

    D)   Gigabit cable

    Answer: Option C

3. Which of the following **BEST** describes a network proxy server?

    A)   It openly connects two distributed systems.

    B)   It adds structure and encapsulation to distributed systems.

    C)   It configures open ports and requests on distributed systems.

    D)   It is used to filter hacker attacks on distributed systems.

    Answer: Option B

LAN, WAN, Wireless, Network Security

Tip #42: Review case study questions where the you must think in a given role (like a network/software person)

If a question provides a hat to wear, do wear it. This mostly refers to case study questions.

Domain: All domains of the CISSP exam.

Subdomain: All subdomains of CISSP exam, Network security.

Subject background: With an innovative testing question, the CISSP exam body often tests the test takers for their "ability to think" or "ability to think practically" in a given situation. After giving a scenario about a security situation, the question asks, "In this situation, if you are the network manager, what is your **FIRST/LAST/BEST/MOST PREFERRED** step?" Note that the question is giving you a hat to wear. In this example, that hat is "network manager." And since you are the network manager, you have to cast aside your personality and real-life work and put yourself in the shoes of a network manager. Once you start thinking like a "network manager," wearing the hat given to you in the question and scenario, the next step is to find what is the **FIRST/LAST/BEST/MOST PREFERRED** way of dealing with the situation.

We often tend to pick an answer from what we know when a certain scenario is projected, but the CISSP question asks how you would react if you wore the given hat as a security professional.

Things to Remember

- Think from the point of view of the given scenario and the person you are projected as, in the question and the scenario.

- Do not select the obvious answer quickly to save time. The most obvious answer could be a wrong answer.

- Removing the verbiage and filtering the superfluous information is the first step in questions involving scenarios.

- Remember what the question is asking. Even if the answer is clearly visible, the question may not be asking for a solution but may be asking what the **FIRST/NEXT/LAST/BEST** step is.

- Note that even in this kind of questions, two answers may be easily eliminated, but you still have to pick the better of the remaining two answers.

Example: The company you work for has decided to move to a new building in downtown to the 7th floor. The 7th floor office space is shared by a cable TV company, a corporate office for a grocery retailer, and a host of medical practice offices of the local hospital. All the companies including yours share common rest areas, closed-circuit television cameras in the halls for safety, and the computer and local area network cabling room. As the company's only network engineer, you first want to visit the network cabling room to make sure that your company's network can be hooked up safely and prevent physical hacking attacks. On your visit, you notice that the network cabling is a zig-zag network of loose hanging cables in a myriad of colors that have accumulated a lot of dust over the years, with flashing lights from network cables on routers, switches, servers, etc. You are also concerned that there is no clear marking of the cabling for which switches or routers belong to which. Despite these problems, currently the network is functioning very well and has no major downtime for any offices on the 7th floor and, in general, to the whole building. It is obvious that the network room needs cleaning, as well as a complete facelift and reconfiguration, to make it accessible easily if a problem arises. This effort also needs cooperation from other offices and some shared funding. After examining this room, what is the **FIRST** step you need to do?

A) Talk to all the other offices in the entire building and ask if they will cooperate about the funding to clean and reconfigure the network room and report the results to your CEO.

B) Make a list of things that need to be fixed in the network room; create a cost-benefit analysis with cleaning, wiring, marking, color coding, updates and other changes; and inform the CEO about the problems and ask for funding to fix.

C) Conduct a risk analysis of using the network room and inform your immediate supervisor.

D) Advise the company's human resources against the move since a broken network in the current scenario can cause major losses to your company.

Analysis: After reading the entire verbiage as a CISSP candidate, your immediate reaction is "phew." Right? Before we delve deep into the question, notice that the question gives you a hat to wear: you are the company's **only network engineer**. This hat implies that you need to think like the network person and see what is practical in this scenario. As a network engineer, what are your options? First, let us consider for a moment the company's move. The question states that the company has "decided to move." It therefore tells you that you did not have a voice in the company's decision to move. You only need to think about this situation as a network engineer and cannot tell the CEO or immediate supervisor why it is a bad idea to move. Nobody asked you if the move is going to be in the best interests of the company. That information about the company's decision to move may sound superfluous, but it applies to the way you need to think while wearing the hat given to you.

The second point of the verbiage is that, though the network room is messy, it is apparently functioning quite well, and there was no mention of frequent or any complaints at all in the question. Therefore, a complete facelift may not be a good idea.

The third important point is that, as a security professional, you do not take drastic actions but do need to carefully examine the situation and come to conclusion of what to do. Once that "what to do" is known, the question is only asking what is the **FIRST** step in that process.

Fourth, as a network engineer, you only report to your immediate supervisor of your concerns and never approach any C-level mangers like a CEO, CFO, or CTO.

Fifth, as a network engineer, you must be familiar that sharing the network room's cables, switches, and routers may be common and comes with its own advantages and disadvantages.

Finally, whether the company incurs losses or derives profits from the move is not a network person's concerns. The network person does not have a role to argue or decide where the company will move. Wearing the network engineer hat gives you only the responsibility of making sure that the company network functions as it should.

Statement: Given the analysis, we can now remove the verbiage and state the question as follows:

The company you work for **has decided to move** to a new building in downtown to the 7th floor. The 7th floor office space is shared by a cable TV company, a corporate office for a grocery retailer, and a host of medical practice offices of the local hospital. **As the company's only network engineer, you first want to visit the network cabling room.** On your visit, you notice that the network cabling is a zig-zag network of loose hanging cables in a myriad of colors that have accumulated a lot of dust over the years, with flashing lights from network cables on routers, switches, servers, etc. Despite these problems, **currently the network is functioning very well** and has no major downtime for any offices on the 7th floor and, in general, to the whole building After examining this room, what is the **FIRST** step you need to do?

Question: The company you work for **has decided to move** to a new building in downtown. **As the company's only network engineer, you first want to visit the network cabling room.** After examining this room, what is the **FIRST** step you need to do?

Solution: Option A is a clear distractor since as a network engineer you do not report to the CEO. Option B has good information about what to do, but those are **not** the first steps you do as a network engineer. Option D is a distractor too since as a network engineer you are not supposed to go to HR and advise them. Option C looks like a possible answer, but let us examine that option too.

The first thing to remember is the hat you are given to wear. As a network engineer, you notice that there are problems to be fixed, but currently the network is functioning very well. So, the very **FIRST** step is to find out what the main problems are, how they may pose as risks, and what the company can do about those risks (since a decision to move was already made). This process of finding the problems, how they can pose as risks, and how the company can tackle those risks is "risk analysis." As a network engineer, you do your job of risk analysis and report it to your immediate supervisor. Therefore, option C looks like the best possible answer for the **FIRST** step in the given scenario, when wearing the hat mentioned in the question.

Review Questions

A great many variations of the questions are possible on any domain and subdomain of the CISSP exam. Some of them are given here as examples:

1. **As a software developer** you have just finished writing the code and want to deploy it on the production server straightaway. Before deploying it on the production server, what should be the **FIRST** step?

   A) Deploy on a test server for testing

   B) Debug the code on a development server

   C) Get access to a production server to deploy

   D) Check the production server security

   Answer: Option B. No software developer can straightaway deploy code on a production server without **first** debugging on a development server. The hat given here is as a software developer. Developers normally are not allowed to deploy software on production servers.

2. As a CEO of the company, what is the **MOST** important factor for physically securing an environment?

   Answer: Protecting human life

3. Your company is well-prepared for an accidental data breach and has everything in place. However, data was breached, and you as CEO were informed by your staff about the breach after they detected the breach and the staff responded by shutting the systems off the network but still kept them running. What is the **NEXT** step you advise your staff to do?

   Answer: Incident response happens in stages: preparation, detection, response, mitigation and reporting, recovery and remediation. Since preparation, detection, and response were done already, the **NEXT** step is mitigation. Did you notice that the underlined words are giving the clues for an incident response? If you did, the answer becomes quickly clear.

Tip #43: Learn various standards used in communication and network security

Remember IEEE Standards 802.xx and which corresponds to which purpose.

Domain: Communication and Network Security.

Subdomain: LAN, WAN, Wireless security, and other protocol details.

Subject background: Table 4-3 gives details of each 802.xx standard. The technologies have been developed from "a" through all the alphabet, but the most used ones are listed.

Table 4-3. *802.xx Standards*

Standard	Purpose
802.1 AE	Defines security infrastructure by providing encryption for data integrity, confidentiality, and authentication.
802.1 AF	Provides key functions for session keys used in data encryption.
802.1 AR	Provides a unique ID for each device. Unique IDs help provide secure data to each device as it comes in through a common cable.
802.1 e	For quality of service (QoS). Provides prioritization of traffic based on traffic classification. When QoS is enabled, the device automatically chooses WiFi Multimedia (WMM) by default.
802.3	Used for Ethernet, which is a set of technologies. Uses carrier sense multiple access/collision detection (CSMA/CD). Supports duplex communication.
802.5	Used for token ring, an older version of networking developed by IBM.
802.11b	Wireless WEP. Uses the DSSS protocol for communication. WEP is considered weak and not very safe. Data speeds up to 11 Mbps.
802.11g	Wireless standard up to 54 Mbps. Backward compatible to 802.11b.
802.11i	Used for WPA2 wireless. Provides encryption protection with the AES algorithm.
802.11n	Works up to the speeds of 5 GHz. Makes use of multi-input multi-output concept to increase data throughput.

(continued)

Table 4-3. (*continued*)

Standard	Purpose
802.11ac	Extension of 802.11n and works in 5 GHz range but throughput increased to 1.3 Gbps. It is backward compatible to a, b, g, n standards.
802.11x	Used for port security (port-based network access control [PNAC]). Provides authentication mechanism to devices wanting to connect to LAN/WAN.
802.15	Standard for wireless personal area network (WPAN) using mostly for Bluetooth and other personal devices. Uses FHSS.
802.16	Broadband wireless access (802 WBA).

FHHS: Frequency hopping spread spectrum. The entire bandwidth is divided into smaller channels or sub-bandwidths to transmit radio signals. When transmitting, the signal hops/changes from one career frequency to another and may move among the bands.Bluetooth frequently uses FHSS.

DSSS: Direct sequence spread spectrum. Th entire spectrum or bandwidth is used for communication.

TKIP, AES: Temporal key integrity protocol, and Advanced Encryption Standard. These two can be used individually or in a combination.

Things to Remember

- Once 802 is mentioned, it is almost always connected to computer networks, either wired or wireless.

- Most wireless network–related questions involve 802.11a, b, i, g, n, and ac models. This can be remembered as "a-big-nac" (akin to "A Big Mac"), and each model is an improvement over the earlier model and mostly backward compatible.

- Token rings were earlier models of computer networks that have since been replaced with Ethernet.

- Anyone who has set up a wireless network at home is probably familiar with router/cable modem setup where one can see the wireless settings for various 802.11 protocols.

Example: A company has a single-cable input from the demarcation point of the Internet service provider. The cable can supply Internet speeds of 200 Mbps. To supply Internet to all the company employees, a wireless network is planned. What is the **BEST** protocol the company can adopt for secure data transactions and high throughput on its wireless network?

A) 802.11b with 5 GHz connections and AES security

B) 802.11ac with TKIP and AES

C) 802.11n with 54 Mbps

D) 802.15 with Bluetooth and WPAN

Analysis: Wireless technologies use 802.11, and thus option D is an automatic distractor in the given list of answers. 802.11b does not work at 5 GHz (works up to 11 Mbps) and is therefore an immediate distractor. Option C is tempting to choose, but it does not mention if additional security is added. But if we look at option B, it has all 802.11n can offer and more. Thus, a careful check reveals the answer as option B. Option C is a close second (but a wrong answer).

Statement: We can remove the verbiage and see that the question can be generalized for any company that plans to use a wireless network. The demarcation point, speed of the Internet, and how many cables are used are all superfluous information. The statement can be as follows:

A company has a single cable input from the Internet service provider. To supply Internet to them all, a wireless network is planned.

Question: What is the **BEST** protocol the company can adapt for high throughput on its planned wireless network?

Solution: Option B since it is also backward compatible to 802.11n. It offers TKIP and AES protection as well over the generic standard along with speed and throughput. Note that on the CISSP exam there are always two answers that can be easily eliminated, but the remaining two are closely correct. One has to choose the "more correct" answer or the **BEST** of the four choices given in the options after identifying the distractors.

Review Questions

Various questions can be asked on the variety of standards, speeds they offer, and other details. Some of them are here:

1. Which protocol or IEEE standard is best for port security and authorization?

    A) 802.11ac

    B) 802.15

    C) 802.1e

    D) 802.1x

    Answer: Option D

2. What replaced 802.5 token ring network?

    A) 804.2 serial network

    B) 802.6 parallel network

    C) 802.3 Ethernet network

    D) 802.11n wireless network

    Answer: Option C

3. What is the full form of TKIP?

    A) Temporary Key for the Internet Provider

    B) Temporal Key Integrity Protocol

    C) Temporary key Integrated in Protocol

    D) Temporal Key Information Protocol

    Answer: Option B

4. Which IEEE standard uses the DSSS protocol for communication?

    Answer: 802.1b

5. Enabling this protocol makes the device WiFi Multimedia (WMM) by default

    Answer: 802.1e

6. Which protocol is the **BEST** for a personal area network using Bluetooth and FHSS?

    Answer: 802.15

Firewalls

Tip #44: Learn the correct but subtle differences in protocols

Remember the protocol differences between EAP and PEAP.

Domain: Communication and Network Security.

Subdomain: Wired and wireless security, Protocols, Network architecture, Firewalls.

Subject background: EAP stands for Extensible Authentication Protocol, and PEAP is Protected EAP. EAP is used in wireless 802.11 and elsewhere. This can be easily observed in wireless router settings menus when one is setting up a WiFi at home. EAP and PEAP are authentication protocols and are sometimes referred as "frameworks." EAP-TLS uses server-side authentication with client-side certificate verification. For a hacker to break this security, though the server can be hacked, a client-side certificate will still be needed to break the entire EAP-TLS. A password is used not for authentication but to encrypt the client certificate for storage. EAP comes in a wide variety of combinations such as EAP-MD5, EAP-POTP (Protected One-Time Password), etc.

PEAP is a protected version of EAP, which is a protocol that encapsulates EAP within an encrypted and authenticated TLS tunnel. PEAP is designed to correct any deficiencies in EAP. EAP assumes that the physical communication channel is secure. PEAP provides security where such physical protection is not provided.

Things to Remember

- EAP is an open standard that uses Transport Layer Security (TLS) and assumes the physical communication channel is well protected.

- PEAP is an extension of EAP that provides security (P = protected) where such physical security is not available.

189

- EAP can be combined with the Radius and Diameter protocols for encapsulating EAP. These are usually for a network access server that forwards EAP packets between 802.1x devices.

- PEAP is a protocol that suggests protection by chaining multiple EAP mechanisms such as EAP-GTC but does not suggest a specific mechanism.

- PEAPv0 (EAP-MSCHAPv2) and PEAP1 (EAP-GTC) are two versions of PEAP.

- PEAP is jointly developed by Cisco, Microsoft, and RSA Security.

- Microsoft Windows XP used PEAPv0.

- Lightweight Directory Access Protocol (LDAP) uses EAP-GTC.

Example: A company wants to implement a network protocol to protect its WiFi communications that use WPA and WPA2 standards. The CEO initially planned to use EAP but is discouraged by the network jockey who recently obtained his CISSP certification and suggested using PEAP that was developed by Microsoft. The CEO is convinced that EAP is fine, but the network jockey made sure that the CEO changed his mind. Why is the network jockey persistent in saying that the CEO is wrong in making the choice of EAP?

A) The CEO is wrong because PEAP is an older version with no known vulnerabilities.

B) The CEO is right because EAP is a newer version with no known vulnerabilities.

C) The network jockey is right because PEAP provides better protection.

D) The network jockey is wrong because EAP is older but still provides the best protection.

Analysis: The information that the network jockey passing the CISSP certification is an added advantage to test taker since it is telling the test taker that the network jockey is right. Second, PEAP suggests in the first letter, *P*, that it is protected. Both EAP and PEAP are used for WPA and WPA2. It is easy to filter the lengthy verbiage and conclude that the network jockey is right.

Statement: A company wants WiFi communications that use WPA and WPA2 standards. The network jockey **who recently obtained his CISSP certification**, suggested using PEAP.

Question: Why is the network jockey persistent in making the choice of PEAP?

Solution: Option C is the correct answer. Option A is wrong because PEAP is newer than EAP. Option B is wrong because EAP is an older version. Option D is wrong because the network jockey is actually right in forcing the CEO to change his mind to opt for PEAP.

Review Questions

A great variety of questions are possible on this topic since it is about network security, which is the backbone for cyber communications. Here are some:

1. What is the difference between EAP and PEAP?

    Answer: PEAP is a protected version of EAP, which "suggests" additional protection with TLS tunnel. PEAP does not recommend any particular method to protect but only suggests protection.

2. On which layer of OSI (or TCP) does the PEAP protocol work?

    Answer: PEAP works on the Data Link layer of OSI (or the Network layer of TCP). The reason is that EAP-TLS is a handshake process that will happen above the Data Link layer. But the handshake needs the cryptographic information that comes from data. Hence, the answer is the Data Link layer in OSI and the Network layer in TCP.

3. EAP or PEAP is mostly used in what communication?

    A) Wired communications.

    B) WiFi communications.

    C) Telephone communications.

    D) EAP or PEAP is no longer used.

    Answer: Option B

4. A company is considering removing the firewall that protects its software and plans to install PEAPv1 developed by the CISCO. What implications can the network and software people expect due to the firewall removal?

    Answer: PEAPv1 is for network communication protection and has nothing to do with software protection. Software firewall removal may still cause viruses to pass through and damage the existing software.

5. PEAP specifically provides a protocol or encryption mechanism of its own to overcome the problems of EAP. True/False?

    Answer: False. PEAP suggests EAP tunneling, which can be done with any combinations such as EAP-GTC or EAP-MSCHAPv0. PEAP is similar to EAP-TTLS.

6. Which version of PEAP is supported by LDAP?

    A)   PEAPv0 (EAP-MSAPv2).

    B)   PEAPv1 (EAP-GTC).

    C)   Both PEAPv0 (EAP-MSAPv2) and PEAPv1 (EAP-GTC).

    D)   LDAP does not support any PEAP versions.

    Answer: Option B

7. What certificate does PEAP use to create a secure TLS tunnel to protect user authentication?

    Answer: Server-side public key certificates

8. A company wants to use EAP with the WEP standard for wireless communication. If possible, they are interested in migrating to PEAP with WEP. Is this a feasible solution?

    Answer: No, WEP is weak and has more vulnerabilities and is not used with EAP or PEAP. EAP and PEAP are more suitable for WPA and WPA2 (with other combinations such as TKIP, etc.)

Network Attacks and Countermeasures

Tip #45: Understand the structure of the IPSec protocol, authentication header, and security payload

Understand the IPSec protocol, Authentication Header (AH), and Encapsulated Security Payload (ESP).

Domain: Communication and Network Security.

Subdomain: Internet protocols, OSI model, Communication protocols.

Subject background: The Internet Protocol Security Standard (IPSec) is a standard architecture approved by the Internet Engineering Task Force (IETF) for setting up a secure channel for information exchange. IPSec uses public key cryptography for encryption, nonrepudiation (signature), and access control (authentication).

IPSec is generally used with the Layer 2 Tunneling Protocol (L2TP) for more security as IPSec/L2TP.

Figure 4-1 gives an overview of IPSec.

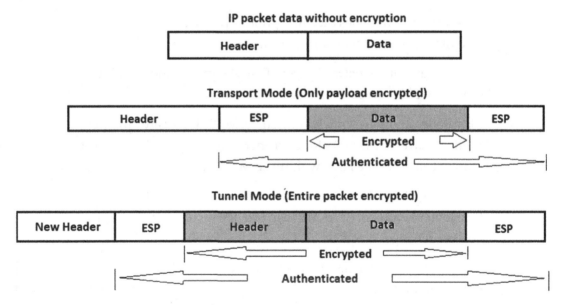

Figure 4-1. *IPSec, ESP, and AH details*

Things to Remember

- IPSec is integral part of both IPv4 and IPv6.

- IPSec relies on security associations (one for each way and always one way).

- IPSec has two main components/protocols: Authentication Header (AH) and Encapsulating Security Payload (ESP).

- AH provides authentication and access control (message integrity and nonrepudiation) and prevents replay attacks.

- ESP provides confidentiality and integrity of packet contents.

- IPSec provides two different ways of operation: tunnel mode and transportation mode.

- Tunnel mode provides encryption of the entire packet including a header. This mode is mostly useful for gateway-to-gateway communication (VPN).

- Transport mode provides the encryption of payload (ESP) only. This is useful for peer-to-peer communication.

- IPSec operates at the network layer of the OSI model and Internet layer of the TCP model.

- IPSec alone cannot be sufficient when network attacks are imminent. Additional layers of security for data encryption can provide the best security. Examples are L2TP with IPSec, WPA2, etc.

- When using IPSec, the Internet Security Association and Key Management Protocol (ISAKMP) can provide security association and key exchange.

- Internet Key Exchange (IKE) provides authenticated keying material for use with ISAKMP.

- AH and ESP can be used together or separately when employing IPSec.

Example: A company employing several contractors allows them to work from home on the company's loaned laptops. Login security is achieved with a username and password. To protect the hard disks, the disk is encrypted in a way that if a laptop is stolen or lost, nobody can read the contents of the hard disk. When the employees are working from home on these laptops, the company needs protect all the data and other information transmitted to and from the laptop to the company's servers. The company wants to employ a security protocol in addition to what is already in place. The Layer 2 Tunneling Protocol (L2TP) will be used to protect the IP traffic. Which is the **BEST** protocol the company can implement for the virtual private network (VPN) for the laptops to connect?

A)   Use PPP with tunnel mode

B)   User IPSec in tunnel mode

C)   User PPP with transport mode

D)   User IPSec with transport mode

Analysis: It is clear that the company wants to implement a good protocol for data since the laptops connect to the servers via VPN. And during the connection, the company wants to protect everything—data and headers and all. Thus, IPSec is a better option that can be used in either transport or tunnel mode. Further analysis can be done by removing the verbiage and coming to the correct answer quickly.

Statement: When employees are working from home on these laptops, **a company needs protect _complete data_ and other information transmitted to and from the laptop to the company's servers**. The company wants to employ a security protocol in addition to <u>what is already in place, Layer 2 Tunneling Protocol (L2TP),</u> to be used on the IP.

Question: Which is the **BEST** protocol a company can implement for the virtual private network (VPN) for the laptops to connect?

Solution: When the complete data with other information needs protection, the straightaway answer is tunnel mode since tunnel mode protects the headers and data and everything else. Since tunnel mode can be done with IPSec and IPSec can be used with L2TP, the quick answer will be option B.

Options C and D are wrong since transport mode only protects data and not everything else.

Review Questions

Several variations of questions are given here:

1. Which part of IPSec provides the **BEST** packet content integrity?

   A) AH

   B) ESP

   C) Either AH or ESP

   D) Both AH and ESP

   E) Neither AH nor ESP

   Answer: ESP provides the best packet integrity.

2. What is the **BEST** way to provide security if only the payload needs to be encrypted when using IPSec?

   Answer: The payload means the data. So, the answer is the transport mode of IPSec provides the best security for the payload if only the payload needs encryption.

3. At what layer of TCP/IP does IPSec work?

   Answer: Internet layer. Note that if the question asks about a layer of OSI, then the answer is "Network layer."

4. Where is IPSec most commonly used?

   Answer: In gateway-to-gateway communication to protect the IP traffic

5. How many connections can IPSec handle?

   Answer: PPTP can handle **only one** connection at a time but IPSec can handle multiple connections at the same time.

6. What mode of IPSec provides "availability?"

   Answer: None. AH and ESP vouch for integrity and confidentiality, but neither of them can guarantee availability.

Tip #46: Review denial-of-service attacks with computer networks

Know about the different attacks, such as smurf, teardrop, LAND, DoS, DDoS, etc.

Domain: Communication and Network Security, Software Security.

Subdomain: Network attacks, Software security.

Subject background: Most of the network attacks are either the DoS type or the DDoS type. If there is a host that provides a service to others, the attacker's aim is to disable the service in one way or the other. This disabling of service is known as a denial of service (DoS). In DoS, there is only one sender involved. Figure 4-2 shows a smurf attack.

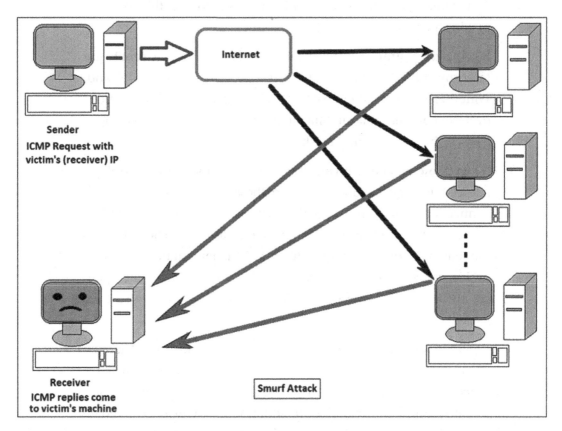

Figure 4-2. *Smurf attack. A single user sends a request with a spoofed IP address to various hosts. Hosts respond to the spoofed IP address, which is the victim's IP address. Smurf is a DoS attack*

In a **distributed/dedicated denial-of-service (DDoS) attack,** the requests come from not a single machine but various machines. This makes the attacker anonymous since the attacker's actual location changes or more than one attacker is often at work, thereby making it difficult to trace the attacker.

Spoofing of IP enables an attacker to stand behind a rogue network and yet use a valid IP address in communication. The valid IP address may actually belong to another third party who is **not** aware of their IP address spoofing.

Things to Remember

- DDoS is a large-scale version of DoS. This means the incoming origin of the attack comes from various sources and unknown IP addresses. All the unknown addresses are either bogus or forged, thereby making them appear real and legal.

- In a **teardrop attack**, mangled and oversized packets are sent to the target machine. Several operating systems such as Windows 95 and Windows NT were vulnerable for this kind of attack. Mangled and oversized packets make it difficult for the host to re-assemble the packets thereby causing a crash.

- A **Syn flood** happens with an attacker sends a flood of TCP/SYN packets with forged addresses. Each of these packets requests a connection from the host, and the host responds by sending "OK, I am ready. Please acknowledge," and opening the connection. But since the sender IP address is forged, the acknowledgment never comes back, thereby keeping the connection half-open. Dozens of half-open connections such as these crash the host and deny service to the real users.

- **LAND attack** (which stands for "local area network denial") happens when an attacker sends a poised packet to the server, which when processed will lock up the host. In a LAND attack, an attacker sends a TCP SYN packet with a host's IP address as both the source and the destination. Thus, the host replies to itself and ultimately locks up.

- In any of the DoS attacks, the main aim of the attacker is to disable the service a host provides. The service can be a web service, credit card processing, telephone answering service, or even day-to-day phone (telephone denial of service [TDoS]).

- A web service or application usually has a limited number of sessions, and if those sessions are tied up, the service will not respond. If the sessions are all starved or tied with the service forever, the service will eventually die of starvation (web crash). This is known as an **R-U-Dead-Yet (RUDY)** attack.

- The main reason the attacks happen is due to neglecting the open ports (not protecting) in a network router or device.

- The idea of the attacker is to gain access to one of the internal machines and create a username or login name as an administrator and from there do anything to disable the service or steal the data (such as credit card numbers, PII, etc.).

- There is no known permanent fix to any attack since attackers get more innovative by the day and since the only solution to prevent DoS or DDoS attacks is to be ready and constantly vigil as long as one owns the network and a host offering some service.

Example: Three attackers are planning to attack a famous banking network. Attacker 1 suggests that they use LAND attack to cripple the bank's network. Attacker 2 thinks that DoS is a better way and the trace of IP address will not find the attackers. However, attacker 3 believes that creating a botnet and widespread attack on the banking network is a better idea. After discussions, all agree to go with the botnet attack. Accordingly, they acquire ten computers from the Internet after checking thoroughly the available open ports. They also establish login credentials on these ten computers. All three attackers load the ten computers with a virus and start sending requests from those computers to the bank's server. On Monday only one computer sends requests, but as days progress, the remaining nine computers join the attack. By the tenth day, all ten computers are sending requests to the bank network at breakneck speed, and the banking network crashes, unable to process the requests.

What attacks did the attackers actually commit on the bank's network?

A) DoS attack, since attackers started with one computer sending many requests

B) LAND attack to disable the bank's LAN

C)   DDoS attack, since several computers are used with spoofed IP
     addresses

D)   SYN/flood attack since the ten computers flooded the bank
     network with requests

Analysis: A quick reading of the verbiage shows that the attackers are using
more than one computer to attack the host and spoofing the bank's network. The ten
computers acquired to use a virus and spoofed IP address to attack the bank's network
are together called a botnet. Botnets are a common group of innocent computers that
are acquired by attackers to send information to a bank. When a botnet of more than one
computer sends requests to a single host to disable a service, it is called DDoS.

Statement: Three attackers are planning to attack a famous banking network.
After discussions, all agree to go with the botnet attack. Accordingly, they acquire
ten computers from the Internet after checking thoroughly for available open ports. All
ten computers are sending requests to the bank network at breakneck speed, and the
banking network crashes, unable to process the requests.

Question: Removing all the verbiage, the question can be extracted as follows:

By the tenth day, all ten computers are sending requests to the bank network, and
the banking network crashes, unable to process the requests.

What attacks did the attackers actually commit on the bank's network?

Solution: The obvious answer for this question is option C. Option A is not correct
since more than one computer is used. Option B is not correct since in a LAND attack
a request is sent with the same source and destination address. Option D is not correct
since syn/flood needs half-open connections after receiving a request.

Review Questions

Some of the questions on this topic and its variations look as follows:

1.   What is the main and the **MOST** probable avenue for an attacker
     to exploit a network?

     Answer: Open ports

2.   What type of attack concentrates on the limited number of
     available sessions?

A) DoS attack

B) DDoS attack

C) RUDY attack

D) Syn/flood attack

Answer: Option C

3. In which attack does an attacker send a request to a host, making the host talk to itself as the sender and receiver and crash?

    Answer: LAN denial (LAND) attack

4. What is the difference between a DoS attack and a DDoS attack?

    Answer: In a DoS attack, a single sender (with a spoofed IP address return address of victim) sends requests to several machines that respond with those requests to the victim. The victim's machine is thus locked up quickly with those requests. In DDoS, the attacker uses dozens of machines with spoofed IP addresses to avoid detection.

5. From the network logs, what can one find to determine a DoS or DDoS attack?

    Answer: In the case of a DoS attack, the network logs will show that a request comes from a single location, whether the location is traceable or not. In a DDoS attack, the network logs will show repeated inquiries from various locations all sending requests simultaneously.

6. What attack reveals several half-open communications?

A) SYN/flood attack

B) LAND attack

C) Virus attack with same IP address

D) Teardrop attack

Answer: Option A

Tip #47: Know various classes of network abuse and their meaning

Understand network abuses and classes.

Domain: Communication and Network Security.

Subdomain: Network attacks and countermeasures, Secure network design.

Subject background: Table 4-4 gives details of all classes of network abuse.

Table 4-4. *Classes of Network Abuse*

Class	Details
A	Legitimate user gains higher-level access and pretends to be a high-level access user. Considered as masquerading. Use of higher access is unauthorized/illegal.
B	User utilizes the network for nonbusiness/not allowed purposes (depends on rules of the organization).
C	Eavesdropping. Can be either active (tampering the channels to create a covert channel) or passive (monitor/listen to transmission).
D	Denial of service or other interruptions.
E	Network intrusion, spoofing, piggybacking, backdoor attacks, etc.
F	Probing that could be used to find the roadmap of network with a sniffer.

Things to Remember

- Attacks on a network are second-stage crimes since abusing the network itself is a first-stage access. The first-stage access that is unauthorized is classified as shown in Table 4-3.

- Class A can fall into the category of the Bell–LaPadula model of no read up and no write down, as well as the Biba model of no read down and no write up. Accessing data from any level to any other unauthorized level is class A misuse.

- Class B has a fine line in that if permission is granted by the employing organization to access data or a website for nonbusiness purposes, then it is not a misuse. This can be done when an organization specifically deals with subjects such as pornography, email hacks, etc.

- Class C, like class B, is dependent on the organization and the rules that were agreed upon.

- Classes D to F are more serious misuses that could have dire consequences when found out.

- Attacks can be either on hardware or on software. They can also be physical on a physical asset sitting idly in an office.

Example: A newly hired employee overhears a conversation between two managers in a bank and obtains the password of an administrator's account. Logging into the account, the employee escalates his own need to know/least privilege account to administrative account level to gain access and later hacks the bank to transfer money into another private account. What kind of network abuse has the employee committed at **WORST**?

A) Class C abuse

B) Class F abuse

C) Class A abuse

D) Class E abuse

Analysis: Note that the employee might have committed more than one abuse. The question is asking about the **WORST** abuse of all the abuses committed in the given situation. Considering the question, we know that the employee first overheard the conversation either directly, indirectly, or by eavesdropping. This is class C abuse. Second, the employee logged into the administrator account and elevated his own privileges, which is like going up a level of authorization without proper permissions. This is class A abuse.

Eavesdropping is a lesser sin than actually using that information to log in and gain higher privileges to steal money. Class F and class E abuses do not fit in the given situation.

Statement: The statement can be reworded easily removing the verbiage as follows:

A newly hired employee **overhears a conversation** and obtains the password of an administrator's account. Logging into the account, the employee escalates his own account to the administrative account level.

Question: An employee **overhears a conversation** and escalates his own account to the administrative account level. What kind of network abuse is the employee said to have committed at **WORST**?

Solution: Class A network abuse is clearly a bigger sin than the class C abuse. Thus, the best answer is option C, which is class A network abuse.

Review Questions

Various possibilities and questions can appear on this topic, and some of them are listed here:

1. An employee hired by a company is allowed to check his private email on the company's server. However, the employee takes this permission as a universal rule to visit any website and does his shopping on Amazon.com. What network abuse might this user have committed?

   Answer: Class B abuse. Using business equipment or the business network for nonbusiness purposes.

2. An attacker using a smurf attack causes an organization-wide DDoS, and the network is shut down for more than five hours causing financial losses to the organization. What class of network abuse can this be classified as?

   Answer: DoS and DDoS attacks fall under class D network abuse.

3. An attacker is trying to find open ports on a server. After probing around for hours, the attacker has a complete network idea of the organization. Using this network idea as a roadmap, he wants to utilize the open ports and send free junk mail from the open server to some people. What network abuse might the attacker have committed?

   A) Class B abuse (nonbusiness purpose)

   B) Class F abuse (probing the network)

   C) Class E abuse (roadmap of the network)

   D) Class C abuse (creating covert channel)

   Answer: Option B. Note that class E does not give a roadmap of the network.

4. Which network abuse model can be compared to the Bell–LaPadula model in which the rule "no read up, no write down" occurs?

   Answer: Class A

5. A computer security firm's physical building has a double door access card entry where each employee scans the ID card to open the door. If an employee enters the opened door following another employee, without scanning any ID card, what abuse can this **BEST** be considered as?

   A) Class A abuse

   B) Class D abuse

   C) Class E abuse

   D) Class K abuse

   Answer: Though this is not a computer network abuse, it can still be considered as abusing a security system by piggybacking. Thus, the answer is option C, which is class E abuse. Note that some software virus attacks that use a backdoor can be considered as abuse in the class E category.

6. What are the levels/classes of network abuse known as?

   A) Six levels: levels P, Q, R, S, T, U

   B) Four levels: levels I, II, III, IV

   C) Six classes: classes A, B, C, D, E, F

   D) Four classes: classes I, II, III, IV

   Answer: Option C

CHAPTER 5

Identity and Access Management

In this chapter, you will learn how identification, authentication, and authorization work in tandem; about the use of biometrics; and about access control categories and related attacks.

Access Control Categories and Attacks

Tip #48: Learn the types of access controls, their definition, and how they are managed

In this section, you'll learn about access controls, DAC, MAC, subjects, object authentication, proofing, and role- and rule-based access control.

Domain: Identity and Access Management, Security Operations.

Subdomain: Rule-based access controls, Access control categories, Access control attacks.

Subject background: Access control dictates how a subject (a person or an entity) can access an object (a resource). Access control is required in information technology and in security because a company or an organization cannot allow everybody to access everything in their resources. In general, the best rule for access is least privilege, giving people the minimum access required to perform their job successfully.

Access control is generally one of three different types: discretionary, mandatory, and role-based. For IT systems, software programs control how and what rules are embedded into each of these access types. These programs can be in the kernel or in any other area that is controlled by the security policies of the organization.

© R. Sarma Danturthi 2020
R. S. Danturthi, *70 Tips and Tricks for Mastering the CISSP Exam*,
https://doi.org/10.1007/978-1-4842-6225-2_5

Things to Remember

The CISSP exam will have at least three to four different questions on this topic, and it is important to understand each access control and how and why it functions.

DAC is discretionary access control. It is based on the "discretion" of the system owner. The owner can change who can and who cannot access the systems depending on how much the owner trusts the user. A user who does not have access can gain access after spending a few months in the company and gaining the confidence of the owner, or an already allowed user can be stripped of his access due to bad behavior or misuse. In short, the owner of the system decides who has the access to the systems. The big drawback of DAC is that once access is allowed, the risk for exploitation is high since an allowed user can do almost anything on the allowed systems. It is also possible to limit the access to a few functions rather than giving full access. DAC normally gives full control for the subjects on the objects they create.

Mandatory access control (MAC) is dependent on a subject's clearance level (secret, top secret, etc.) and the object's sensitivity labels. Clearances are matched to labels to decide who can access what. MAC is usually applicable when the confidentiality of data is required. The MAC model also implements the rules depending on a subject's need to know. If some information or access is not required, the access is not given.

Role-based access control (RBAC) is used when a subject is given a particular role to perform. RBAC is also called nondiscretionary access control since subjects are grouped into roles depending on their job function. For example, a bank teller does not have full access to the entire cash repository in the bank, and a normal software developer does not have access or permission to deploy code on a production server. Another form of RBAC is task-based where a subject may perform an action with the help of another (dual control).

Rule-based access control (RuBAC) is designed based on specific rules of the company policies. These rules are usually created based on a series of decisions in software with if/then statements. An example is a virus protection program that works with a number of known stored signatures. The program checks the files for a known virus (if that virus matches) and either allows or blocks the files.

Content-dependent access control is a finer version beyond MAC and DAC. It means that even if a subject is allowed to access a database or system, the subject is further filtered depending on the content of the file to allow access. An example is that a supervisor may be able to access employee records to check the hours logged but may not be allowed to see the medical records of the employee (due to privacy concerns).

Context-based access controls have a different set of rules, usually the time-of-day rules. An example is to allow access to a user from Monday to Friday in the working hours, but when the user tries to log in on Saturday or Sunday, the access is denied.

Subjects have security clearances/capability lists, and objects have sensitivity labels. The main aim of the access control mechanisms is to protect the CIA triad of security.

Discretionary access control is identity-based and usually depends on the group/membership a subject has.

In a large organization, where there is a huge employee turnover, RBAC is usually set up. In nondiscretionary access control, a central authority determines the control access. RuBAC is usually implemented in firewalls and access controls lists with rules.

In MAC, an access control matrix determines which subject can access what object at the highest level (being able to access a high level automatically means access is allowed below that level too).

Example: A company wants to use two different access controls. The first control wants to limit the access of subjects depending on their clearance level, which is granted at the discretion of the owner. The IT systems are given sensitivity labels depending on the sensitivity of data they process or store. The access control matrix to match the clearances and labels is updated regularly as well. Once this first access is given, the second access control limits users from reading the files stored depending on the data stored in the files. A write access is never allowed except for the owners at this second access level. What two access controls are **BEST** suited to the scenario described?

A)   Discretionary access control and mandatory access control

B)   Discretionary access control and context-based access control

C)   Mandatory access control and content-based access control

D)   Mandatory access control and context-based access control

Analysis: Simply, the company wants two access control mechanisms. The first one is based on clearances and labels (MAC should come to mind immediately). The word "discretion" is a clear distractor. The second access control depends on the content of the files. Thus, content dependent access control is best suited.

Statement: Removing the verbiage, we can read the question statement as follows:

A company wants to use two different access controls. The first control wants to limit the access of subjects depending on their **clearance level**. The IT systems are given **sensitivity labels**. The second access control limits users from reading the files stored depending on the **data stored**. What two access controls are **BEST** suited to the scenario described?

Question: The first control wants to limit the access of subjects depending on their **clearance level** and **sensitivity labels**; the second access control limits users to files stored depending on the **data stored**. What two access controls are **BEST** suited to the scenario described?

Solution: Option C is the correct answer. Option A is wrong since both MAC and DAC are not implemented at the same time. The secondary access control required for the company is an access control beyond MAC or DAC. Context-based access control is for checking the time of day and does not apply in this scenario, thus making options B and D incorrect answers.

Review Questions

Some of the questions and their variations are listed here:

1. For a large corporation with high employee turnover, which access control is **BEST** suited?

   Answer: RuBAC is best suited for a company with high employee turnover.

2. What is the **BEST** reason access control is implemented?

   A) To meet the security triad of CIA

   B) To limit access to secure systems

   C) To allow access to secure systems

   D) To exert supervisor control on employees

   Answer: Option B

3. If a company wants to limit access to their IT systems after work hours, what access control is **BEST** suited for the situation?

   Answer: Context-based access control

4. Which access control uses sensitivity labels and security clearances?

   Answer: Mandatory access control (MAC)

5. What access control is best suited for a group of users with similar roles who are all given access uniformly and grouped depending their identity?

   A) Discretionary access control (DAC)

   B) Mandatory access control (MAC)

   C) Role-based access control (RBAC)

   D) Task-based access control (TBAC)

   Answer: DAC is given for a group depending their identity. So, the answer is option A. Note that the word "roles" is a clear and dangerous distractor because though the users have similar roles, the access is given differently.

6. A firewall to protect the network has at least 200 virus signatures placed in memory to detect any virus-based attacks. To thwart a virus-based attack, what kind of access control is **BEST** suited in a firewall?

   A) Content-based access control (CBAC)

   B) Mandatory access control (MAC)

   C) Rule-based access control (RuBAC)

   D) Virus-based access control (VBAC)

   Answer: Firewalls operate on rules (also known as virus signatures) put in the software to block viruses. Thus, the correct answer is option C.

7. In any mandatory access control, what do subjects and objects have, respectively?

   A) Subjects have sensitivity labels, and objects have clearances.

   B) Subjects have clearances, and objects have sensitivity labels.

   C) Subjects have access/discretion, and objects have all rules that allow access.

   D) Subjects have rules to access, and objects have access/discretion.

   Answer: Option B

Biometrics

Tip #49: Biometrics Access mechanism that operates on "what you are."

The authentication methods can range from a simple username/password combination to the most advanced biometric screening based on the physical traits of a person.

Domain: Identity and Access Management.

Subdomain: Access control, Identification and authentication, Biometrics.

Subject background: The following methods are usually involved in access control and authentication. Identification is the first step, followed by authentication and authorization.

Basic authentication is usually done by a username and password. This is the **WEAKEST** form of authentication where identification can be easily stolen by attackers.

The **Digest type** of authentication is done by challenge and response. Digest is usually performed by sending a session key that is valid for a limited period of time. Online banking and some websites use this method for more security. A digest is a hashed string and reproducible.

Integrated authentication is usually done via Active Directory where usernames and identities are stored. Lightweight Directory Access Protocol (LDAP) is also an option for integrated authentication. Before a user is given authorization, the user's credentials are stored on the LDAP or Active Directory for checking. The main problem with integrated authentication is to update the directory regularly and maintaining it.

Certificate-based authentication is usually done via a user's public key certificates (X.509). The certificate authentication may use TLS/SSL, which is a basis for secure websites with HTTPS. Certificates can be stored in the certificate authority (CA). Certificates are also used in digital signatures and email exchange.

Forms-based authentication is another method used on Internet web forms. Until the form is submitted, the user is not evaluated. A form can use basic authentication, a key, or a secret code among a variety of other methods.

Token-based authentication gives authorization for a single source or multiple sources upon basic authentication to a user. A token issued after validating the identification can be used by the user for accessing a resource. A token is a second layer of security over basic authentication. Tokens are not necessarily reproducible and are very random.

Smart cards are the newest way of logging into systems with proper ID and authentication. However, smart cards usually combine a PIN/fixed token to further validate a user. A smart card can be used for multiple purposes such as main gate access, building access, storage access, or system access in full or in part.

Biometrics are the best but least used forms (due to the costs) of authentication for a device or system. Apple iPhone's face recognition, the fingerprint scanner used in some keyboards, and palm/retina/iris scans for building entry are all examples of biometrics.

Things to Remember

- The basic username/password is the weakest form of identification but is the most widely used.

- A 100% match on a biometric scanner is usually considered a fraud since there cannot be a perfect scan of a living being's physical traits that change from time to time and due to various uncontrollable circumstances.

- Biometric scanning is usually the most expensive but more accurate.

- Biometric authentication falls into the area of what you are (Type 3).

- False rejection rate (FRR, which is Type 1) and false acceptance rate (FAR, Type 2) are important factors in biometrics.

- FRR means falsely rejecting a truly recognized good authentication.

- FAR means falsely accepting a bad authentication as correct.

- Crossover error rate or equal error rate (CER/EER) is where the FRR meets the FAR or where the FAR equals the FRR. It is well-suited for comparing two biometric solutions/devices.

- Access time for a typical biometric scanner should be less than or equal to six seconds (or ten subjects per minute).

Example: When a user tries to log into his bank account with a username and password, a bank's website sends an eight-digit code to the user's cell phone to be input on the bank's website as a second step to authenticate the user before authorizing access of the accounts. What kind of authentication does the eight-digit code serve?

A) Digest authentication

B) Digital code dual authentication

C) Integrated authentication

D) Token-based authentication

Analysis: The question clearly states that the bank's website is using two-step authentication. The final question after the initial verbiage is what authentication does the eight-digit code serve? So, we can conveniently forget about the first kind of authentication that the bank website requires since whatever is the first authentication (web forms, basic username/password) is augmented by the second, an eight-digit code sent by the bank's website. The code sent by the bank's website is usually a token that is valid for a few hours only. Once we understand that the second authentication is done via this token (an eight-digit number sent on a cell phone), we can easily eliminate the distractors and pick the correct answer. Note that the bank sent a token, and the token can change every time the user logs in; therefore, it is **not** a digest.

Also, note that there is no such thing as digital code dual authentication given in option C.

Statement: A bank's website sends an eight-digit code as a **second step for authentication**.

Concentrating on the basic question, we can easily understand that the authentication process asked for is only for the second step, which is an eight-digit code entry on the bank's website.

Question: What authentication does the eight-digit code serve?

Solution: Option D is the correct answer since the code sent by the bank is a token valid for a time frame to authorize the user who tries to log in with another basic form of authentication.

Review Questions

Several possible questions include biometric authentication, Active Directory, LDAP, and so on. The following are some examples:

1. In biometrics, the point where the false acceptance rate (FAR) equals the false rejection rate (FRR) is called:

    A) Differential error rate (DER)

    B) Crossover error rate (CER)

C) Accept reject rate (ARR)

D) Biometric error rate (BER)

Answer: Option B

2. A company decides that it wants to store all the identities of the users in a location and use the location either internally or remotely to authenticate the users. Any user who is not in the list will be denied entry to a system. The company also has a person who regularly updates the list to add, drop, and modify users. What authentication mechanism is the company planning to deploy?

    Answer: Integrated authentication (Active Directory or LDAP)

3. A false acceptance rate (FAR) is defined as:

    A) When correctly identified users are falsely rejected

    B) When incorrectly identified users are falsely accepted

    C) When incorrectly identified users are truly accepted

    D) When correctly identified users are truly accepted

    Answer: Option C

Identification Authentication and Authorization

Tip #50: Understanding the process of access control management from identification to authorization

Learn the clear difference between identification, authentication, and authorization.

Domain: Identity and Access Management.

Subdomain: Identification, Authentication, Authorization, Proofing, and Credentials.

Subject background: Identification is a process of uniquely recognizing a user (unique recognition) with a username, email, or some form of identity. Identification is the **first step** in allowing a person to do something. Authentication is the process of validating the identity provided. During authentication, the system validates a username, a password, a passphrase, and a fingerprint or such. Authentication is the **second step** in allowing a person to work on an IT asset or system. The last and **third step** is authorization. Authorization tells the user that the provided identification was authenticated, and the user is now allowed to operate the system or the IT asset. What exactly a user is authorized to do on an IT system depends on least privilege, separation of duties, and other related policies and guidelines followed by an organization. Accountability is the way to trace an action of the user and determine whether it was actually performed by the user (nonrepudiation) and, if so, why the user has performed it.

This three-step process demonstrates that any user who is authorized is also identified and authenticated, but not vice versa. Once authorized, a user is not given all the powers to deal with anything on an IT system. Authorized people are governed by the policies and procedures that are in place according to the job duties, least privilege, and other rules set forth.

Data stored in smart cards such as common access cards provides the identification, and a user has to provide a PIN or passcode to be authenticated by a server or IT asset.

Things to Remember

- Identification can be done in a variety of ways such as recognizing a facial image, a fingerprint, an email address, or a user/system-generated unique ID.

- Authentication is a way of validating the identification to prove that the person trying to use the IT asset is actually a valid person/system.

- Identification and authentication provide entry into an IT system but do **not** give superpowers to do whatever one likes on the IT system.

- Authorization is the last step of allowing a user to operate an IT asset.

- Identification and authentication can have one simple process or can demand more than one way of questioning and confirming that the user is genuine. For example, an identification process can ask for a user ID and another form of ID such as an email address, username, etc. Likewise, authentication can be in more than one way. Whether the system uses a single identification and authentication process or uses more than one method depends on the policies of the organization implementing it. When two or more steps are required for authentication, it is usually called a two-factor or multifactor identification/authentication process.

- Security is more enhanced with multifactor authentication than using a single-factor authentication, but multifactor authentication can be time-consuming and expensive.

- The processes of identification and authentication are also sometimes called:

    a)   Something you know, or Type 1 (for example, a password, a passphrase, or a PIN)

    b)   Something you have, or Type 2 (for example, a passport, an access card, a token)

    c)   Something you are, or Type 3 (for example, a fingerprint, a facial image, a palm scan)

- The least secure way of identification and authentication is to use an email address and password, but this is the basic process that is most widely used.

- Authorized users are usually tracked via logs to make sure they are not misusing their authorizations and crossing the red lines. This tracking is known as accounting. For any misuse, an authorized user is accountable.

- Identification, authentication, authorization, and accountability are designated by IAAA.

Example: A new biotechnology firm wants to implement a multifactor authentication system that tracks users entering the entrance doors with an access card. The card can be used to open closets that store IT assets such as backup tapes, disk drives, and other company proprietary documents. The access card can also be used to log in to a workstation and perform file transfer, use email, etc. When accessing any system, what are the **BEST** possible factors the company can utilize for multifactor authentication?

A)   What a user has and the user's ability to do with it

B)   What a user is and what the user knows

C)   What a user has and the user's access card

D)   What a user is and the user's palm scan

Analysis: When we read the question, we find that the main idea of the firm is to implement two-factor authentication. Two-factor authentication normally has two different factors, not the same type of factor twice. Read each answer given closely and compare them with Type 1 (what a user knows), Type 2 (what a user has), and Type 3 (what a user is). Two-factor authentication combines Types 1 and 2 or Types 2 and 3 or Types 1 and 3. It may be useless to combine one type of factor with another factor of same type. Option A stated a factor has a "user's ability to do with it," which is actually not a factor. Other options given need to be screened out the same way to pick the correct answer.

Statement: A new biotechnology firm wants to implement a multifactor authentication system.

Question: Which option given has "the **BEST** possible factors the company can utilize for multifactor authentication?"

Solution: Option A is invalid since a user's ability is not a Type 1, 2, or 3 factor. Option C combines the same type of factor twice: what a user has and his access card. Both come under what a user has or Type 2 factor. Option D is like a Type 3 factor combined twice. Both Options C and D seem to have two factors, but they are the same type and cannot be technically called multifactor authentication in practice because they are two factors of same type. Thus, option B is the **BEST** possible solution since it states "What a user is and what the user knows," which are Type 3 (something you are) and Type 1 (something you know).

Review Questions

Several variations of this topic are possible. A few of them are given here:

1.   What is the second step in the process of authorizing a user into an IT asset such as a file system or a workstation?

     Answer: In the identification, authentication, authorization, and accountability (IAAAA) process, the second step is authentication.

2. Authorizing a user to use an IT system can be **BEST** said as:

A) Giving access of the full file system and workstation to the user

B) Giving some access on the server and full access on the workstation

C) Giving only the lowest needed access for the user anywhere

D) Letting the user decide what access the user wants and where he wants it

Answer: The obvious answer is option C because once the user is identified and authenticated, he should be able to get access to the system only to an extent he is required to access to complete his job function. Any other access is considered an overflow, which can endanger the IT system and its security.

3. Which of the following is the **LEAST** secure way of authenticating a user?

A) Access card and a fingerprint

B) A smart card and token

C) Username and a password

D) Palm scan and a PIN

Answer: The least secure way is to use a username and password since they can be easily stolen and hacked. So, the answer is option C.

Tip #51: Learn the meaning and use of various markup languages related to IT systems

Learn the meaning of markup languages, SOAP, OpenID, and other software details.

Domain: Security Engineering, Software Development Security.

Subdomain: Testing, Authentication, Development of security controls, Markup languages, Built-in authentication and identification.

Subject background: Markup languages have evolved from a typical GML to sophisticated versions such as XML, SAML, and SPML. There are dozens of markup languages, and you can even create your own new markup language with new rules.

The evolution of markup languages is GML > SGML > HTML > XML > XHTML. The most widely used markup language is XML, which is used in web services and applications on the Internet.

Things to Remember

- **XML**: Extensible Markup Language has no prespecified tags, and you can create your own tags.

- **HTML**: Hypertext Markup Language has predefined tags, and only those tags must be used.

- **SPML**: Service Provision Markup Language is used for user management and account creation/removal, etc. It is an XML-based framework. It allows data authorization and can be used to easily set up user interfaces on web services and Internet applications.

- **SAML**: Security Assertion Markup Language. This is an open standard used to exchange authentication and authorization data between two parties, usually the identity provider and the service provider. SAML is also an XML-based markup language.

- **Service**: This is functionality that can be accessed remotely or may be able to make changes when requested. An example is retrieving a credit report online or accessing a bank statement by a manager updating it.

- **SOA**: Service-oriented architecture is a style of software design in which services are provided by various application components. SOA uses interoperable services among multiple environments.

- **SOAP**: Simple Object Access Protocol is a messaging protocol for exchanging information in web services and computer networks. It uses an XML information set. SOAP allows one to invoke running processes to authenticate, authorize, and communicate using XML.

- **OpenID**: This is an open standard for authentication. OpenID does *not* rely on a central authority to authenticate a user's identity. It might allow third-party authentication.

- **OAuth**: This is an open standard for access delegation. It is a way to grant users access to websites, applications, etc., without giving any password information. This issues access tokens to third-party clients with approval of the resource owner. It works with HTTP.

- **Federated ID**: This links a user's electronic ID stored among multiple and distinct systems to work as single sign-on (SSO). It issues tickets or tokens that are trusted and validated across many systems and organizations.

- **Centralized ID**: This is a unified ID management system. It helps minimize an organization's workload when authenticating a valid user.

- **Decentralized ID**: ID attributes are not visible for exchange or verification, and one single ID cannot be used for various services. Each service needs its own verification system.

Example: An organization wants to develop a web service that can supply an Excel worksheet with data in various columns when a request is made. The technology expert in charge suggests using an XML format for the web service data supplied to the users. What is the **BEST** reason the technology expert suggested XML data on the web service?

A)   An XML file has the same tags as HTML.

B)   XML files can be read only by programmers.

C)   XML files universally readable.

D)   XML files are encrypted and safe.

Analysis: All XML files are text files that are readable in any plain-text editor. XML has its own tags and does not use HTML tags. Given these facts, we know that options A, B, and D are incorrect. Importantly, XML files are readable by many programs and applications such as Excel, Visual Studio, text editor, databases etc. The great convenience with XML is that it can be directly converted to a table or into any other data format the programmer/user wants.

Statement: Removing the verbiage, we can state the question as follows:

An organization wants to develop a web service to provide data in an Excel worksheet. The technology expert in charge suggests using XML format.

Question: What is the **BEST** reason for providing XML data on the web service?

Solution: Option C is the best option since data is easily readable by humans and machines as well. Tags in XML are self-created and do not have to conform to any rules.

Review Questions

Many questions can be asked on these topics. Some of them are listed here:

1. What is the full form of SPML that is used by user management?

    A) Service Protection Makeup Language

    B) Serial and Parallel Mode License

    C) Service Provision Markup Language

    D) Service Provided by Main Line

    Answer: Option C

2. Which markup language is a predecessor to XML?

    Answer: HTML

3. Which language is **BEST** suited for account creation/removal and user management?

    A) XML

    B) SPML

    C) SAML

    D) SOAP

    Answer: Option B

4. Which of the following open standards is **BEST** suited for access delegation to grant users access to websites, applications, etc., without giving any password information?

    A) Federated ID

    B) Centralized ID

    C) OAuth

    D) OpenID

    Answer: Option C. Note that OpenID is a clear distractor given the other details in the question.

5. Which of the following is a messaging protocol for exchanging information in web services and computer networks?

    A) Simple Object Access Protocol (SOAP)

    B) Service And Network Protocol (SANP)

    C) Message Protocol for Computer Service (MPCS)

    D) Simple Internet Message Protocol (SIMP)

    Answer: Option A

6. Which form of ID management is **BEST** suited for mainframe computers?
    Answer: Centralized ID management is best suited for a mainframe. It simplifies the organization's workload.

CHAPTER 6

Security Assessment and Testing

In this chapter, you will learn about the intricacies of assessing a security loophole or weakness, and you'll learn about testing strategies along with how to securely process data.

Assessment and Test Strategies

Tip #52: Learn the concepts of security assessment and how to find and fix vulnerabilities, risks, and threats

In this section, you'll learn about vulnerabilities, exposure, risks, and threats.

Domain: Security, Asset Security, Risk Management. In fact, vulnerability is an area that can fall under any domain either in software or in hardware.

Subdomain: Software security, Security architecture, Designs, Solution elements, Assessment and test strategies, and Risk minimizing.

Subject background:

Remember the following definitions to get a clear understanding of the topic area. This can be memorized easily as **VERT-WOLD**.

V: Vulnerability is also known as a	**W**: Weakness
E: Exposure is also known as an	**O**: Opening that can be exploited
R: Risk is also known as a	**L**: Loss or potential likelihood of loss
T: Threat also known as a	**D**: Danger

Things to Remember

- A **<u>threat agent</u>** is a person or employee who is causing the attack.

- A **<u>threat vector</u>** is a program such as an email or virus that runs on the IT system to disable it.

- A vulnerability that exists may or may not be exploited unless an attacker finds an opening or exposure.

- Even if there is an exposure, a vulnerability may not be exploited if the attacker has no financial or other related interests (such as using open ports to send email, etc.)

- A danger or threat can happen if an attacker or threat agent loads a threat vector. This can be described as "a threat agent loads a threat vector to exploit a vulnerability that creates a possible exposure in an IT system."

- The IT system can be either software or hardware.

- Software vulnerabilities are far more complex and occupy a wider range than hardware vulnerabilities and exposures.

- There will never be a perfect 100% foolproof system without a single vulnerability.

- Risk can never be eliminated altogether. It can be reduced, transferred, tolerated, or ignored. **There is no such thing as zero risk.**

- Reducing risk is done with implementing corrective measures such as antivirus, patching with updates.

- Risk transfer is done by purchasing insurance whereby a third party takes care of damages and financial losses.

- When all possible risk is either reduced or transferred, the remaining residual risk is said to be tolerable risk, which is monitored regularly.

- Risk that does not cause much damage in any form is said to be the risk that can be ignored. This is the residual risk after all possible measures are taken to reduce the risk and transfer it to a third party by buying insurance.

Example: A cable service company providing Internet to customers as an Internet service provider (ISP) found that it had a software bug that allows faster speeds of Internet to subscribers who actually pay a lower price for slower speeds. The software bug was not noticed until a hacker exploited it with a clever software set up on his modem and published it in his blog. It was not until several months later that the ISP found it and wanted to correct it. The cable company first tried to minimize the software problems, but when it was not sufficient, the ISP purchased insurance for the loss of income. It took nearly two years before the bug was almost eliminated, but some five or ten smarter subscribers still hacked the ISP in new ways. The ISP noticed these but let them go since they did not lose a huge portion of their income.

What is the **BEST** name one can give to the risk avoidance the ISP has adopted?

A)   The ISP transferred the risk to the insurance company.

B)   The ISP minimized and/or eliminated the risk completely.

C)   The ISP minimized the risk to a tolerable level.

D)   The ISP ignored the risk the first two years and then eliminated it.

A couple of variations of this question can happen with the same narrative as follows:

- What was the threat vector/agent in this situation?

- The threat that the cable company faced can **BEST** be called what?

What caused the vulnerability for the ISP?

Analysis: Reading the verbiage is a pain, but we will notice that the question at the end is asking how the ISP dealt with the risk. First, they ignored the risk, and then they tried to correct the software bug to minimize the problems. When it did not completely remove the risk, the company also purchased insurance to compensate. Thus, after finding the problem, the ISP worked systematically to minimize the risk to a tolerable level because even with the lowest possible risk, some were still exploiting it, but the company chose to let it go. We can assume that the company will continue to adapt this method and may improve its performance and thereby remove the risk in the long term.

Statement: The statement can be rearranged as follows:

An Internet service provider (ISP) found that it had a software bug that allows faster speeds to subscribers who pay a lower price. The cable company first tried to minimize the software problems but purchased insurance for the loss of income.

Question: What is the **BEST** name one can give to the risk avoidance the ISP has adopted?

Solution: Option C is the best answer in this case. Option A is wrong because the insurance company did not buy insurance first, and when it bought insurance, it did not completely eliminate the problem. Option B is wrong since no risk can ever be completely eliminated. It can only be minimized. Option D is partially right in that it ignored the problem first, but then it minimized the risk to a tolerable level and was never able to eliminate it.

For the next three questions, the answers are as follows:

What was the threat vector/agent in this situation?

The threat vector is the software setup/patch on the modem. The threat agent is the hacker or end users who used this method of exploitation.

The threat that the cable company faced can BEST be called what?

The threat is the danger. The ISP lost money, and thus the threat was the financial loss.

What caused the vulnerability for the ISP?

Vulnerability is a weakness. The weakness was in the ISP-provided software, which was exploited first by the hacker and then by the other end users.

Review Questions

Some possible questions about VERT-WOLD are listed here:

1. Select the **MOST** accurate statement.

    A) The threat vector creates a threat agent to exploit an exposure created by a vulnerability.

    B) The threat agent creates a threat vector to exploit an exposure created by a vulnerability.

    C) An exposure created by a vulnerability is exploited by a threat vector.

    D) A vulnerability created by an exposure is exploited by a threat agent.

    Answer: Option B

2. What factor creates an exposure in an IT system that can be exploited?

    A) A vulnerability

    B) A software bug

C) A hardware bug

D) A threat

Answer: Option A

3. When insurance is purchased to accommodate losses arising from a risk due to a software bug, what is said to happen to the risk?

A) The risk is reduced.

B) The risk is eliminated.

C) The risk is transferred.

D) The risk is not affected.

Answer: Option C

4. What is the other name for an exposure?

A) Threat

B) Opening

C) Vulnerability

D) Risk

Answer: Option B

5. A company that develops software wants to create a zero-risk software package. What is the **BEST** possible option for the company?

A) Create software with the best software experts with lots of experience

B) Outsource software development and transfer the risk to a third party

C) Risk can never be made to zero; reduce risk to a tolerable level

D) Inform the end users that using the software has some risk

Answer: Option C

6. A threat or danger can have two components. What are they?

    A) A threat agent and a threat medium

    B) A threat agent and a threat vector

    C) A threat vector and a threat time period

    D) A threat time and age of threat

    Answer: Option B

7. What is the **BEST** term for a potential likelihood of loss?

    A) A vulnerability

    B) A threat

    C) A risk

    D) A weakness

    Answer: Option C. In the VERT-WOLD acronym, "L," or loss/potential likelihood of loss, corresponds to "R," or risk.

Security Process Data: Management and Operational Controls

Tip #53: Learn various types of controls to understand and implement in asset/data management

Controls can be preventive, detective, corrective, compensating, recovery, or deterrent.

Domain: Asset security, Security Engineering, Security Assessment and Testing.

Subdomain: Data controls, Security controls, Access controls, Management and Operational controls, Physical controls, Natural controls, and Environmental controls.

Subject background: Controls are put in place to prevent, detect, correct, or compensate for a vulnerability or a possible threat. Controls are put in place before an audit if the managers can find a need for them or after an audit when the auditor recommends a measure. Controls are required for electronic data as well as physical buildings and assets to prevent theft, possible threats, or incident/events.

Controls themselves can be electronic, physical, or any other form such as standards, guidelines. Controls can be applied or just recommended for data at rest, data in motion/transit, or data in use. Since the most important asset an organization has is its data, all these controls are necessary protect the data.

Controls can be applied individually or in combination as the management deems fit to protect the data and information assets.

One control can fall into more than one category.

Things to Remember

- **DAR** stands for data at rest, which is on a tape, disk, or another stable location from where it can be picked up easily when required.

- **DIT** indicates data in transit. Transit can be online or offline. Online transit can be on a network, the Internet, or a shared drive.

- **DIU** specifies data in use. Data in this state is <u>most difficult to protect</u> even with encryption or other controls.

- **Data retention** dictates how long the data is retained by an organization after it was collected. Several guidelines dictate the length of time (like Safe Harbor, GDPR, etc.) that the data can and should be retained.

- **Data remanence** is what remains after data is cleaned up. Disks must be cleaned at least seven times before they are made sure that the data is completely erased.

- Controls can be applied to data, physical security, or any electronic asset as deemed necessary.

- **Preventive controls** make an attempt to avert the user from committing a theft, causing an incident, or thwarting a hack.

- **Detective controls** identify when an attack happens, and they may or may not stop the attack from happening. If detective controls are used to only detect an attack, the attack needs to have other controls in place to thwart it. Alarm in libraries that alert the front desk when an intruder tries to steal a book or DVD is an example of detective control. Audits also are detective controls.

- **Corrective controls** are controls that try to correct a bug. An example of a corrective control is antivirus software. The antivirus software can detect a virus and remove it from the infected files. Corrective controls may also help prevent a recurrence of an event or incident.

- **Compensating controls** are also called alternative controls. If an original control is too expensive or time-consuming to implement, then any other control that can temporarily do the job can be implemented. In such a case, the temporary control is a compensating control. Examples of compensating controls are the separation of duties, regular reviewing of logs, and audit trails. These are more like using a plan B when plan A does not work.

- **Recovery controls** can reclaim an original piece of information. Examples are backup and restores, antivirus software, database clustering, etc.

- **Deterrent controls** discourage an intruder. Locks, security cameras, alarms, fences, and security warnings fall into this category.

- **Administrative controls** are access controls with rules, standards, guidelines, and training. These are applicable to everyone equally.

- **Logical/technical controls** are those put with software, hardware, or any other possible technology to protect an organization's assets.

- **Physical access controls** protect access by people. Gates, locked doors, windows, lighting, video cameras, and such fall into this category.

Example: In a surprise audit, it was found that the local credit union has failed to notice discrepancies that allowed a manager to steal thousands of dollars of customers' money. By the time an audit found the discrepancies, the manager had left the bank months ago and had no contact details, thereby forcing the bank to absorb the losses. What kind of control can the surprise audit be termed as?

A) Logical and corrective control

B) Administrative and detective control

C) Physical and deterrent control

D) Administrative and recovery control

Analysis: Notice from the answers given that two different controls are combined in all the options. First, we need to find what kind of control an audit is. An audit is an administrative control that happens after the management agrees that an external entity should poke its account books. An audit can be logical or technical if it is done with software or other ways of scanning. But it was not stated that the audit used any software. Thus, we can assume that the audit is administrative and looked through the account books to detect discrepancies manually. Importantly, audits do not correct the mistakes (option A). An audit is also not a physical control (option C) and will try to find an error after browsing through the books. An audit also does not recover anything (option D).

Statement: If we remove too much information given, we can deduce that the question is asking about an audit that happened and what kind of control an audit is. The question can be written as follows:

A credit union has failed to notice discrepancies that allowed a manager to steal thousands of dollars of bank customers' money.

Question: What kind of control is an audit?

Solution: The audit did not warn anyone before the losses. Neither did the audit deter the manager who stole the money. It only detected the discrepancies months after the event happened. Nobody could find it earlier. Since the audit was done after the administration deemed an audit as a necessary control, the answer has to be option B. All other options are wrong.

Review Questions

Some of the other questions about controls can be as follows:

1. To prevent intruders from entering the facility, a sign posted on a small physical metal board on the outer fence of a nuclear fission material processing company reads as "Warning: Trespassers will be prosecuted to the full extent of federal and other applicable government laws." What kind of control is the sign posted on the fence?

    A) Physical control

    B) Caution control

C) Deterrent control

D) Preventive control

Answer: Option C. A sign is not a preventive control. The words "prevent" and "physical" in the question are clear distractors tied to options D and A.

2. A bank's locker to store money and valuables lies behind a series of four locked doors, each with a different combination of two electronic keys to be entered by two different people. What kind of control are the locked doors of the bank?

A) Dual and combination controls

B) Physical and logical controls

C) Compensating and recovery controls

D) Logical and dual controls

Answer: Option B. The word "dual" is a distractor tied to two people opening doors.

3. What kind of control is a wide-panning, adjustable zoom camera that records people who enter and exit an office building?

A) Logical and compensating control

B) Physical and detective control

C) Logical and deterrent control

D) Physical and compensating control

Answer: Option B

4. A company's backup and restore mechanism put in place in the case of a natural disaster like an earthquake occurrence **BEST** falls into what category of control?

A) Deterrent control

B) Environmental control

C) Restorative control

D) Recovery control

Answer: Option D

5. Even with all the best controls put in place and working, which of the following is the **MOST** difficult to protect?

A) Data at rest

B) Data in motion

C) Data in use

D) Data in archive

Answer: Option C

6. Which of the following **BEST** describes data at rest?

A) Data going from the server to a user on the client

B) Data sent from the server to another server

C) Data on a network drive shared by users

D) Data in desktop computer files currently being sorted

Answer: Option C. Option D is data in use since it is currently being sorted. Options A and B are data in motion/transit.

7. A temporary solution to encrypt a file to protect data is **BEST** described as a:

A) Corrective control

B) Deterrent control

C) Complementary control

D) Compensatory control

Answer: Option D. Hint: Note the wording "temporary solution."

CHAPTER 7

Security Operations

In this chapter, you will learn tips about incidents, digital crime, incident management, investigations, digital forensics, eDiscovery, disaster recovery, business continuity planning and backup, and recovery strategies.

Investigations, Digital Forensics, and eDiscovery in the Case of a Data Breach

Tip #54: Learn about digital forensics, eDiscovery, and investigation methods in a breach

Domain: Security Assessment and Testing, Security Operations.

Subdomain: Investigations, Support and requirements, Digital forensics, Recovery, Awareness.

Subject background: When a hacking attack or breach happens, collecting evidence about how the breach happened is important. The process of collecting this information is called digital forensics. Forensics in general is both digital and analog and may contain fingerprints and other physical evidence.

Forensics is also used for recovery, data collection, reporting, and follow-up. The forensics team can include a variety of people including police. The tools used in forensics can be specialized such as software, digital cameras, etc.

Things to Remember

- The tools or methods used in forensics used in data collection and discovery are important, and the process must always be documented since the evidence has to be genuine.

- Utmost care should be exercised to not change evidence in the case of a breach/theft of information.

© R. Sarma Danturthi 2020
R. S. Danturthi, *70 Tips and Tricks for Mastering the CISSP Exam*,
https://doi.org/10.1007/978-1-4842-6225-2_7

- The people handling the digital forensics should have proper training for the job.

- When handling the evidence, the person should take full responsibility for handling digital and all other evidence.

- **MOM** means the "motive," "opportunity," and "means" of a crime.

- Motive is a factor that finds out the "why" or "who" of the breach or attack.

- Opportunity describes the "where and when" of the attack.

- Means is the ability or tools of the person who did the breach/attack.

- MO is the modus operandi of the crime, in other words, the process of how the crime happened.

- **Locard's principle** states that a person who attacks/hacks always leaves something behind (forgetfulness, intentionally, a signature, etc.) and takes/steals something. Depending on this principle, an investigator can usually find some clues.

- Forensic analysis and investigation has several steps: identify, preserve, collect, exam, analyze, present, and report/decision.

- If a hard disk needs to be scanned, the investigator has to analyze the entire disk space including the slack spaces, the full spaces, and the leftover blank spaces.

- **Chain of custody (COC)** is a process that indicates how the evidence is collected, analyzed, transported, and preserved. COC must be followed in strict terms or the court may reject the evidence as inadmissible. A full-blown criminal case can fall apart to nothing if COC is not maintained correctly.

- Evidence should be marked correctly with the name, date, time, and all possible other details. Care should be taken in handling the disks, tapes, etc., so that the data is not affected by magnetic fields or such that may cause the data to become corrupt.

- **eDiscovery** is a systematic method of producing the evidence to the court or legal bodies. eDiscovery does not necessarily mean only the product but can relate to even email communicated in and around the company that is related to the product.

- The evidence presented to the court must be relevant (related to the incident), reliable (fact), and sufficient. Irrelevant information is not admissible in court.

- **Entrapment** is not legal or ethical. It is a way of inviting users to do something. The user may not know that what he is doing is legal or illegal (for example, it is not the user's fault if they click a link that offers free lottery ticket entries).

- **Enticement** is a legal and ethical method of inviting an attacker to do something. An example is to create a honeypot and let the attacker in by leaving connections and ports open.

- **Exigent circumstances** means seizing related evidence found on-site where the judge may have the final say in deciding if the collected evidence is admissible or not. For example, an attacker's computer did not have any record of remotely connecting to a server, but the hard disk found in another location of the attacker's property may have evidence.

- **Proximate causation** is omitting something intentionally that can cause a consequence. An example is not implementing a firewall and letting a virus/hacking attack happen.

- **Due care** is also known as "duty care." Due care is to do all responsible actions to make sure the risk is reduced/tolerable.

- **Due diligence** is the process of checking what the risks are and knowing them.

- **A prudent person** carries out both diligence and due care.

Example: A company has created a website for Internet sales, and there is also a honeypot to invite attackers in order to track them to a location and record their actions. The honeypot contains open ports and unused services that look tempting for an attacker to use and exploit the company. When an attacker logged in to the honeypot, all his actions were recorded, and the evidence was hurriedly collected and moved around the company staff as proof. The staff was not aware of the legal procedures to be followed and added more compelling data to the tracks of the attacker. As data was passed from one staff member to the other and finally to law enforcement, it became large and had only the final date of compilation and company name. Law enforcement was informed, and the data collected was given as proof. When presented in court, however, the judge found that the evidence was not admissible since it did not contain the proper information. What made the judge decide that the data collected was not admissible?

A)   eDiscovery was not admissible.

B)   The chain of custody was incomplete.

C)   Proximate causation was applied to the website.

D)   Entrapment with a honeypot is illegal.

Analysis: The main problem seems to be that the staff of the company added all the data they could to the existing file (evidence) and never put their name, date, what changes were made, or how the data was collected in the process. The final file that was produced contained only the final date and company name. As the file passed from one person to another among the staff, the important information of who collected it, how it was collected, etc., was not recorded. In other words, a proper chain of custody was absent clearly.

Mentioning of "honeypot" in the question is a distractor since option D shows it was entrapment. Honeypots are enticements and are completely legal. There was no entrapment involved in the given scenario.

eDiscovery is a process of finding all the details about the crime and submitting them to the legal authorities on request; it is admissible when done properly. So, option A is not the answer. Proximate causation is obviously wrong since the evidence collected was directly from the company staff and on-site and the process itself was legal, thereby making option C a wrong answer.

Statement: A company has created a website with a honeypot. When an attacker logged in to the honeypot, the **evidence was hurriedly** collected and moved around the company staff as proof. The staff **was not aware** of the legal procedures to be followed and added more compelling data to the tracks of the attacker. As the data was passed around, it had only the final date of compilation and the company name. The judge has found that the evidence **was not admissible** since it did not contain the proper information. What makes the judge decide that the data collected was not admissible?

Question: The **evidence was hurriedly** collected. As data was passed around, it had only the final date of date of compilation and the company name. The judge has found that the evidence **was not admissible**. What makes the judge decide that the data collected was not admissible?

Solution: The proper chain of custody was not followed, making the evidence inadmissible. The information about who changed what, when it was changed, what was originally found and recorded, and all other related signatures, names, etc., was completely missing from the file. The correct answer is option B: the chain of custody was incomplete.

Review Questions

Several twists and turns in the legal language in this domain and subdomain can make a simple question look complicated. Some of the questions are listed here:

1. What is the **BEST** description of the prudent person concept?

    A) A concept that understands what is due diligence

    B) A concept that conducts due diligence and implements due care

    C) A concept that a person acts wisely in a given circumstance

    D) A concept that implements due care

    Answer: Option B

2. A law enforcement officer checking the home laptop of an attacker could not find any evidence on the hard disk, but when leaving the house of the attacker found a USB drive that was later found to have some evidence of attack. It was presented in court, and the judge later allowed the USB drive as evidence to prove the attack. This situation is **BEST** known as:

    Answer: Exigent circumstances

3. What is eDiscovery?

Answer: The systematic process of collecting and producing data in a crime to produce to the court

4. What does Locard's principle state?

A) An attacker steals/takes something and leaves no evidence.

B) An attacker leaves evidence and steals/takes nothing.

C) An attacker steals/takes evidence and leaves something.

D) An attacker leaves something and steals/takes something.

Answer: Option D. What is left by attacker can be used as evidence but attacker doesn't necessarily leave any evidence. This is the reason Option B is wrong.

5. When looking for a suspected attacker/hacker, it is important to consider MOM. What does MOM stand for?

A) Means, occasions, and motives

B) Motives, opportunities, and means

C) Means, occurrences, and motives

D) Motives, occlusions, and means

Answer: Option B

6. What is the **NEXT** step after collecting evidence in forensic analysis?

Answer: Forensic analysis has the following steps: identify, preserve, collect, exam, analyze, present, and report/decision. The **NEXT** step after collection is "examination."

Tip #55: Understand the salami attack, diddle attack, etc

Domain: Security Operations, Software Security.

Subdomain: Administrative management, Secure data, Investigations, Software attack.

Subject background: Some definitions of the terms are given here.

Salami attack: If a few pennies are shaved from accounts without significantly being noticed by any account holder, it is called a salami attack. The attacker is usually an insider who has access to several accounts. The insider steals a few pennies from all accounts and deposits the money in their own account. This is usually very delicate work and undetectable. The usual solution is to enforce mandatory vacation, rotation of duty, and maybe the least privilege rules. Salami attacks can also happen by a store's front-desk clerks who steal from the cash box regularly without being noticed.

Data diddle attack: This is a form of attack where the attacker changes data/ information. One example is modifying a file by small amounts and increasing the modifications slowly over a time to finally corrupt the file or deleting the file itself. The diddling attack can be verified with some kind of file integrity check on a regular basis. Note that the diddling attack changes the stored file's data and is thus an active attack. The file integrity check can also be used to create a log of file changes.

Mandatory vacation: Employees are forced to take vacation so that another person can work in the same position to detect any abnormalities.

Rotation of duty: Employees take turns in their work to do duties that are varied among available work shifts and are regularly rotated so that all employees are aware of all the work and no employee can completely secure command of one type of job only.

Things to Remember

- A salami attack directly steals cash or money, whereas data diddling is changing the information in files gradually.

- Both salami and data diddling attacks are **incremental attacks** since the attacker slowly gains confidence and starts stealing more and more.

- Suggested practices such as rotation of duty, mandatory vacations, and least privilege to avoid salami and data diddling are to be tailored to each situation. One method alone may not be entirely sufficient to avoid the attacks.

- Since data diddling involves changes to files, a log needs to be kept for logging data such as who opened the file, what modifications were made if any, what actions were completed at the end of the work, and the date and time when the file was accessed and modified. Having more than one log, such as one log for reading and one log for modifications, is also helpful.

Example: A credit card company has several customer service representatives (CSRs) who take calls from the users and check the card usage, balances, etc. The CSRs also have privileges to modify the customer data in files depending on a customer request for more credit amount, claims about unauthorized payments, removing charges not known, and so on. The company discovered that there were several errors in the data, and customers complained of paying more money than they owe. On investigation it was found that almost all the CSRs were data diddling with the customer files. What precautions should the company take for recording the changes in the credit files of customers by the CSRs?

A)   Keep the CSR privileges, but warn them not to diddle with the credit files of customers.

B)   Revoke the CSRs' full privileges, but keep the credit files up-to-date.

C)   Keep CSR privileges to only read the credit files, and any edits to credit files should be referred to another manager or upper-level employee.

D)   Implement job rotation and mandatory leave for all CSRs.

Analysis: Note that every member of the team of CSRs was involved in data diddling, per the given text. Thus, mandatory vacations or job rotations may not help rectify the problem. This kind of attack is an insider attack where everyone wants a piece of the pie. Thus, removing the privileges is an option. But removing all privileges prevents the CSRs from even reading the data when a customer calls. Thus, changes should be made in a way that only by upper-level employees can do edits to the credit files.

Statement: The verbiage not required can be deleted, and the statement can be made as follows:

A credit card company discovered that **<u>almost all the CSRs</u>** were data diddling with the customer files.

Question: What precautions should the company take for recording the changes in the credit files of customers by the CSRs?

Solution: The obvious answer would be to pick option C. Option D is wrong since almost all CSRs were found to be involved in stealing in the internal attack. Option B is wrong since removing all the privileges of CSRs will make then unable to open any credit record of the customers. CSRs can have the "read-only" privilege on the files. Option A is wrong since the warnings may or may not work always. Even if they work for a specific time period, the CSRs who are used to stealing data will find new ways and continue to steal.

Review Questions

1. What should be stored for data integrity when a file is accessed/ changed?

   A) Original file and log of changes made to the original file

   B) Original file, new file, and log of changes made to the original file

   C) New file and log of changes made to the original file

   D) Log of changes made to the original file only

   Answer: Remember that the more information we have about an attacker and the methods, the better. Thus, option B is the correct answer.

2. What is the best solution for a salami attack?

   Answer: Rotation of duties and/or mandatory vacation, whichever works

3. What is the main purpose of file integrity checks?

   Answer: To make sure that the file is not modified without authorization. File integrity must always follow with a detailed log of who made what changes in the file.

4. Can a data diddling attack be prevented by implementing least privilege?

   Answer: Yes, it can help prevent the data diddling attack by refusing authorization for the user to make changes, but least privilege alone may not prevent the attack. It should always be used in combination with other possible remedies.

5. Why is least privilege helpful?

   Answer: In least privilege, the employee is given the minimum required permissions to successfully perform their job duties. Thus, even if the employee wants to steal or make some undesired modifications, the employee may not have access to perform those duties.

Incident Management: Incident, Remediation, and After-Incident Review

Tip #56: Understand how good the evidence must be and the steps in handling the information and reporting

Domain: Security Operations, Asset Security.

    Subdomain: Investigation, Chain of custody, Incident handling.

    Subject background: When a system breaks down for whatever reasons, an investigation is done to find the root cause and to avoid it in the future. If there is a crime, then the investigation must concentrate on collecting good evidence to show and prove the occurrence of the event. While collecting the evidence, it is important to remember that evidence must be authentic, accurate, complete, convincing, and admissible. Otherwise, the entire investigation process can fall apart.

    Things to Remember

- MOM is motive (who, why), opportunity (when and where), and means (capabilities of criminals). These are the basic terms to remember in an investigation.

- **MO is the modus operandi** (how the crime was done) of the criminals. This can also be said as the process the criminals are accustomed to follow in their work. If the MO (tools used, behaviors, what is left over, etc.) can be identified, it can lead to the criminal since each criminal follows a particular MO.

- **Admissible** is a term used in a court of law. If the evidence is admissible, it must follow certain rules. Evidence cannot be produced from thin air. Authentic evidence, if not properly collected and followed by legal procedures, may not be admissible.

- **Incidents** are when damage occurs (see Tip #11). Damage might occur due to a variety of reasons such as disasters and natural or manmade catastrophes.

- **COC, or chain of custody,** is a process that records how the evidence was collected, analyzed, transported, preserved, and presented to the required authorities. Not only the physical evidence but even the electronic or computer evidence can be modified/corrupted by negligence. Evidence, even when collected in bits and pieces, must also be sealed and marked with the date, signature, and name of the collector as it moves/transfers from one person to another and one location to another.

- **Evidence** is what is available for the investigator to collect that is original and that will be admissible in a court of law. Please note that what is admissible in court can change depending on the evolution of computer crimes and the development of new laws by the legislative branches of the government.

- **Investigation** refers to looking for a cause of the trouble. One of the biggest headaches is to collect evidence in a proper manner while finding the root cause with minute details and proper documentation. Inadvertent mistakes or purposeful negligence can cause the entire process to fail and the losses to be irrecoverable.

- **Forensic investigation** consists of the identification, preservation, collection, examination, analysis, presentation, and decision processes.

- **Exigent circumstances** are when the law enforcement can seize evidence when they feel that the evidence is under a threat or is going to be damaged. Examples are a suspect reformatting the hard disk, cleaning the crime area of any possible fingerprints, etc.

- **Enticement** is when a person is provided a venue to commit a crime. This is a legal and ethical process. An example of enticement is to put in a honeypot for a network system to track the actions of a hacker. In this case, the hacker intended to attack but is diverted to a honeypot, which is not a valid system but gives the impression of a valid system.

- **Entrapment** is neither legal nor ethical. This does not prove that the hacker has an intent but is instead lured to commit a crime. An example of entrapment is to provide a link to the user to download free software. The user has no intent to download anything but came to the system and is lured by the free software. In this case, it is hard to prove that the attacker has an intent.

- **Lifecycle of evidence** includes identification and collection, storage, preservation, transportation, presentation, and return to owner processes.

Example: During a court session, the evidence presented by the local law enforcement officials (LEOs) when a hacker stole data from a company was rejected by the 58-year-old judge who said that the evidence lacked a particular and important factor. The local LEO argued that the evidence was authentic, accurate, complete, and very convincing. The judge was not convinced and threw out the case. Why did the judge consider that the case lacked evidence?

A) The hacker has the right to hack any open systems, and it is not a crime.

B) The evidence produced by the LEO meets almost all the factors but is not admissible.

C) The FBI has the sole jurisdiction of computer systems, not the local LEO.

D) The 58-year-old judge is not well versed in the new generation of computer crimes.

Analysis: Reading the question, it becomes quickly clear that the evidence presented was authentic, accurate, complete, and very convincing but clearly lacked the last item of "being admissible." The rest of the statements in the question about the judge's age and others, are distractors and superfluous information. The judge's age was given in the question to match with option D, but clearly that is not the answer.

Statement: Removing the additional information, the statement can be constructed as follows:

The evidence presented was rejected by the judge. The local LEO argued that **the evidence was authentic, accurate, complete, and very convincing**. The judge was not convinced and threw out the case.

Question: What factor caused the judge to consider that the case lacked evidence?

Solution: Option B is a clear favorite. Option A is a distractor because designing an open system does not give an invitation to a hacker to come and exploit it. Any hacking is illegal if it can be proved with correct evidence. Option C is a distractor too since any law enforcement can investigate a crime, transfer it to other departments, or work in tandem with others. Option D is also a distractor since the age of the judge is never a factor to understand the law.

Review Questions

Some of the other questions can be as follows:

1. The law enforcement agency suspects that the evidence at a crime scene can be modified by a suspect and thus asks a judge to issue orders to seize the crime scene area. What is the name of this order that a judge can issue in these conditions?

   Answer: Exigent circumstances

2. The lifecycle of evidence consists of which **CONSECUTIVE** processes?

   A) Identification, storage, preservation, transportation, presentation, return to owner

   B) Transportation, storage, preservation, presentation, return to owner

   C) Preservation, transportation, identification, chain of custody, presentation

   D) Storage, preservation, identification, transportation, presentation, discard

   Answer: Option A

3. Why is chain of custody considered the **MOST** important in gathering evidence?

   A) The chain of custody clearly demonstrates the responsibilities of evidence handlers.

   B) The chain of custody proves that the evidence is admissible.

   C) The chain of custody is a government-required mandate in evidence collection.

   D) The chain of custody proves that the suspect is really guilty of the crime.

   Answer: Option B

4. When browsing a website, a normal user clicks a link that promises a free version of the Microsoft Office software. The software when downloaded tracks the user and reports to local law enforcement. The process of luring a normal user in this way for a free software download is called:

A) Entrapment

B) Enforcement

C) Entitlement

D) Enticement

Answer: Option A. The user had no intention to get the software but was lured.

Preventative Measures: Malware Prevention

Tip #57: Remember different types of viruses, detection, removal and levels of their operation.

Domain: Software Development and Security, Security Operations.

Subdomain: Security in software development lifecycle, Enforcing software security, Source code vulnerabilities, Malware prevention.

Subject background: Virtual and digital media provide various ways to impregnate a program and steal data or personally identifiable information (PII). Some programs just test the strength of an application and try to crash it for fun, whereas most programs are designed to steal and cause trouble for the end user. These programs come in various shapes and sizes and even as attachments to email. These programs are called viruses, malware, spyware, and by many other names. Unfortunately, these programs keep evolving rapidly as the digital world expands beyond our comprehension.

Computer malware has the primary components of addition, avoidance, eradication, replication, trigger (at a point of time), and payload (does what it is supposed to perform).

Things to Remember

- A virus is a program or a small executable code that infects or causes undesirable behavior in software. Viruses depend on a host application (such as an email program or Microsoft Office program) and <u>cannot</u> replicate by themselves.

- A **stealth virus** hides any modifications it has done on files/systems and on booting records. This is can be indirectly done by modifying the file monitoring programs to show that nothing was modified. It is a way of fooling a user into thinking that everything is fine on the system.

- **Logic bombs** are pieces of code inserted into the program to run at a particular time on a particular day. Assume that there is a bad manager who regularly causes trouble for a programmer writing an application. The manager wants to demonstrate the program in a conference on April 23 between 11 a.m. and 4 p.m. The programmer can write code that the program does not function on this particular date and time but will work fine on any other date and time. The manager who is unaware of the logic bomb would never know why it did not work on April 23 during the conference times.

- **Trojan horses** are programs that do one thing that is visible to the user but do a different job in the background. For example, they may work as a patch for a program, but in the background, unknown to the user, they may steal data and pass it to some other host.

- **Worms** are self-replicating viruses. Some viruses need a host application to replicate, but the worms do not need any. These are self-contained programs. **Stuxnet**, which was created purposefully to disrupt the Iranian nuclear program, is an example of a worm.

- A **rootkit** attempts to gain administrative privileges first to upload tools that run at startup to gain control of the system. Since the attacker gets administrative access, he can get access at any time and modify anything on the system.

- A **multipart virus**, as its name indicates, has several parts installed at various locations of the file system. It may affect the boot sector and other files. Because it exists in various locations, it can spread quickly.

- **Script viruses** are made of scripts in the VBScript or JavaScript language. They also come as a package that prompts users to install it. When installed, the scripts merge with the original software such as Microsoft Office and cause trouble for users. They also spread via email when infected files are exchanged in email.

- A **meme virus** is a type of email message that is forwarded or sent by users/systems when users/systems receive and forward emails to others. These are more a nuisance than a problem. Chain letters that ask users to send the email to a few more people and sales gimmicks fall into this category and are generally considered to be junk email. Note that some of these junk mails may contain **phishing attempts** that take the user to a website that may attempt to steal PII.

- A **polymorphic virus** is a malware program that morphs itself into different forms and thereby evades detection. It may use various encryption and decryption methods, and the detecting program may need to run several times to detect all existing versions of the virus.

- **Spyware/adware** is a software program that collects information about the user and uses it for malicious purposes. Adware may not use the data for malicious purposes but to show nuisance advertisements regularly, like pop-ups that ask the user to click a HTML link.

- **Botnets** are a group of computers where some malicious software is installed. Bots (also known as a group of robots) transmit data regularly to a central point (attacker) that will analyze the data and use it for malicious purposes.

- **Driveby downloads** are automatically scheduled to be downloaded when the user visits a website and does not even click any link.

- **Macros** are a kind of malware inserted into programs that allow macros (e.g., Excel). For fear of getting a virus is the main reason why unknown macros should not be used.

Example: A user visits a website to check the news, and while he is reading the news, a program was automatically downloaded without the user's knowledge. At a later date when the user opened the file system, he found that the file system was modified and his user data was being passed to another external computer without his knowledge. What kind of virus might the user have downloaded?

A) A logic bomb downloaded by a driveby download

B) A script virus directly downloaded

C) A multipart virus by direct download and installation

D) A Trojan horse by driveby download

Analysis: Since the program automatically downloaded without the user's consent, and without asking the user, it is a driveby download. The program is also passing the data in the background, which says that the virus it is working as a Trojan horse.

Statement: A user visits a website, and a program was automatically downloading. At a later date, his user data was being passed to another external computer without his knowledge.

Question: What kind of virus might the user have downloaded?

Solution: The virus downloaded automatically, which means it is a driveby download. The virus also passes information in the background, which is typical of a Trojan horse. This gives a clue that the answer is option D. Note that the wording "at a later date" is a distractor to say it is a logic bomb. But the virus is not running at a specific time and date.

Review Questions

Various questions can be asked on the topic as follows:

1. A programmer writes an application inserting a piece of macro script that runs on March 21 at 12 p.m. and disables the entire file system in the background, unknown to the front-end user. What kind of virus can this piece of macro be **BEST** described as?

    A) Macro virus

    B) Logic bomb

    C) Script meme

    D) Macro worm

    Answer: When it runs at a particular time and date, it is a logic bomb, so option B is the correct answer.

2. What does a rootkit malware be **BEST** said to hide when it gets installed on a Windows computer?

    A) Rootkits hide infected files at the operating system level.

    B) Rootkits hide a process, a registry item, or a file.

    C) Rootkits work on the kernel and hide the kernel.

    D) Rootkits hide the operating system files.

    Answer: Rootkits can hide a process, a file, or a registry item. So, the correct answer is option B.

3. What is a virus that replicates itself called?

    Answer: Self-replicating viruses are called worms.

4. What kind of virus needs several rounds of checks to see whether the virus remains in other forms over the entire file system?

    Answer: A polymorphic virus needs several detection loops.

5. Which virus is **MOST** difficult to detect?

    Answer: Root-level operating system viruses and those that exist in hardware/firmware are the most difficult to detect.

Change Management Process

Tip #58: Understand the types of data used for testing purposes and how to prepare test data

In this section, you'll learn about test data, how to mimic it to resemble production data, and how to get sanitized production data for test purposes.

Domain: Software Development and Security, Security Operations.

Subdomain: Software development, Software environment, Testing software, Data security, PII security, Sanitation, Destruction of data, Change management process.

Subject background: It is a general practice in software development that there are different machines or environments to develop, test, and deploy software. The servers themselves can have one or more of clusters where the code can remain or run. Switching of code from one cluster to another is random to avoid a hacking attempt.

But as long as the code remains on a server, a programmer can access it on one of the server's clusters.

A developer can connect their desktop to a development or test server via a network connection without physically moving from one office to another for access. A developer has access only to the development area and can do all they want on that machine/server/cluster while doing the software development work. Once development is complete, they can also do the unit testing on their own machine and create an installation package to be put on the test machine.

The process of development, test, and deployment to production is a systematic process monitored usually by the change management board, sometimes called the change advisory board (CAB). A developer has access **only** to a development environment, a tester has access **only** to a test environment, and the deployment person has access **only** to a production environment, and all three have to work in tandem for the software to work successfully.

Note that the development environment has development tools such as Java's Eclipse or Microsoft's Visual Studio. But the test environment will not have development tools and will have only the bare-bones framework to "run" the developed code. This bare environment is sometimes called a petri dish framework used only for testing the program. A tester, if bugs are found in the software, only records the bugs and passes them back to the developer but cannot correct the bugs or even debug them because his environment is a bare-bones one.

Once the software is ready to be tested, the developer creates a test package and passes it to be installed on the test machine. As said earlier, the test machine can be a virtual machine and has the bare-bones environment (like the .NET Framework only) to run the software.

The process of going from development to test and back to development can happen in more than one round and can take several days or even months. A tester also will have no idea why the software is crashing or showing an error because the tester has his own tools to test the software and cannot debug it.

The development and test machines and servers are usually on private IP addresses (see Tip #37) and are accessible privately only on the internal servers of the organization. The production server is a public server where the executable code is exposed or distributed to the general public or to a restricted number of third-party users via the Internet.

A tester does/should not have valid production data to test. It is the developer's responsibility to create "production-like" data and supply it to the tester (a tester can create this data too) to test the software. The production-like data can be artificially created (to protect the PII) or can be pulled from production and modified. If the data is pulled from a live production machine and modified, it is called sanitized production data.

Once testing is complete, the completely corrected development package is now ready for deployment to production, subject to the rules of the CAB such as date of deployment, rollout, etc.

Things to Remember

- Production data has to be always kept as production data and cannot be copied to test or development machines "as is."

- Development and test servers have their own data sets to test the code, and the data on these servers can be either the same, similar, or different.

- Production data can be sanitized (modified to remove the PII) to make it available to development and test servers for use.

- Test and development servers are usually on a private IP address, which is not available to the public via a web browser.

- There is more than one way to create or modify a sanitized production data set for use on development and test servers.

- A production server with live valid data contains a minimum bare-bones configuration such as a runnable .NET Framework to run the required program.

- A test server mostly resembles the production server but with a sanitized data set.

- A development server contains all the development tools a programmer requires and the sanitized data set for the programmer to develop fully functioning code.

Example: A developer writing an application has a need to unit test his code on the development server, package the application to the test server, and when testing is successful, deploy the same application without changes on the production server. The production server carries the live data that will be used by the application. However, the developer has to first use some kind of data that resembles the production data for his unit testing and use similar data on the testing machine for the tester to verify. The tester does not have access to the production data, which is handled by the deployment division. The tester goes to the deployment division to ask for a sample of production data for testing the application. What kind of production data should the deployment department provide the developer or tester?

A)   The actual production data but only a few sample data items

B)   Sanitized/modified production data but only a few sample items

C)   Full production data on USD drives or DVDs, depending on how much data it is

D)   Part production data on USD drives or DVDs, depending on how much data it is

Analysis: Looking at the verbiage, we find that the developer just needs a data set to test his application on his machine and on the test machine. The best data to test/modify/edit/delete will be a sample of sanitized production data. Obviously, the production dataset in its entirety can be very large, and providing the entire dataset is a moot point due to obvious reasons. Part production data may or may not be able to serve the complete purpose of testing. Additionally, copying production data to USBs or DVDs poses a risk of a loss of media. One should never expose the production data for testing on any environment.

Statement: The tester goes to the deployment department to ask for a sample of production data for his own use.

Question: Removing the entire verbiage, the basic question is the last sentence of the entire statement, which can be rephrased as:

What kind of production data should the deployment department provide the developer or tester?

Solution: Only option B makes sense as a correct answer.

Review Questions

Some of the options for the topic can be as follows:

1.   Which is a correct IP address for implementing a production server?

A)   192.168.9.223

B)   10.18.225.255

C) 147.293.253.28

D) 147.29.23.225

Answer: Option D

2. Why is sanitized production data used on test and developmental servers?

   A) Sanitized production data resembles the actual data but protects PII.

   B) Sanitized production data removes all PII and the format completely.

   C) Sanitized production data does not resemble anything and protects PII.

   D) Sanitized production data is another name for actual data copied from the production server, so there is no difference between production data and test data.

   Answer: Option A

3. Pick the **MOST** accurate statement from the options.

   A) Production data is the most accurate, so it can and should be copied to the test and development machines for test and development purposes.

   B) Production is the most accurate, and it should always be sanitized before copying to the test and developmental environments.

   C) Test and development data items can be combined with production data and deployed on production servers, so to save time and money, an application can be developed, tested, and used directly in production.

   D) Test, production, and development servers must contain three different types of data and formatting, since they all have different executable code that responds to individual data needs.

   Answer: Option B

4. A data table on production database server has Social Security numbers (SSNs) and names of users. The table is updated daily at night. A developer doing an update to the application that accesses this data table wants to test her application with sanitized production data. What is the best way to sanitize production data?

A) Copy the data table from production to development and remove the SSN and name columns of the copied data table.

B) Copy the data table from production to development and randomize the SSN and name columns of the copied data table.

C) Copy the data table from production to development and randomize the SSN column, but remove the name column of the copied data table.

D) Copy the data table from production to development and remove the SSN column, but randomize the name column of the copied data table.

Answer: Option B

5. Can development and test have identical data?

Answer: Yes, as long as both the development and test machines are on private IP addresses that are not accessible to the public, they can have sanitized versions of production data, but the same sanitized data can exist on both the development and test servers.

Recovery Strategies: Backup, Multiple Operation Sites

Tip #59: Know the types of backup strategies for recovery and security in backup/recovery

Find the twist, if any, in the question before you answer. Read the given statement carefully and read what is asked about full/differential/incremental backups. The statement and the actual question may contradict each other to create subtle confusion.

Domain: Security Operations.

Subdomain: Recovery strategies, Backup.

Subject background: Data or information collected by an organization is the most valueable asset an organization canhave.It needs to be protected and in case of a loss, be backed up on a secure drive or in location from where it can be recovered and restored easily. There are various methods of back up and recovery. Backup can be a full back, an incremental backup up or a differential backup that are scheduled to run a daily, weekly or monthly basis. Archive bit is an important factor to remember when backing up the data. Depending on the needs of an organization these backup processes are selected and scheduled.It is also important to know that back up can be on a tape, a disk, a USB or another form of memory that can be stored on site or offsite. There are several strategies adopted for selecting the back up device.

Things to Remember

- There are three basic methods of backup: full backup, differential backup, and incremental backup. Of these, only a differential backup does **not** touch (set, reset, or change) the archive bit.

- An incremental backup backs up files that were changed since the last backup of any type.

- Incremental backups are done to save time.

- A differential backup backs up files that were changed since the last full backup.

- Differential backups are done to save on the number of backup disks/ media needed.

- A full backup backs up everything without worrying about the type of the last backup.

- A full backup takes the longest time and memory but has everything needed for full restoration.

- Figure 7-1 demonstrates differential and incremental backup methods.

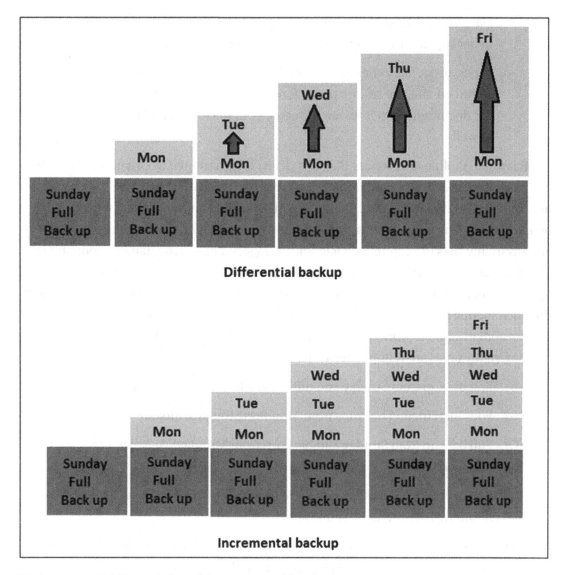

Figure 7-1. *Differential and incremental backups*

- Backing up data is a basic way of saving data on a retrievable/ recoverable medium. In the case of a disaster, the data can be fully loaded back to the IT systems.

- The data custodian is responsible for doing the backups.

- The backup methodology may be set by an organization's policies, standards, and procedures as required.

- Data owners/C-level managers such as CEO, CISO, etc., have no role in backup processes other than establishing a policy or standard.

- Tapes, disks, and other backup media are usually utilized and stored off-site, the restore procedures are well documented and the documentation is reviewed regularly to make required changes as well.

Example: Prolific & Visionary Backups (PVB) Inc., stationed in Orlando, Florida, has established a data backup methodology on tapes for its data services. The backup creates full backups on Sunday at 6 p.m. and differential backups on weekdays at 6 p.m., with no backups on Saturdays. During the hurricane season, which usually occurs from April and invariably lasts to September/October, a category 4 hurricane named Bloom hit the city, and the data center was automatically shut down by the environmental controls set up on-site on a Thursday at noon due to flooding. When the center opened, it was found that incremental backups were done to save time due to the onset of the hurricane. PVB's data custodian came to work on Saturday to restore data from backups.

How many tapes are required for PVB to restore the data on Saturday at 9 a.m.?

A) Full backup from Sunday and differential backup from Wednesday

B) Four incremental backups from Monday through Thursday

C) Full backup from Sunday and backups from Monday, Tuesday, and Wednesday

D) Full backup from Sunday and three incremental backups from Monday, Tuesday, and Wednesday

Analysis: There is a lot of verbiage in the question that can be removed as follows and make the statement clear and easy to understand:

Statement: Prolific & Visionary Backups (PVB) Inc. creates full backups on Sunday at 6 p.m. and differential backups on weekdays at 6 p.m., with no backup on Saturday. The data center was automatically shut down on Thursday at noon. When the center opened, it was **found that incremental backups were done** to save time. PVB's on-call data custodian came to work on Saturday to restore data from the backups.

Question: How many tapes are required on **Saturday at 9 a.m.**?

Notice the last two sentences of the statement. Usually PVB Inc. does differential backups, but due to the onset of the hurricane, it did the incremental backups. This gives a clue to picking the correct answer. **Any option with "differential" backup can**

therefore be eliminated. This leaves us with options B, C, and D. Now, depending on what we know of backup methods from Figure 7-1, we can use reason to deduce an answer.

Of the three remaining options, option B can be eliminated because incremental (or for that matter, differential) backups alone cannot restore the data. We will need a full backup from some earlier time. Though the question states that differential backups are "usually" done, with the onset of the hurricane, PVB did only the incremental backups to save time. This gives the clue that option C can also be eliminated. If we read option C carefully, we notice that it does not mention what type of backups from Monday/Tuesday/Wednesday are being used.

Solution: We are now left with option D. Is option D the correct answer? Before deciding that as an answer, we can verify that for the given situation, we need a full backup first, followed by incremental backups for every day after that full backup, until the system shut down. Thus, we need one Sunday full backup and incremental backups of Monday, Tuesday, and Wednesday. This proves that the answer is indeed option D.

Review Questions

Variations on the question on the actual CISSP exam will look like the following, with the same statement verbiage:

1. How many backups does the custodian actually need for complete data restoration on Saturday at 9 a.m., if there were no hurricane?

   Answer: In this case, the center did not shut down since there was no hurricane. It means that the custodian has Sunday's full backup and every day's differential backup in his possession. He would simply need the Sunday full backup and the Friday differential backup.

2. When does the archive bit get reset in the backup process if the senior management decides to switch the daily backups from differential to incremental?

   Answer: The answer would be every time a backup is made. Why? Because we know that either full or incremental backups reset the archive bit. Only the differential backup does not touch the archive bit.

3. When does the archive bit get reset if there is no hurricane?

> **Answer**: Only when the full backup is done on Sundays since the differential backup does not touch the archive bit. This is because if there is no hurricane, PVB does differential backups on all weekdays, no backups on Saturday, and a full backup on Sunday.

Disaster Recovery Processes and Plans

Tip #60: Request to fix an issue, time allowed and its impact on business

Understand the time required to fix an issue and the maximum tolerable downtime (MTD) for a task depending the criticality of the task and operation.

Domain: Security Assessment and Testing, Security Operations.

Subdomain: Disaster recovery, Business continuity plans, Disaster recovery process and plans, Business impact analysis.

Subject background: MTDs for the business operations are listed in Table 7-1. Note that these are guidelines only and change their definitions depending on the situation. For example, in case of an earthquake or tornado, every task at hand can be classified as "critical," whereas in some situations like a sudden labor union strike, a few things can be critical and others can be classified into other areas.

Table 7-1. *Generic Rules for Allowed Time to Fix an Issue*

Type	Addressing Time
Nonessential	30 days
Normal	7 to 10 days
Important	72 hours
Urgent	24 hours
Critical	Minutes to hours

Things to Remember

In the case of a disaster, human lives matter the most. Once that factor is taken care of, the next things that need attention are the most critical functions of a business.

Maximum tolerable downtime (MTD) is also known as the maximum period time of disruption (MPTD).

The main task of business impact analysis (BIA) is to identify the critical functions (that need to be restored first). Even before restoring the critical function, the **FIRST** and most important thing is to consider human lives.

Usually **nonessential things** include losing an Internet connection to a building and services that deal with physical facility such as plumbing, carpet replacement. But the same items can be classified as critical if the business loses huge money (say $100,000 per week) due to a loss of incoming orders when the Internet connection no longer is available or a visitor cannot be allowed inside the building to buy any item.

Service level agreements (SLAs) also impact how a service can be classified since an outsourced service such as an Internet connection by a cable company might be governed by an SLA that promises to restore the connection in three to five days or some other time frame.

Anything and everything must be considered that can have a detrimental effect on the company's business when classifying operations in a BIA.

Disasters can be due to human factors, natural factors, or environmental factors.

The **restoration team** gets an off-site facility ready and working soon. They also use the backups to do the needed data or information restore.

The **salvage team** is for working at the original site of the disaster.

The **recovery team** helps in preparing the systems and environment and in helping set up the alternate location/site. This team has the knowledge to build a fully working alternative site in the case of a disaster.

Notice the subtle difference between the recovery team and the restoration team.

Example: Ahead of a disaster, all the information systems were shut down, and the employees were asked to stay at home until further notice, thereby taking care of all the human lives. The paychecks to employees will be automatically deposited, and there were no worries about paying bills to vendors either. What is the **FIRST** action for the business after the disaster is over?

A)   Save human lives

B)   Restore critical functions

C)   Recover the facility

D)   Salvage the facility

Analysis: Notice that in any disaster the **FIRST** important thing is to take care of human lives. But in this question human lives were said to have been taken care of already. Thus, option A is a distractor. The first action the business should take care of is to restore the critical functions of the business.

Statement: Ahead of a disaster, all the information systems were shut down, and the employees were asked to stay at home, thereby taking care of all human lives.

Question: Ahead of a disaster and to take care of all human lives, what is the **FIRST** action for the business **after** the disaster is over?

Solution: Option B is the correct answer since the question statement said that the human lives were already taken care of ahead of the disaster. Paychecks can be sent later, and they are not critical functions though important. They can be done in 24 hours (urgent), 72 hours (important), or even 7 to 10 days (normal) with the cooperation of employees.

Note that recovery and salvaging may be required functions for a business, but they are not the **FIRST**. The first actions are those that restore the critical functions of the business. Recovery and salvaging are the functions that can be carried out later. The salvage team can also be involved in using the backups to get systems working at the original facility and also to send them back to the backup facility for future use.

Review Questions

Variations of the questions are as follows:

1.   Who is responsible for the recovery of the original business site?

A) Recovery team

B) Restoration team

C) Salvage team

D) Rebuilding team

Answer: Option C. At the original site, it is always the salvage team's work.

2. After the disaster was over, the original site was fully prepared for operations. What should an organization **FIRST** ensure before moving into the original facility?

   A) Make sure that the critical functions are restored

   B) Ensure the safety of employees

   C) Ensure that the local authorities approve the facility

   D) Test the original facility

   Answer: Option B. Since the disaster was over already, before allowing the employees to go into the original facitlity, the **FIRST** responsibility is to ensure the safety of everyone who enter the facility because the original facility may still have some unexpected problems.

3. What is the time frame an important business operation should be addressed in?

   Answer: 72 hours

4. If a business operation needs to be restored within minutes to hours, it should be classified in the operations as:

   A) Immediate

   B) Critical

   C) Urgent

   D) Essential

   Answer: Option B. There are no "immediate" and "essential" operations.

5. What is a service level agreement (SLA)?

   A) Document stating that service will be restored as and when possible

   B) Agreement signed by a business owner and service provider about a service provided for a one-time or recurring price

C) Agreement signed by the salvage party to restore a critical service

D) Mutual verbal understanding of two parties about how they cooperate with each other in doing or developing a service

Answer: Option B

Business Continuity Planning and Exercises

Tip #61: Learn various acronyms and first steps in disaster recovery, business continuity, etc.

Master the acronyms for threat models, risk assessment, attacks, system development lifecycle (SDLC), and disaster recovery planning (DRP), among other models.

Domain: Security Assessment and Testing, Security Operations, Security and Risk Management.

Subdomain: DRP processes and plans, Risk management concepts, Risk analysis.

Subject background: Figure 7-2 gives the acronyms for some of the models.

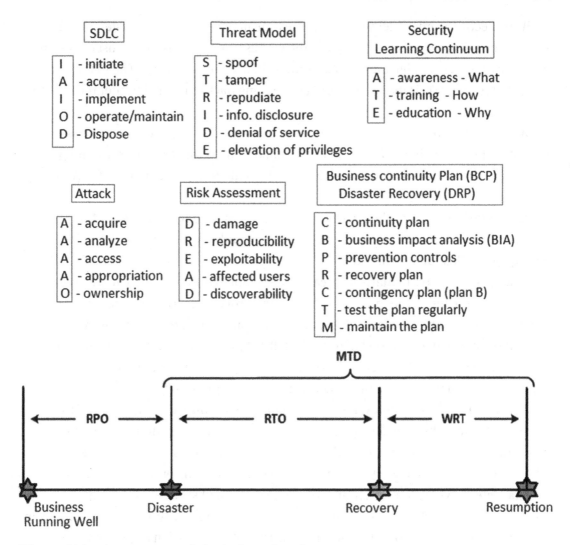

Figure 7-2. *Acronyms and depiction of various terms*

Things to Remember

Each process has specific steps, and they follow an order. In Figure 7-2, the following definitions apply.

SDLC: Sometimes SDLC can be interpreted as software development life cycle, but with disaster recovery and business continuity areas, we can also call it as system development life cycle.

RPO: Recovery point objective. This represents the maximum acceptable data loss for an organization, measured in terms of time. This also tells how long the company can afford to be down before the business starts suffering. In other words, this is the company's overall resilience for loss of data. The main thing to remember is that RPO points to data loss.

RTO: Recovery time objective. This is the time needed to bring all systems back online <u>after a disaster strikes</u>. This is also the earliest time the business must be restored or the maximum time a business remains unavailable after a disaster. The main point to remember is that RTO is the time to bring everything back to normalcy after the disaster strikes.

WRT: Work recovery time. Before the system goes back to production successfully, the restored systems should be tested and verified. WRT is that time to verify and pull the business back to production successfully. The main thing to remember for WRT is restoration.

MTD: Maximum tolerable downtime. MTD is the sum of RTO and WRT. This is the maximum time the business can be interrupted without causing unacceptable consequences (loss of income, etc.).

The CISSP exam particularly tests candidates about DRP/BCP and can ask questions about each of the individual processes, the overall process of a DRP, or what step comes after a particular step. For example, a typical question can be presented like, "When is the contingency plan developed in the BCP/DRP plan?" or "How often is the BCP/DRP plan tested to maintain it correctly?" Likewise, in the attack methodology, a question can be given as "At what stage does an attacker do the appropriation?"

Note that Figure 7-2 is an example of the many acronyms a candidate needs to remember for the CISSP certification exam. But a mere memorization does not help the exam taker. It is important to understand the basic methods, to know how each subsection of the method works, and to have a good idea of the entire nomenclature.

Example: A cyber attacker aiming to induce a denial of service sends a ping command as an initial step to find out details about a computer system. Upon finding an empty and unprotected port, the hacker wants to exploit it. At what stage can the attacker usually claim ownership after sending the initial ping command?

A) Immediately after receiving results of the ping command

B) After receiving the ping command and analyzing the results

C) In the final step after appropriation of the system

D) After accessing the system via unprotected port

Analysis: Closely reading the question more than once reveals that the question is asking when the ownership will occur and after what step in the attack process. From the Figure 7-2 and attack methodology of AAAAO, we know that ownership occurs as a final step and before the appropriation. In an attack methodology, the initial steps are pinging, finding open ports, accessing, analyzing, and acquisition.

The final step is ownership, but the question is asking after what step the ownership happens. Thus, we can find that after appropriation, the final step of ownership happens. In other words, a hacker can completely own the system when all the other steps are complete.

Statement: A cyber attacker sends a ping command as an initial step. **After what stage can the attacker usually claim ownership?**

Question: <u>After what stage</u> can the attacker usually claim ownership?

Solution: Notice the first three words that give a clue about the answer. Option C is a straightforward answer for this question. Options A, B, and D are not the correct answers because pinging alone does not give full details of a system to a hacker. If the hacker can access the system via a port, he may be able to compromise it to some level but may not be able to claim ownership of the system.

Appropriation is a method of seizing the system or getting a full handle on the system to create accounts, modify passwords, or do anything that a hacker wants to perform. Once a hacker can seize the administrative access to a system, he can delete existing accounts and create his own and delete or modify files, etc. At this point, he will be able to claim ownership of the system.

Review Questions

Some variations of the previous acronyms will look as follows:

1. Maximum tolerable downtime (MTD) is a sum of:

    A) Recovery point objective (RPO) and work recovery time (WRT)

    B) Recovery point objective (RPO) and recovery time objective (RTO)

    C) Recovery time objective (RTO) and work recovery time (WRT)

    D) Recovery point objective (RPO) and minimum data loss time (MDLT)

    Answer: Option C is the correct answer. There is no MDLT defined per se.

2.   What are the factors in a security learning continuum?

A) Education, training, and experience

B) Professionalism, education, and awareness

C) Observation, learning, and education

D) Awareness, training, and education

Answer: Option D is the correct answer.

3.   How often does a disaster recovery/business continuity plan (DR/BCP) need to be tested to keep it up-to-date?

A) Once when plan is ready and in six to nine months thereafter

B) At least once a year and whenever a need arises

C) As and when the DR/BCP team has time and a need to test

D) Two or three days before the disaster warning is issued

Answer: Option B is the correct one. Plans must be tested at least once a year and also when there is a need like an important update is made or a new policy/rule is created.

4.   A candy business making hard candy produces 3 million candies in a normal day of production. Due to a fire, the plant was shut down on Monday. The fire department cleared the debris and gave a final green light for the company to start production by Wednesday. The company was able to tolerate the data loss until Wednesday. But initiating the production systems back to normal took 36 hours, and after the systems are back up, testing the systems took another 18 hours before going to production at full throttle. What is the work recovery time (WRT) and maximum tolerable downtime (MTD) experienced by the candy company?

A) The WRT is 54 hours, and the MTD is 18 hours.

B) The MTD is 54 hours, and the WRT is 18 hours.

C) The WRT is 36 hours, and the MTD is 18 hours.

D) The MTD is Monday to Wednesday plus 54 hours, and the WRT is 54 hours.

Answer: Option B is the correct answer since the question is asking about times **after** the disaster stuck. From Monday to

Wednesday there was no production, but the company was able to accept the data loss. Monday to Wednesday is thus the recovery point objective (RPO). Once given the green light on Wednesday, the company's RTO was 36 hours, and the WRT was 18 hours. The MTD is a sum of the RTO and the WRT, which is 54 hours.

Tip #62: Know the exercise types for BCP

Domain: Security and Risk Management, Security Assessment and Testing.

Subdomain: Disaster recovery, Business continuity plans, Testing and refining DRP/BCP.

Subject background: A disaster recovery plan (DRP) or a business continuity plan (BCP) generally goes through a refining process before a final plan is put in place. The plan is also updated and checked at least annually and as necessary. This means the plan can be updated anytime when required but must be checked and updated as needed at least once a year.

Disaster recovery is about how quickly a company can bounce back from a disaster and how safely the human life can be protected, etc., after a disaster strikes. A disaster can be a terrorist attack, a manmade problem, a fire, or even a natural disaster such as an earthquake or flood.

Business continuity is about how the company can resume full-fledged operations after a disaster strikes.

Before, after, and while keeping an organization up-to-date and running, a disaster plan is necessary to be put in place, tested regularly by various methods, and kept up-to-date. This is the main reason why several testing types are required for the plan.

Things to Remember

- A **simulation test** is a kind of walk-through test. A team of people are invited to the test, given a set of circumstances to participate and to find the response to such a situation. Most of the simulation test is a kind of mock test. The response is observed by another set of people who suggest improvements after the test is complete.

- A **full test** is actually a "live test." This means the testing is done after the plan is ready and when a normal disaster happens. This could shut down the organization or at least disrupt the day-to-day processes. Full test is hard to conduct since at the time of actual disaster, a test may not be carried out, and an organization needs to actually survive the "live-wire" situation. It is also next to impossible to find participating people who can help do this test during a disaster and extremely difficult to get the buy-in from the owner of the organization, since during the test, the lives of people can be in danger, which can in turn cause a flurry of lawsuits later.

- A **parallel test** is a test that is suitable if the organization has more than one live plant in two or more locations. In a parallel test, both plants would be running at their full strength but all the employees of first location are moved to a second location for testing. In this way, while the employees test one location as a live test (as described in full test), the second location is in full working force, without disrupting production.

- A **read-through test** is a group meeting wherein the participants are provided a handout and everyone is made aware of how they should respond in the case of a disaster.

- A **tabletop test** is somewhat an extension of the read-through test. This is sometimes called a **structured walk-through test**. In this test, participants meet in a group meeting, led by a testing manager who plays the situation of disaster and directs how each one should respond in the case of a disaster. The manager may or may not give the details of the plan ahead of the meeting.

- **Sandbox testing** is a way of creating a sandbox situation and testing the actual test as if it were a live situation. A sandbox is a kind of facility or application that looks similar to a production facility. But a sandbox does not actually produce anything. In such a situation, the participants can do anything and learn how to respond in a disaster situation. This test or the sandbox itself does not have any consequences on the actual production. This is mostly used in large IT systems dealing with large databases and applications.

- A **maintenance test** is done to regularly update an existing test. A maintenance test needs to be done at least once annually. It can also be done as and when necessary depending on changes and as the management deems necessary.

- An organization's disaster recovery plan is a necessary and exhaustive document that needs to be in place and updated regularly. While creating a disaster recovery plan is a great thing, implementing it well and training the staff to understand and implement the plan is equally important for the day-to-day health of an organization.

Example: A confectionary factory producing chocolates for children has four plants in a city, and two of the plants are in the same location. The company has a disaster recovery plan (DRP) that was recently created since the two plants situated in the city are on the seismic belt that is prone to frequent earthquakes. The company now wants to do a test that initially tests the DRP and completes the test in the future in case of a natural disaster. What test can the company opt to do on the DRP as an initial test that could lead to final and better testing for live-wire production?

A) Do a live-wire parallel test on the second site

B) Do a read-through test only

C) Do a tabletop test and update participants

D) DRP needs training and not testing; just save the DRP document

Analysis: Looking at the verbiage, the question is asking about the "initial test" for the created DRP. It is not asking what test is required, what test can actually severely test the DRP, or any other type of meeting. The question's verbiage can be removed, and the question can be rearranged as follows.

Statement: A company has a disaster recovery plan (DRP) recently created since the two plants situated in a city are on the seismic belt. The company now wants to do a test that **initially tests** the DRP.

Question: What test can the company opt to do on the DRP as an initial test ?

A) Do a live-wire parallel test on the second site.

B) Do a read-through test only.

C) Do a tabletop test and update participants.

D) The DRP needs training and not testing. Just save the DRP document.

Solution: Option D can safely be eliminated first because it is obviously wrong. Every DRP needs testing and maintenance. Option A is wrong because live-wire testing is not for initial DRP testing. Live-wire testing can disrupt one plant, and it is not done in the initial stage of the DRP. Options B and C are very close, but if we reconsider what the question is asking, we can infer that the tabletop test is not the initial test. A tabletop is a kind of extension of the read-through test. That tells that the "initial test" should be a read-through test, which is option B.

Review Questions

A lot of variations can occur on the CISSP exam about this topic. Some of them are listed here:

1. What is another name for a structured walk-through test?

    A) Read through the structures test

    B) Initial first test of structures

    C) Tabletop test

    D) Test that uses programming structures

    Answer: Option C

2. How often does the DRP need to be updated?

    A) Once a year only

    B) Once a year and as necessary

    C) Every six months

    D) Only when updates are necessary

    Answer: Option B

3. What is a mutual assistance agreement (MAA) between two companies?

    A) It is an agreement that helps each other in the case of a disaster.

    B) It is an agreement of business deals to supply the items required.

C) It is an agreement that each company stores its DRP with the other company.

D) It is an agreement that both companies create one DRP that works for both.

Answer: Option A

4. Which of the following is a man-made disaster?

   A) Power outage

   B) Earthquake

   C) Floods and rains

   D) Meteor shower hit

   Answer: Option A

5. Which of the following is a natural disaster?

   A) Vandalism

   B) Software failure

   C) Structural failure

   D) Tsunami

   Answer: Option D

6. Hurricane Katrina in the United States caused a lot of damage to the US economy. Katrina is considered what type of disaster?

   A) Man-made disaster

   B) Natural disaster

   C) Hand of God

   D) Environmental problem

   Answer: Option B

7. What is the main reason for a DRP to be maintained regularly?

   Answer: To keep it up-to-date for the ever-changing environment and train the staff accordingly so that the staff can respond in the most realistic way on the day of disaster

Tip #63: Understand hot, cold, and warm sites, as well as reciprocal agreements, etc., for IT operations

Domain: Asset Security, Security and Risk Management, Security Engineering.

Subdomain: Disaster recovery, Business continuity, Site and facility design.

Subject background: Every organization, whatever the size, should have some kind of disaster recovery plan (DRP) for backup, daily operations, and getting back to business if a disaster strikes. For the DRP to work, there are several options such as arranging for a hot site, cold site, warm site, or at least having a reciprocal agreement with another company.

A **cold site** is just a building with no other facilities such as equipment, data backups, or anything. It can just house a few employees and may have basic furniture for people to sit, but nothing beyond that. Other than housing the employees and making sure they are present, a cold site may not serve any other purpose than having meetings and discussions. It may take several weeks to months to bring the cold site work to full business operations since it involves purchasing or borrowing IT equipment, installing hardware and software, and bringing up the site to business operations.

A **warm site** usually has more than what a cold site can offer. It may have IT equipment or mobile technology such as laptops and such but is not fully functional. To restore the full service of the business, a warm site needs data, software, and other details. In other words, to make the warm site functional for restoring some or all business operations, it may take a few days of hard work to bring up the IT systems.

A **hot site** is a mirror image of the actual business operations site. It can come around and start business operations in a matter of minutes to hours. It already has everything required for the business to function and up-to-date data. This is the most expensive option for a business site since it needs to be up-to-date with the data from actual business site. Websites such as Amazon, Walmart, and others that sell online have this kind of sites in case their primary site goes down.

A **reciprocal agreement** is a document signed with another company that agrees to host the company in the case of a disaster. The main problem with this kind of agreement is that the other company should have similar equipment and compatibility for the data to let the company work and bring operations together. The proximity of the company signing the reciprocal agreement may or may not have a say depending on the IT operations. If the operations are required locally or virtually, that factor may decide the location of the company signing the agreement. This agreement is also risky if both companies are in the same area and are affected by the same disaster.

Before a company goes into reciprocal agreement with another organization, pros and cons of previous agreements with other organizations if any would need to be considered in detail. The DRP also needs to be updated if any circumstances change or if the agreements or sites go void or become incapacitated due to any reason.

Things to Remember

- Hot sites, warm sites, and cold sites are recommendations in the case of a disaster and are not mandatory for any company to have.

- A company can have all four (hot, cold, warm and alternative) types of arrangements or none depending on their financial and other capabilities.

- A reciprocal agreement does **not** guarantee everything in the case of a disaster. It is an agreement to provide facilities if the other company is willing and capable at the time of disaster.

- While drafting a reciprocal agreement is very inexpensive, implementing it can be a different headache altogether.

- The selection of a site is a compromise between cost and need.

- A hot/cold/warm site can be several miles away or can be in the same area.

- An **alternative site** is usually a different facility where the original staff can be relocated for a few days. But an alternative site cannot be a permanent site since the business operations must return to the original site when the disaster is over. The most important consideration in selecting an alternative site, is to see if the alternative site is affected by the same disaster.

- Testing for a live disaster test is also known as a full interruption test.

- A **service bureau** is a contracted site that can be available quickly, and testing may be possible at this site. This can be an expensive option because of the nature of the contract and may or may not be available during all emergencies. The availability depends on the contractor's own ability to provide facilities.

- A **mirror site** provides parallel processing and is an instant failover/switch to companies that cannot tolerate any downtime.

Example: A software development company with millions of dollars in turnover per year has a hot site and a warm site in different areas of the same city, which is on a seismic belt known for regular earthquakes and other natural disasters such as summer cyclones and tornadoes. The company decided not to choose a cold site but wants to investigate the details of an alternative site. Which of the following is the **MOST** important consideration for selecting an alternative facility suitable for software and IT development operations when developing a disaster recovery plan and salvage plan?

A) Proximity to the primary site to be operational as quickly as possible

B) Distance between the alternative site and the company's customers

C) The alternative site unlikely to be affected by the same disaster

D) The alternative site's ability to become operational within a few hours

Analysis: From the verbiage, we can find that the question's primary intent is to ask the main consideration in selecting the alternative site. Thus, except the last sentence, the rest of the verbiage mainly serves no purpose other than saying that the company is big and has more money to opt for an alternative site. Those factors can indirectly tell the reader that the company needs to be operational quickly and does not want to lose any time (or incur any financial losses).

Statement: The given question can be pruned as follows:

Which of the following is the **MOST** important consideration for selecting an alternative facility when developing a disaster recovery plan and salvage plan?

Question: Which of the following is the **MOST** important consideration for selecting an alternative facility?

Solution: Option D is incorrect since the main purpose of the alternative facility is to become operational very quickly. Option B is wrong too since a software company does not need to have close proximity physically with a customer. Software distribution can be online, and all the company may need is a working Internet connection. Option A is wrong too since the primary site and the alternative site need not be physically closer for software development. The main consideration is that if the primary site goes down due to an earthquake or other natural disaster, the same disaster should not affect the alternative site. This is because business operations can be conducted uninterrupted from either the primary or alternative site. Thus, the best answer is option C.

Review Questions

The following are some of the questions on this topic:

1. A document between two companies that agrees one company to provide facilities to the affected company in the case of a disaster (but not guaranteed) can **BEST** be described as:

   A) Business exchange agreement

   B) Disaster exchange agreement

   C) Reciprocal agreement

   D) Alternative exchange agreement

   Answer: Option C

2. Which of the following disaster recovery sites is the **MOST** difficult to test, validate, and bring to action in the case of an earthquake that affects a whole city?

   A) Alternative site

   B) Warm site

   C) Mobile site

   D) Cold site

   Answer: Option D

3. Who is the **BEST** person to direct short-term recovery actions immediately after a disaster?

   A) Chief executive officer (CEO)

   B) Chief information officer (CIO)

   C) Disaster recovery manager (DRM)

   D) Disaster information department (DID)

   Answer: Option C. Option D gives a name of the department (if something like this exists at all) that gives information only but cannot direct or declare a disaster.

4. During disaster recovery for a company that has primary and alternative sites, which of the following is the **MOST** important consideration?

   A) Safety of the humans

   B) The amount of loss a disaster can cause

   C) Location of alternative site (AS) and if the AS is also affected by the same disaster

   D) Salvaging the original site as soon as the disaster ends

   Answer: Option A. Under any disaster, the most important consideration is to save the lives of the humans. Everything else is secondary.

5. Which of the following sites is the **MOST** mandatory requirement for an organization in the case of a natural disaster?

   A) Alternative site.

   B) Cold site.

   C) Warm site.

   D) There is no mandatory requirement.

   Answer: Option D. Nobody forces a company to have a mandatory site, but it helps the organization to recover quickly after a disaster strikes.

6. A company would like to hire a contractor who can provide the facility with some equipment, preferably with a quick response and availability. Which of the following sites **BEST** suits the company's requirement?

   A) Alternative site

   B) Cold site

   C) Service bureau

   D) Reciprocal agreement

   Answer: Option C

7. What is the most important factor in a mutual agreement between two companies?

   A) Only one company provides facilities to the second company.

   B) Each company has sufficient facilities to support the other company.

   C) Both companies agree to support each other in the case of a disaster.

   D) Both companies decide whether to support or not at the time of disaster.

   Answer: Option B. Option D is wrong because the DRP must be in place **before** a disaster happens, not when the disaster happens and in the last minute. Note that option C is the agreement itself but not the required factor to consider in a mutual agreement.

CHAPTER 8

Software Development Security

In this chapter, you will learn tips about software development, various development models, the SDLC, testing, and effectiveness in software security.

Software Security: Development Lifecycle, Cohesion and Coupling

Tip #64: Clearly understand the terms cohesion and coupling for software modules

Domain: Software Development and Security.

Subdomain: Security in the software development lifecycle (SDLC), Cohesion, Coupling.

Subject background: Modern software is usually developed using an object-oriented programming (OOP) methodology, which defines classes, objects, methods, encapsulation, and inheritance.

Things to Remember

- Cohesion is the extent to which one or more parts of a single module are related to each other. It also indicates how these individual parts work together to make the single module more efficient. In other words, "The entire software package has greater importance than the individual modules/libraries." An example is a basketball team or a software development team. A team can do better things than a single member can achieve.

© R. Sarma Danturthi 2020
R. S. Danturthi, *70 Tips and Tricks for Mastering the CISSP Exam*,
https://doi.org/10.1007/978-1-4842-6225-2_8

- Coupling refers to the direct or indirect relation one module has with others. If one module is totally dependent on another module (one cannot function without the other), they are said to be tightly coupled.

- OOP is effective with either strong coupling or high cohesion and depends on how the module or classes are designed.

- A general rule of thumb is that each module should have high cohesion and low coupling. This implies that a module can function independently of the other modules and has an effective functionality within itself (as a stand-alone module).

- Cohesion and coupling may correspond to the SDLC, but the questions on the CISSP exam will indirectly ask about these terms differently (see example below).

- The key terms to learn here are **cohesion**, which is how a module/team works by itself effectively, and **coupling**, where more than one module is required and specifies how each module is linked to the other module.

Example: Cohesion and coupling are used invariably in the software development lifecycle (SDLC). Say you are working in a team of software developers, and your supervisor calls for a meeting and mentions that he wants to form a new team named SealTeam for an upcoming contract where the developers are completely isolated from the other teams. He also mentions that the team has 20 members who interact with each other in a weekly meeting and give him progress reports every Friday. For SealTeam, what **MUST** be the basic requirements?

A) High cohesion and high coupling

B) High cohesion and low coupling

C) Low cohesion and high coupling

D) Low cohesion and low coupling

Analysis: Notice that the question briefly mentions the SDLC when talking about cohesion and coupling, but the actual question is about the team and not about the software itself. Once the team is mentioned, we know that the individuals have to work together (as a team) to make the project a success. The statement also mentions that the developers in the team are completely isolated from the other teams. This implies the team has to stand alone and not depend on any other teams or members. Let's rephrase the question and remove the information not needed.

Statement: Your supervisor calls for a meeting and mentions that he wants to form a new team named SealTeam, where the developers are **completely isolated from the other teams**. He also mentions that the team has **20 members who interact with each other in a weekly meeting**.

Question: For SealTeam, what **MUST** be the basic requirements?

A)   High cohesion and high coupling

B)   High cohesion and low coupling

C)   Low cohesion and high coupling

D)   Low cohesion and low coupling

Solution: A team working by and interacting within itself, has high cohesion among its members and low coupling when each member works independently and team is not dependent on other teams. So, the straightaway answer is option B. The other three answers are just a mix of the words high and low. This is the main reason that you should clearly understand the terms and the technology for the CISSP exam.

Review Questions

Some variations of the question are as follows:

1.   Traditional computer languages use external libraries to make software efficient. External libraries can be added with `import` and `using` statements, or via directives at the top of the module, without which the module cannot function effectively. When such statements are used to create a module, what is the created module **BEST** said to have?

     Answer: When a module being designed depends greatly on external libraries, it is said to be tightly coupled. Note that nothing about cohesion is mentioned in the question and thus should not even be considered.

2. You are creating a two-person control for office security, where each person must enter a preselected password or PIN to open the entrance of a gate. How can this two-person control **BEST** be described?

   Answer: It is a tightly coupled security system since both must enter a PIN.

3. Taking a cue from the cohesion and coupling of the SDLC, if we apply these terms to a family consisting of a wife and husband, what term can this family be said to have?

   Answer: A family unit made up of a wife and a husband has a tight cohesion to the family. Note that the question is asking about the "family" as a module and **not** what happens between the wife and husband. A tightly cohesive family is a close unit and functions better. On the other hand, if the question asks how the wife and husband are connected, the answer would be that they are tightly coupled.

4. You have written an OOP module that imports a runtime dynamic link library (DLL) to display Adobe PDF documents on your web page. Without the DLL, your module displays a runtime error. What is your module said to have?

   Answer: High coupling to the DLL. Note that your module is **not** highly coupled to the PDF files or documents but is coupled to the DLL.

5. At what stage of the software development lifecycle (SDLC) do you decide on the cohesion and coupling between class modules?

   Answer: In the design phase, after the requirements are collected

Various Software Development Models

Tip #65: Remember the SDLC models such as agile, waterfall, and spiral, and understand their features

Domain: Software Development Security, Asset Security.

Subdomain: Software development models, Information classification.

Subject background: In software development, SDLC is an acronym for software development lifecycle, which is a process or a set of actions for developing new software or modifying an existing piece of software. The lifecycle is the evolution of the software or information system (IS) from the beginning to the final deployment and continued use or disposal of software. Security is the main aspect of the SDLC since any vulnerability can be easily exploited by hackers to steal information or valuable data. Security aspects for software need to be considered as early as the project's initiation and as late as the disposal phase and at every stage in between these two phases.

The Open Web Application Security Project (OWASP) is an online nonprofit community that produces free articles, methodologies, documentation, tools, and other technologies for web application security. OWASP aims to raise application security and helps in the SDLC as well.

The SDLC has several steps: requirements gathering, design and test planning, coding, testing, deployment, and maintenance. Each group may have several individual smaller steps. For example, the testing group may have the following steps: do unit testing, select a testing plan and create testing documentation, select a tester, select a testing environment, complete the test, document the testing results for the development group, and adjourn for the next cycle of testing after the bugs in the results are corrected (until no more bugs can be recorded or successful testing is complete).

Things to Remember

Each organization has a unique model of the SDLC that it follows religiously. Some may follow more than one model.

- **Waterfall model**: In this model, one phase follows the next phase only when the previous phase is complete. There is no going back, like a waterfall where the falling water can never go back to the top. This means the software requirements, once finalized, are set in stone until the completion. Any changes (to any phase of this model in general) will require a new project. Once a phase is completed, there is no room for changes to that completed phase.

- **V-model**: This is similar to the waterfall model but with a twist. Each phase in the V-model has a verification step with testing. This is also known as the verification and validation model. Remember that it is similar to the waterfall model and thus it is difficult to go back to the previous phase from a current phase.

- **Iterative model**: This model does not wait for the requirements to be ready before it starts. It sets to design the model depending on the roughly available requirements or even phantom requirements and creates a working version. As requirements, testing, and other things evolve, each phase is revisited, and the product is improved. Thus, it takes many iterations before a final and good product can be produced (by several iterations). But the advantage is that there is a product (good or bad) as early as possible.

- **Spiral model**: The spiral model, as the name indicates, starts with whatever is available and evolves as time progresses. It is an advanced variation of the iterative model but improved. The spiral model can be and often is customized with user feedback. The main problem with this model is that since we are in a spiral, there may be no ending, and the product can be delayed forever.

- **Big bang model**: This is the most ideal model when there are just one or two developers who want to develop the software right away. There are no rules to plan, test, or develop. The developers do the coding right away, and there may not be any documentation at all. A majority of the time is spent on development rather than the other steps of the SDLC.

- **Agile model**: This is a kind of iterative model, but at each stage there is a product released. When a product is released in a stage, it always contains improvements over the previous version. Agile quickly delivers various versions of the product over a time period and is flexible to incorporate changes for each release. Each release is an independent version of the same software but with several improvements and the customer interaction/requirements. The disadvantage of this model is that if the customer has no clear ideas of the product, the customer will end up with various versions of a useless software product.

Selecting which model to implement depends on the environment, budget, size of the team, and various other factors such as delivery time and project constraints.

Example: A software company starting in the garage of a house with just two employees is aiming to develop an app that can be used on both iPhone and Android devices. The immediate requirement is to create the app and deploy and then follow a rigorous and traditional software model. Which software model **BEST** suits the company?

A) Waterfall model

B) Big bang model

C) Agile development model

D) Spiral model

Analysis: The question describes a modern software development company. It starts with one or two employees in the garage of the house and grows quickly with each evolution. The requirements are not captured, not well documented, and not even tested directly with different testers. Everything first is aimed at creating the app and getting it out to users. Any bugs found in the app will be corrected in the next release. The wording "two employees" should give you an idea of what model the company follows.

Statement: A software company with **just two employees** is aiming to develop an app. **The immediate requirement is to create the app and deploy**. Which software model **BEST** suits the company?

Question: Which software model **BEST** suits the company with two employees and an immediate requirement to create the app and deploy?

Solution: The model may initially look like the spiral model, but the wording of "two employees" should point us to the correct answer of option B. In a big bang model, employees are few, and the requirement is to get the product out as soon as possible. There are no rules or documentation for the first release until the company is successful.

Review Questions

Various questions on this topic are listed here:

1. In which software development lifecycle model are several versions of the software released quickly one after another, each improving or changing the earlier version?

A) Big bang model

B) Spiral model

C) Agile model

D) V-model

Answer: Option A. "software released quickly" are the words to note to pick the correct answer.

2. What is the **FIRST** step of the software development lifecycle?

A) Designing and writing the code

B) Planning and collecting requirements

C) Planning the testing process

D) Planning and organizing a team

Answer: Option B

3. Which software model has the ability to run on iterations, with each iteration watched closely by the customer, and may have the ability to slowly run out of control?
    Answer: Spiral model

4. At what stage of the SDLC is security **MOST** important?

A) At the beginning of the software development lifecycle

B) Just before the deployment of the software product

C) During the rigorous testing of the developed software

D) At every stage of the software development lifecycle

Answer: Option D

5. Which model is similar to a waterfall development model but needs verification and validation at every phase of the model?

A) Iterative model

B) V-model

C) Agile model

D) Big bang model

Answer: Option B

Software Security Effectiveness: Auditing, Risk Analysis

Tip #66: Remember encapsulation, polymorphism, OOP, polyinstantiation, and abstraction concepts

Domain: Security Operations, Software Development Security, Asset Security.

Subdomain: Software development tools, Object-oriented programming, Identifying source code vulnerabilities.

Subject background: Object-oriented programming (OOP) deals with hiding data by various methods. Hiding data effectively is also known as **encapsulation**. This is accomplished by declaring variables, classes, and their methods as `public`, `private`, `protected`, `friend`, and others. Effective encapsulation is the main objective of OOP along with an easy division of data and code into classes, subclasses, derived classes, and methods.

A method with one name in OOP can have the same name with different parameters to accomplish a different job. Though methods can have the same name and override each other, each method needs to have a unique set of parameters, called a **signature**.

There can be a few main classes, but several classes can be derived from a combination of one or more main classes. This deriving of subclasses from main classes is called **inheritance**. Some languages such as C# do not allow sub-classes to be derived from multiple classes (called **multiple inheritance**).

When multiple inheritance is required in programming languages that do not allow multiple inheritance, interfaces are used instead of classes.

Things to Remember

Class: This is a set of properties, variables, and methods. Classes can be public (visible to all), private (not visible to others), or protected (visible to the main class, which is the **parent** of the derived class, or **child**). A class can also be considered a group of dissimilar objects all packed together and can describe a physical object of the real world. For example, class **Human** can have variables to indicate gender, age, date of birth, first name, last name, medical data like blood pressure, blood glucose, etc. It can have methods that can calculate the age variable depending on today's date. It can also have a method to warn when the blood glucose variable goes above 120.

Method: This is a function or a subroutine of a class that can be `public`, `private`, or `protected` and can operate on the variables of the class in which it is defined.

Derived class: This is the child class where it gets permissions from the main class (on what variables can be used, cannot be used, etc.). A boy class be derived (from the main Human class) and can share some methods and variables. The sharing of variables or methods from the main class to the derived class is purely optional and at the discretion of the code requirements.

Interface: This is a bare-bones subclass with only the names of the methods mentioned and can be used for singular or multiple inheritance. They are like an alter ego of a child class. A child class contains full descriptions of methods and their code but an interface only has names of methods but no code inside the methods.

Polymorphism: This is, as the name suggests, the ability to override classes that have the same name for various methods when required. This means a parent class and a child class have methods by the same name but respond differently depending on the input supplied. If one type of input supplied invokes a parent class's method, then another type of input can invoke the child class's method, thereby giving two different results. In other words, one object with the same name can morph itself to act as another. **Morph** means to transform into another form.

Instantiation: This is the process of initiating or creating a class variable once a class is defined. When a class is defined, it cannot be used straightaway. A variable of the defined class needs to be declared or instantiated to use the class as an object. If class is a theoretical concept used to describe an object then the instantiated class variable is a physical object.

Polyinstantiation: This is the process of creating more than one variable with the same name and yet both the created variables behave in a different manner. This is mainly used in database (DB) systems when various people share data and the data needs to be protected. Usually in a DB, a row of data called a **tuple** has a primary key that uniquely identifies each row. With polyinstantiation, two rows can be made to have the same primary key, and each row is shown to the user depending on the user's security clearance level. In other words, polyinstantiation is a way to fool the general public with dummy data, whereas the actual data is protected since the general public does not have the security clearance to access it. The actual data is supplied only to users with the proper clearance level.

An **application program interface (API)** is a kind of software library that can be imported for reuse. An API specifies how software components work with each other. The APIs can be in any language, and the program that uses the API does not need to be in the same language as the API. The advantage of an API is that the code can be reused, and the programmer who is utilizing the API does not have to know how the code inside the API works or what language it is made of.

Example: A large software engineering company is designing an application program interface (API) with hundreds of main classes, sub-classes made from main classes, interfaces and derived classes. When all classes are completely designed, the company will use them with object-oriented programming (OOP) logic. What is the process of creating objects from declared classes or derived classes **BEST** called?

A) Polymorphism

B) Instantiation

C) Inheritance

D) Encapsulation

Analysis: All the verbiage mentioned is about what a software company is planning to do but it is completely irrelevant to the question. Except the last sentence in the question everything is superflous information. In a simple way, the question is asking the name of process that creates obects from classes, whether these classes are main or derived classes. Inheritance, polymorphism and encapsulation are for designing classes. Instantiation is like creating a physical bicycle object that can be used when a blue print paper plan of bicycle is available.

Statement: What is the process of creating objects from classes and derived classes **BEST** called?

Except the last sentence, everything in the question is superfluous. Classes and derived classes are created as part of OOP, and the question is actually asking what the name of the process that creates objects from declared classes is. In OOP, an object of a type class is created once the class is declared and ready to be used.

Question: What is the process of creating objects from classes and derived classes **BEST** called?

Solution: Polymorphism is not a process of creating objects from declared classes. Thus, option A is wrong. Inheritance is a way of deriving another class with an existing class. Encapsulation is a process of hiding data or methods effectively. Thus, options C and D are wrong too. Option B is instantiation, which is the process of creating an object from a class. In other words, an object is created (instantiated) or comes to life when we declare a variable name of the declared class type. Instantiation is creating an object of a particular class type.

Review Questions

Variations of the OOP concepts are as follows:

1. What are considered the **BEST** principles of object-oriented programming (OOP)?

   A) Encapsulation, polymorphism, inheritance

   B) Creating classes and subclasses

   C) Polymorphism and polyinstantiation

   D) Polyinstantiation and encapsulation

   Answer: Option A. Option B is wrong. Polyinstantiation is not part of OOP; it is a technique used in databases to protect secure data from unnecessary leaks.

2. What are the **BEST** advantages of object-oriented programming (OOP)?

   Answer: Modularity, reusability, and granularity within programs

3. A programming language such as C# or Java doesn't allow multiple inheritance from more than one class. If the programmer still want to use multiple inheritance, what are the **BEST** options the programmer has?

   A) Use polymorphism

   B) Use interfaces

   C) Use polyinstantiaton

   D) Use encapsulation

   Answer: Option B is the correct answer.

Tip #67: Remember the exact rules of race conditions, as well as the difference between time of check (TOC) and time of use (TOU) in software hack attacks

Domain: Software Development and Security, Security Engineering.

Subdomain: Specific and special software attacks, Software security effectiveness.

Subject background: Time of check (TOC)/time of use (TOU) is a special type of attack in which the hacker delicately dissects the steps a system uses to complete a task and poisons those steps depending on the timing of events by introducing a new step or by altering the steps the process follows.

Things to Remember

- TOC/TOU needs precise timing between steps to cause an attack.

- Time of check (TOC) is the step where some rule is checked (for example, to see if the file is writable).

- Time of use (TOU) is the step **after** the rule is checked to use that rule (for example, if the file is writable, put something in the file).

- One way to prevent TOC/TOU attacks is file locking or permission locking. Another option is to implement exception handling.

- TOC/TOU can happen mostly in mainframe Unix systems but can also happen in any concurrent systems if the process is not well taken care of.

- Increasing the number of checks, using checks very close to the use, and not allowing bindings of files (immutable) are other methods to mitigate TOC/TOU attacks.

- Reducing the window of vulnerability is possible by the methods mentioned above, but still an attack is not impossible unless permissions are truly immutable.

- Creating a process as an atomic process (all or nothing) and not allowing other processes to interrupt the run is also a better way to prevent TOC/TOU attacks.

Example: A concurrent process of identification, authentication, and authorization is being implemented on a website. When a user logs in, authorization will be carried out after validating the user for privileges. The validation process can take up to 25 seconds since the front-end web page has to communicate with the server via the Internet. A hacker found this loophole to log in and access a web form to modify some data in that time frame of 25 seconds. The hacker's authorization, if found may be revoked within 25 seconds, which is the time it takes for the web page to make a round-trip to server. If the hacker's authorization was revoked within 15 seconds, the revoking point of time can be **BEST** described as:

A) Time of check (TOC)

B) Time of use (TOU)

C) Race condition time (RCT)

D) Time for round-trip (TRT)

Analysis: Notice that the entire question has verbiage to explain a lot of things. Among these are two distinct values: TOC and TOU. It is important to know the difference between the two: when the hacker can get the form to check if it is editable and when he is able to write the form back to the server. When he submits the form, he is using the data to make changes. And it takes about 25 seconds for the web page to refresh. But the process that authorizes the user/hacker was revoked after 15 seconds, which indicates that at the time of use (when he is trying to make the change), the authorization was revoked. Time of check is when the user logs in successfully and sees if modifications are possible.

Statement: A concurrent process of the identification, authentication, and authorization process can take up to 25 seconds. A hacker can log in and access a web form to modify some data in that 25 seconds. And his authorization may be revoked in that 25 seconds.

Question: If the authorization was revoked in 15 seconds, the revoking point of time can be **BEST** called as?

Solution: Option B is the correct answer since the user tried to use the changes that were made earlier. Option D, time for a round-trip, is wrong and like option C is a distractor. Option A is close, but it is not the time of check. Time of check is when a rule is made, such as identification but not authentication, but the actual authorization is implemented after the changes are submitted. In other words, the changes made on the web form are "used" (TOU) in the authorization process to determine privileges.

Review Questions

Various types of questions are possible on this topic. Some of them are listed here:

1. A TOC/TOU hacking attempt **MOST** usually requires any:

    A) Website to enter data

    B) Concurrent processes

    C) Changes in computer time

    D) Parallel processes

    Answer: Option B

2. What is the **BEST** method to avoid a TOC/TOU hacking attempt?

    Answer: Increase the number of checks and do not allow file bindings

Tip #68: Understand auditing, file changes, logs, the process of file changes, and auditing

Domain: Security Assessment and Testing, Software Development and Security.

    Subdomain: Audit logs, Files, Backup, Archive bits, Software security effectiveness.

    Subject background: Auditing file/record/database changes is important in many industries such as credit card companies where a customer's usage is recorded. The changes recorded cannot be erased and should be kept in order of date or time of occurrence or both.

    Things to Remember

Files that are important cannot be changed or modified by anyone. If file changes are needed, a log must be kept, and the logs need to be audited. Auditing in such a case should be an automatic and routine task that may run daily, weekly, monthly, or all of these.

Files should also be ready for manual auditing at any time the organization needs or a third party demands (such as an attorney, law enforcement agency, etc.).

The following are some ways to keep a log, the file, the changes in the file, and the archive bits: 1) save the new file after changes, save the old file before changes, and record the date and time, who changed, and other details in the log; 2) save the changes alone in a separate file, keep the file before changes, and record the date and time, who changed what, and other details in the log; 3) save the file after changes, overwriting the original file, and record the details in the log; 4) combine the previous three methods with the archive bit changes and record them to the log; 5) for more security, back up the files before and after changes on a separate drive that is not accessible to everyone on a regular basis ; 6) even if files and data are not changed, if the file is accessed (read/written or attempted to read/write), and a log should be kept about who tried to access what along with the date and time.

Audit logs help in finding violations of privacy, access, and changes attempted or made.

Audit logs themselves should never be deleted but backed up for future use.

Audit logs are mandatory for employee and system accountability. Most databases such as Oracle and SQL Server have audit logs that can be checked manually or with a program, automatically and routinely.

Advanced audit functions can be used and included in logs for compliancy and regulatory uses (if possible and required) to help prevent fraud.

Audits and audit logs are usually audited by a third party in the case of fraud.

In Microsoft Windows, group/domain policies can help set up permissions and record activity.

Clipping level is a tolerable number of violations an organization is willing to allow a user/system to commit/happen. Beyond the clipping level, violations are not tolerated. Clipping levels help prevent fraud before something major breaks down the entire process.

Assurance level is a level of trust a product can provide. Operational and lifecycle assurances are part of the assurance level and continuous process evolution and improvement.

Example: A credit company keeping records of customers has a company policy implemented for tracking changes to the customer records/files. The policy states that the clipping level is 3 for customer service representatives and 2 for managers. Audit files are regularly backed up and deleted when they are no longer required. The customer records are also backed up on a drive with the archive bit that is accessible to managers only. Managers also have the permission to delete audit logs and modify customer records as they deem fit. After four years of operation, the company was cited for fraud and was asked to pay for damages done to the credit card customers. What steps could the company have taken to avoid the fraud?

A)   The clipping level set for customer representatives and managers was not adequate.

B)   The company should have hired a third party to audit files, logs, and activities.

C)   The company should have never allowed managers to modify/delete logs or files.

D)   All credit companies are cited for fraud, and it was not avoidable.

Analysis: After reading the verbiage given in the question, it should be immediately revealing that a major problem in the company is to allow the managers to do whatever they want with the customers' records. Whether the records are audit logs or anything, nobody, including the CEO, should delete the audit logs. When fraud happens or is about to happen, audit logs have a record of who is accessing the files, doing the changes, and such. In this instance, the log files might be backed up but are probably modified and regularly deleted by managers. It does not matter whether the people deleting the logs are trusted or disgruntled managers in the company. It is possible for the CEO and managers to combine forces and cheat customers like the companies Enron and Worldcom did.

Statement: A credit company keeping records of customers has audit files that are regularly backed up **and deleted when they are no longer required**. **Managers also have permission to delete audit logs** and modify customer records as they deem fit. After four years of operation, the company was cited for fraud.

Question: What steps could the company have taken to avoid the fraud?

Solution: The obvious problem is the managers' ability and permissions to delete logs. Any manager could have modified (with or without support of the CEO and other C-level managers) the log files or deleted them. Option C, therefore, is the correct answer. Option A is not relevant in that the clipping levels are not a problem. Option B is not relevant since the audit can be either internal, external, or both. Option D is not correct because every company has to take care of possible fraud in the age of cybersecurity and take the necessary steps to protect the company and its assets, both software and hardware.

Review Questions

Several variations of questions are possible on this topic. Some of them are listed here:

1. Which of the following is part of the continuous evolution and improvement process?

    A) Quality assurance

    B) Quantity assurance

    C) Lifetime assurance

    D) Lifecycle assurance

    Answer: Option D

2. Why is setting up a clipping level important?

    A) It helps detect fraud.

    B) It helps the new employees learn.

    C) It is a standard defined by credit card companies.

    D) It is required by law.

    Answer: Option A

3. What is the best way to detect fraud that might have happened a couple of year ago?

    Answer: Audit the logs that were backed up

4. In Microsoft Windows, what process might help set up privacy and file auditing?

    Answer: Group/domain policy

5. How often should the audit logs be deleted?

    A) Audit logs should be backed up and deleted once a month.

    B) Audit logs should be backed up and deleted per company policy.

    C) Audit logs should be backed up and deleted once every three months.

    D) Audit logs should be backed up but never deleted.

    Answer: Option D

Acquired Software Security Impact

Tip #69: Learn the intricacies of SQL injection, involved technologies, and the possible remedies

Domain: Software Development Security.

   Subdomain: Security in the software development lifecycle, Development of security controls, Acquired software security impact, Software testing.

   Subject background: SQL injection can happen from a web page where an end user is supposed to enter some data. While a textbox provided for a username or email is expected to take only those values as input, there is no guarantee that anyone who accesses the web page or application will enter the required input. Rather, a hacker can enter a long SQL string that can be processed by either the client or the server. This means a text box expecting to receive a particular type of input, such as email address, username, day or birth, SSN, or any other information, must conform to the format of the input so that the user cannot type any other data than the required input. This can be done by validating the input, such as checking for numeric data of nine characters only for an SSN and rejecting any other input as invalid. An apostrophe character (" ' ") plays an important role in SQL when supplying data for SQL statement clauses such as DELETE, INSERT, UPDATE, and SELECT (DIUS). In the absence of the input data check, a hacker can use the SQL's special characters to exploit the back end database. SQL injection can be prevented with input data validation, by checking for special characters (that are important for database-related operations, such as $, @, ', among others). It is always a good idea to check the inputted data both on the client and server sides of an application. SQL injection is not necessarily limited to an application on the Internet. It can happen on a client-server application or a stand-alone application.

   Things to Remember

- A Structured Query Language (SQL) injection is an attack on the database when the programmer forgets to put validators both on the client and server sides for textboxes that are expecting some user input.

- If the user input in a textbox should be an existing and registered username, it can be compared to the existing usernames in the database, as follows:

```
SELECT * from users_table where Username = ' " + username_entered_
in_TextBox + " '; "
```

- A hacker, instead of just inserting a username, can insert SQL code such as **" ' OR '1' = '1 "** in the input without the starting and ending double quotes, which will make the server-side SELECT statement as follows:

```
SELECT * from users_table where name = ' ' OR '1' = '1'; " (note
that the starting and ending single quotes are in our select
statement and the hacker knows it or can guess it easily).
```

- Now the input entered or 1=1 evaluates to TRUE and makes the database interpret the entire command as follows: "When the user input is as entered or TRUE." Thus, even if the user did not enter a valid, expected username, the SQL command will run and give supply some data back to the hacker. So, an important point to remember is that the single quote character is a notorious one to allow in a textbox.

- Validators for every textbox where user input is expected are mandatory and must be used to evaluate the user input. Note that the validators can be on the client side (either on the browser or as an added script).

- Client evaluation does not completely remove the SQL injection and other attacks. Therefore, a second option to be implemented is to evaluate input again on the server side where the code is processed.

- In general, SQL injection attacks target the database, and therefore the best option to protect resources is to do several checks at various points and on the database side.

- Database-side protection can be achieved by using stored procedures. They help the programmer avoid inserting code pages when dealing with a database.

- Every database system such as Oracle and SQL Server allows stored procedures to be written and evaluated before being deployed to the server.

- Hackers can do worse damage when the input is not checked and can completely modify the database or get full access. One example is when a hacker introduces the following code:

  ```
  " ' OR '1' = '1 ; Drop table users_table;"
  ```

  which will translate to completing removing users_table. When such liberal access is obtained, the hacker will proceed to create a new table with a username and full grants for the entire database and can steal anything.

- SQL injection is a serious attack that can jeopardize the entire server, not just the web page or application and has far-reaching complications.

- A SQL injection attack is an example of how a small opening or a vulnerability left by a programmer's mistake/oversight can cause heavy damage to the database servers, which can be taken over by an attacker.

Example: When designing a website with commercial credit card transactions to buy groceries online, the programmer Ozzie Ozone put a first page that asks for users' email addresses and passwords. New users can register for an account, and returning users can directly log in. There are two textboxes and a log in button on the first page: one textbox for email address and one textbox for passwords. On the second page that opens when the user logs in correctly, there are several textboxes for entering the grocery items. On how many pages and textboxes does Ozzie Ozone have to put validators to prevent SQL injection attacks?

A) Only for two textboxes (email address, password) on the first page

B) On both the first page and second page for all textboxes displayed

C) Only on the second page's grocery items textboxes after successful login

D) Only for the username textbox on the first page and the grocery list textboxes on the second page

Analysis: SQL injection can be done from any page and from any textbox if there is no validator properly checking the entered input. Since the first page has two textboxes, both need validators to prevent SQL injection. Note that the question says that there is a way to create a new user on this page. This means even if the hacker cannot do SQL injection on this page, he can create a new account and access the second page. In such a case, he can access all the textboxes of the second page as well and force a SQL injection attack from that page. Thus, every single textbox on the second page also needs validation to prevent SQL injection.

In general, any textbox that a user can insert text into needs to be validated for SQL injection because while the programmer is expecting simple text, a hacker can enter anything else to compromise the application and steal data and information.

Statement: Programmer Ozzie Ozone put a first web page that asks for users' email addresses and passwords. New users can register for an account, and returning users can directly log in from this facing page. There are two textboxes and a button on the first page. On the second page, there are several textboxes.

Question: On how many pages and textboxes does Ozzie Ozone have to put validators to prevent SQL injection attacks?

Solution: The simplest solution is to put validators on every page for every text box. So, the answer is option B. Option A does not work since if only facing-page textboxes are prevented from SQL injection, a hacker can create an account and log in to access the second page. And once he accesses the second page, he can still introduce SQL injection attacks from the second page. Option C is not correct because SQL injection can be introduced on the first page if the input is not validated. Option D is wrong because from the password text box SQL injection is still possible.

Review Questions

Variations of the question will look like this:

1. Which character, clause or statement is the **MOST** important in SQL injection?

    A) Single quote character (')

    B) Double quote character (")

    C) `WHERE` clause of Structured Query Language (SQL)

    D) `SELECT` statement of Structured Query Language (SQL)

Answer: The correct answer is option A though options C and D look close. A hacker can obviously introduce many of the SQL features such as SELECT and DELETE and WHERE clauses, but the most important character they should first introduce is the single quote character.

2. What method is the **BEST** way to avoid SQL injection attacks?

   (i) Prevent free text of unlimited length in all textboxes of user input

   (ii) Validate user input with client-side script

   (iii) Validate user input on server-side code

   (iv) Use stored procedures on the database server

   A) (i) and (ii) only since SQL injection happens on the client side

   B) (ii) and (iii) only since SQL injection is prevented by checking the client- and server-side code correctness and validation

   C) (i), (ii), (iii), and (iv) since all these steps are important to prevent SQL injection

   D) Only (i) and (iv) since SQL injection does not need client- and server-side validation

Answer: The correct answer for this is option C since every effort must be done to secure a server and database; and this includes preventing unlimited free text (option A), using client-side script validation (option B), validating user input again on the server side (Option C), and also using stored procedures on the database side (Option D).

3. When a programmer forgets to corroborate user input on a web page, giving a hacker the ability to create a SQL injection attack, it is called:

   A) Bug in the client code

   B) Bug in the web page

   C) The website's vulnerability

   D) SQL injection attack

Answer: Option C. The website has created an opening (exposure) for an attack and presents a weakness and thus is called a vulnerability (weakness). The fact that the website allows any input is not a bug in the code. The ability of the website to take any input is a weakness that a hacker can exploit.

4. What principle is **MOST** useful while creating user accounts in the database to prevent SQL injection attacks?

    A) Principle of code validation

    B) Principle of least privilege

    C) Principle of user's secret clearance

    D) Principle of least resistance or effort

Answer: Option B. Reread the question to understand that it is asking about the **MOST** useful factor when creating database accounts. When creating a database account for a user, the most important factor to take into consideration is the users' privileges. If the users are not privileged to get access to all parts of the database or only to some aspects of the database, the principle of least privileges dictates those terms. For example, when a web page that is accessing the database to pull information from the database is created, only the SELECT privilege is granted to the user, rather than giving the full access of SELECT, DELETE, INSERT, and UPDATE. Thus, the principle of least privilege is the **MOST** important factor.

Tip #70: Remember various types of software tests, their use and intent

Domain: Software Development and Security, Security and Risk Management.

   Subdomain: Software testing, Acquired software security impact, Acquisition of new software.

   Subject background: Software testing is used in a variety of ways by a variety of people and is necessary for creating accurate software. Software testing can be functional (testing the program's behavior against the requirements) and nonfunctional (testing the program's behavior against the code's intent). Functional testing can be as follows:

A **unit test** is done by the developers in the early stages when code is developed to see whether each unit of the code works as required. If code passes unit tests, it does not mean the code is ready to be deployed. A unit test only confirms that each code unit works independently.

An **integration test** verifies that the components of one program unit work with the other unit without causing any problems for both units and that the units work together as specified in the design. An example of integration testing is the development of a big API interface by a group of programmers who develop their modules individually. When a final package is built, these modules should work together without causing any problems. Note that in integration testing, one module will integrate with the other to form a final package.

A **smoke test** is conducted after a software version is released to ensure that the built version is stable. For that reason, this is sometimes called build verification testing.

A **sanity test** makes sure that all major functions of the software actually work. A sanity test usually happens after the smoke test is successful.

A **system test** is done after the entire software is built and deployed in a platform where it can be tested to see whether it functions independently.

Fuzz testing involves sending large amounts of malformed data to break a piece of code and checks whether the code can withstand such data.

An **interface test** deals with data exchange and evaluates the exchange process for a flawless and smooth operation. An interface is an exchange point between two systems or a system and a library and/or hardware. Examples of interfaces are PCI cards for frame grabbing, scientific control, or a graphic user interface (GUI) and a library such as Oracle Data Components (ODC) for Microsoft's Visual Studio software. In the first case, the system and the card should exchange data well, and in the second version, the ODC must communicate with Visual Studio to transfer data back and forth with the back-end Oracle database. The interface test basically checks that these data exchanges have no problems when working in tandem. In interface testing, the modules remain independent but work in tandem with each other.

A **regression test** demonstrates that the changes made to one section of code do not adversely affect the already working code modules that never required any changes.

A **beta or acceptance test** is almost the final stage of testing a software package and ensures that the code meets the customer requirements to the full satisfaction.

Things to Remember

- At any stage of software testing, the code and final deployment package may go back to the developer for modifications when the testing gives an indication of failure.

- Nonfunctional test methods include the following: performance testing, load testing, stress testing, volume testing, security testing, compatibility testing, install testing, recovery testing, reliability testing, usability testing, compliance testing, and localization testing.

- Make sure you know the clear difference between integration testing and interface testing.

- Alpha testing is done in the initial stages by the software development teams, whereas beta testing is done by anyone and everyone who wants to use the software after it is deployed on a public test server.

- A deployment or release of the software package after successful beta testing can still unearth bugs that were not found in all the other testing phases. These bugs will normally be corrected via service packs, updates, and requests for code changes (RFC).

- Software bugs are usually fixed and delivered via updates.

- Service packs contain several updates and fixes in a single release.

Example: A group of programmers developing a dynamic link library (DLL) write code to develop individual modules that comprise a single package. When these modules are combined, they want to test one module against the others in the package. After the modules' testing is complete, the package itself is deployed against another application programming interface (API) to see whether the software package and API can work in tandem. What tests do the programmers have to complete for the package modules and the data exchange with the API?

A) Interface testing for package modules, integration testing for the package and API

B) Integration testing for package modules, interface testing for the package and API

C)   Unit testing for package modules, system testing for the package and API

D)   Alpha testing for package modules and beta/acceptable testing for the package and API

Analysis: The question is somewhat complicated in that it asks for two different testing processes. The first process is that programmers want to test their individual modules with each other, and the second process is to test the entire package (composed of all the individual modules) against another package that is ready to run the API. The API is not developed by the programmers but is supposed to be available to them according to the question. In other words, the second process is to see how the in-house developed package works with the external API as a whole.

The first test is an insider test with individual modules, and the second test is an out-of-the-box test of the package in its entirety with an external API. Removing the superfluous information, the statement of the question can be constructed as follows:

Statement: There are individual modules that comprise a single package. First need is to **test one module against other** in the package, and the second need is to test the entire deployed against another application programming interface (API) to see whether the **software package and API can work in tandem**. What tests do the programmers have to complete for the package modules and its data exchange with the API?

Question: What tests do the programmers have to complete for the package modules and for the data exchange with the API?

Solution: Option B is the correct answer. The question clearly is asking for two different testing methods. The first is to test each module against the others before combining or integrating them into a single package), and the second is to test this bundled package against another interface. In the second case, the package and API will remain independent but will work with each other in tandem (interface). Thus, the answer is option B. Option A is wrong because interface testing is not done for individual modules. Option C is wrong because unit testing is done by each programmer for their own module. Option D is wrong because alpha testing is done by programmers after they combine the modules and test the package on an independent machine. Alpha testing is done for the entire package, not for individual modules. Likewise, a beta/acceptance test is done when the package is believed to have passed all the tests and is released to the public for a trial run.

Review Questions

A great variety of questions are possible for the software testing methods. A few of them are given here:

1. The C-level managers have decided that no formal testing is required for their software packaging and want to directly release a beta version and test the application as a whole. Despite this decision, what testing do the programmers still have to do on their own part?

   A) Interface testing

   B) Unit testing

   C) Regression testing

   D) Fuzz testing

   Answer: Option B. Unit testing is always done by the coding team even if the formal test processes are not required.

2. After fixing four newly found errors, the new software package released showed some errors that were not seen earlier in an area of code that functioned correctly before fixing those four errors. What testing process could have unearthed these new errors that the test team forgot to conduct?

   Answer: Regression testing. Regression testing checks to see if a change made to fix a known error created additional, unwanted and new errors in the code.

3. The testing team wants to feed a large amount of automatically generated data to a software package to see whether it crashes. What is this testing called?

   A) Case studies testing

   B) Real-time testing

   C) Fuzz testing

   D) Gamma sanity testing

Answer: A large amount of data is normally done with fuzz testing. Option C is the correct answer.

4. What is a programmer's way of finding errors and correcting them called in software?

    A) Bug testing

    B) Debugging

    C) Smoke test

    D) Weeding

    Answer: Option B

5. A company released a new service pack for its software. What does a newly released service pack usually contain?

    A) Several updated details of the software company's customer service

    B) Single update of the software for a vendor

    C) Several bug fixes of the software for a vendor

    D) An updated service level agreement (SLA) for the vendor

    Answer: Option C

6. What does a structural or nonfunctional software test do **BEST**?

    A) Tests the code's behavior against the given requirements

    B) Tests the program for functions not intended for the business

    C) Tests the program's behavior against code's intent

    D) Tests the code's intent for the user behavior

    Answer: Option C

CHAPTER 9

Practice Test and Answers

1. A company's software product lead decides that his team will not conduct any formal testing for a particular software package as part of the software development lifecycle (SDLC) before deployment. What testing does the developer still have to do before deploying, despite the software lead's decision, to ensure that the developer **BEST** accomplish his own work successfully?

   A) Integration testing

   B) Unit testing

   C) Machine testing

   D) Compatibility testing

   Answer: Unit testing is mandatory for the developer even if the package skips the entire testing phase of the SDLC. The correct answer is option B.

2. The business impact assessment (BIA) team wants to conduct a test and needs data from the database group (DBG). What data should the DBG supply to the BIA team for the **BEST** testing process and results?

   A) Actual production data to reflect the actual impact on the business.

   B) Random data since the assessment is only an estimation and not a reality.

© R. Sarma Danturthi 2020
R. S. Danturthi, *70 Tips and Tricks for Mastering the CISSP Exam*,
https://doi.org/10.1007/978-1-4842-6225-2_9

C) The DBG should not provide any data, and the BIA should create its own data.

D) Sanitized production data since it may closely reflect a realistic situation.

Answer: Option D is the best answer. The DBG never should give actual data to anyone. Random data is useless since it does not reflect a realistic situation.

3. Which of the following is the **MOST** trusted component of an IT system when installing a baseline operating system and required software for a trusted user who already has the required security clearance to access the IT system?

A) Secondary hard disk drive (HDD)

B) Central processing unit (CPU)

C) Universal serial bus (USB) port

D) Classicication Level of the IT System

Answer: Option B since all the other options may not necessarily exist in an IT system

4. Which of the following **BEST** describes the sequence of phases in a disaster recovery program (DRP)?

A) Scope, initiate, plan, test, review

B) Scope, plan, implement, test, review

C) Initiate, scope, plan, test, review

D) Plan, scope, implement, test, review

Answer: Option B

5. A financial institution wants to implement two-way protection for their Internet customers. A username and password form of logging to user accounts is already in place on the Internet. Which of the following is the **MOST** secure as a second form of authentication?

A) A picture message to choose online

B) A CAPTCHA to make sure a human is logged in

C) A one-time password (OTP) sent as a text message

D) A standard prestored question and its answer

Answer: Most secure is the one-time password (OTP); thus, the correct answer is option C.

6. Which of the following is the **BEST** combination for a security kernel?

A) The firmware and software required to run the baseline configuration

B) The software and firmware required to run the complete IT system

C) The hardware, software, and firmware required to run the baseline configuration

D) The software and hardware required to run the complete IT system

Answer: Option C is the correct answer.

7. After developing and successfully testing the software, the development team wants to deploy it on a public facing server. Which of the following IP addresses is **BEST** suited for deployment?

A) 192.168.42.15

B) 172.28.242.59

C) 149.175.42.25

D) 10.234.32.25

Answer: Option C becuase all other options indicate a private IP.

8. A Kerberos mechanism can be used to allow nodes communicating over a nonsecure network. Which of the following is the **PRIMARY** mechanism that Kerberos provides?

    A) Identification

    B) Authentication

    C) Nonrepudiation

    D) Authorization

    Answer: Option B. Kerberos also provides credentials for integrity.

9. A user requested access to a table in the database, and the database administrator (DBA) created a database object so that the user can only read the data from that object. Which of the following is the **BEST** name given to the object created by the DBA?

    A) A derived database table

    B) A table of metadata

    C) A database view

    D) A database join

    Answer: Option C

10. A company has acquired a virus protection system that uses signature-based viruses. With the signature-based virus detection system, which of the following is the **GREATEST** risk to the company?

    A) Only currently or previously known viruses can be detected with the system.

    B) Only newly created viruses can be detected by the system.

    C) Any hacker can easily prevent the virus program from successfully finding the viruses.

    D) Any hacker can easily introduce a new virus into the system.

    Answer: Option A. Signature-based means only known viruses (whose details or signatures are well-known) can be detected.

11. A user sends an email properly adding his signature as a certificate so that the email conforms to the nonrepudiation rules. What certificate **MUST** the receiver of this email have in order to open and read the message?

    A) The receiver's private key certificate

    B) The sender's private key certificate

    C) The receiver's public key certificate

    D) The sender's public key certificate

    Answer: Option D. Private keys are known only to the users. Private keys are used to compose, encrypt and send messages, whereas public keys are published globally so others can read the email correctly. Also, a message composed by a user with his private key can be retrieved/validated only by the public key.

12. Which of the following is the correct way to allow a user to access an IT system?

    A) Logging, verification, access to system

    B) Identification, authorization, authentication

    C) Verification, logging, access to system

    D) Identification, authentication, authorization

    Answer: Option D

13. In which of the following models does a central authority determine which subjects can have access to certain objects based on the organization security policy (OSP)?

    A) Discretionary access control (DAC)

    B) Mandatory access control (MAC)

    C) Nondiscretionary access control (NDAC)

    D) Rule-based access control (Ru-BAC)

    Answer: Option C

14. Which of the following errors occurs when a biometric system falsely rejects the true identification of subjects?

    A) Type I error

    B) Type II error

    C) Crossover error

    D) Type III error

    Answer: False rejection rate (FRR) is a Type I error. Thus, the correct answer is option A.

15. Kerberos authentication deals **BEST** with which of the following?

    A) Identities and confidence

    B) Tickets and timestamps

    C) Timestamps and identities

    D) Tickets and confidentiality

    Answer: Option C

16. Which of the following is the information security risk management standard?

    A) ISO/IEC 27005

    B) ISO/ICE 27050

    C) ISO/IEC 27500

    D) ISO/ICE 27500

    Answer: Option A

17. Which of the following are the **MOST** general disaster events?

    A) Human, system, natural, and environmental

    B) System, human, and environmental

C) Environmental, natural, and human

D) Natural, system, and human

Answer: Option C. Remember the acronym HEN: human, environmental, and natural.

18. Which of the following memory types is the **CHEAPEST** but offers low speeds?

    A) Static random access memory (SRAM)

    B) Dynamic random access memory (DRAM)

    C) Erasable programmable read-only memory (EPROM)

    D) Sluggish read-only memory (SRAM)

    Answer: Option B. Note that option D is an invalid distractor.

19. In cryptography, confusion and diffusion are two properties of a secure cipher. Confusion is to substitution as diffusion is to:

    A) Transmission

    B) Transporting

    C) Transposition

    D) Transformation

    Answer: Option C

20. Which one of the following is the **MOST** appropriate definition of a "security target"?

    A) It is the product that is being tested for security.

    B) It is the documentation that explains function and assurance.

    C) It is the basic profile of the adapted security methodology.

    D) It is a hardened IT product that is already secure.

    Answer: Option B

21. In which of the following Digital Encryption Standard (DES) cryptographic modes does a 64-bit block of input transform into a 64-bit block of output and the same plain text always produces the same cipher text for a given key?

A) Cipher Block Chain (CBC)

B) Output Feedback (OFB)

C) Cipher Feedback (CFB)

D) Electronic Code Book (ECB)

Answer: Option D

22. On finding the company's network attacked and compromised, a network engineer decides to determine the damage, disconnect the compromised machines from the network, and isolate. At this juncture, which phase of the incident response is the network engineer **MOST** likely dealing with?

A) Eradicating or mitigating the damage

B) Recovering from the damage

C) Containing or controlling the damage

D) Preparing to find the damage

Answer: Option C

23. Which software development life cycle (SDLC) model is **BEST** suited for a large company that needs meticulous documentation and verification at every phase, but the requirements are collected only once, and each phase, when completed, cannot go back to the previous phase?

A) Waterfall model

B) Agile development model

C) V-model

D) Large-scale development model

Answer: Option C

24. A product that is semiformally tested and designed can **BEST** be said to have an evaluation assurance level (EAL) of:

    A) EAL 4

    B) EAL 7

    C) EAL 5

    D) EAL 6

    Answer: Option C

25. A newly designed website was hacked by a user from Europe by inserting some commands into the textboxes on a login page that were intended for usernames and passwords. The hacker inserted `delete` commands containing semicolons. What attack might the hacker have attempted to compromise the website?

    A) Internet input attack

    B) SQL injection attack

    C) Textbox injection attack

    D) Website input attack

    Answer: Option B

26. The project group gathers around a conference room to simulate an exercise for testing the business continuity plan (BCP) that has been created. The team does not really have a disaster to test the BCP but simulates the situation. What exercise has the team **MOST** likely created and performed in the conference room?

    A) Mockup exercise

    B) Tabletop exercise

    C) Readiness exercise

    D) Time-lapse exercise

    Answer: Option B

27. A large video streaming company sells videos for users to watch. The company's network consists of several servers placed around the country to provide video clips to the users in an optimal way so that any user looking for a video is connected to the closest available server for a quick and hassle-free connection. The company's network is **BEST** called what?

A) Local area network

B) Content distribution network

C) On-demand network

D) Media distribution network

Answer: Option B

28. The management of IPv6 addresses is delegated to what entity?

A) Intranet Assigned Naming Authority

B) Internationally Assigned Numbering Annotation

C) Internet Assigned Numbers Authority

D) Immediate Annotated Numbering Action

Answer: Option C

29. In what layer of the TCP model does the binary data of 0s and 1s get converted to electrical signals that are fit for transmission on the electric cables?

A) Physical layer

B) Presentation layer

C) Network layer

D) Application layer

Answer: Option C. Note that the question is asking about the TCP layer. When the question is about the OSI layer, then the answer is option A.

30. Which of the following is **BEST** suited for certificate-based authentication?

    A) X.590

    B) X.509

    C) X.550

    D) X.950

    Answer: Option B

31. Which of the following **BEST** identifies the ethics of ISC²?

    A) Promote profession, act honorably, provide diligent service, and assist society

    B) Provide diligent service, active in profession, protect society, and act honorably

    C) Prepare for honors, active in profession, proof of service, and accolades in society

    D) Protect society, act honorably, provide diligent service, and advance in profession

    Answer: Option D

32. What memory addressing directly specifies the data that is being operated on in the instruction itself?

    A) Direct addressing

    B) Specific addressing

    C) Immediate addressing

    D) Register addressing

    Answer: When data is directly mentioned in the instruction, it is referred to as immediate addressing. Therefore, the correct choice is option C.

33. Which of the following sites has a hookup for basic telephone, Internet, HVAC, and electric power and can be set up with the **LEAST** financial burden and is **MOST** common?

    A) Hot site

    B) Alternative site

    C) Service bureau

    D) Cold site

    Answer: Option D

34. Which of the following is the **BEST** definition of a service level agreement (SLA)?

    A) Agreement signed by managers in two different companies to support each other

    B) Agreement signed by two internal groups of the same company

    C) Agreement signed by two different government service departments

    D) Agreement signed between two service providers to a user group

    Answer: Option B

35. Next-generation addressing (IPng) is also known as:

    A) IPv4

    B) IPv8

    C) IPv6

    D) IPv5

    Answer: IPv6 is known as next-generation addressing. Option C is the correct answer.

36. Which of the following sites provides analogous processing for a company that cannot tolerate long periods of downtime?

    A) Mirror site

    B) Hot site

    C) Alternative site

    D) Failproof site

    Answer: Option A. Note that "analogous" processing means parallel processing.

37. In the displacement or offset method of addressing, the following instruction was executed: ADD Register2, [Register1]+200. ADD stands for addition, and 200 is the displacement or offset. What does Register2 contain after the instruction is executed?

    A) Sum of contents of Register2 and Register1.

    B) Sum of contents of Register2, contents of Register1 plus 200.

    C) Sum of contents of Register2 and content of memory pointed by address {Resigter1 plus 200}.

    D) Register1 will remain unchanged.

    Answer: Option D is a actually mentioning about Register 1, but it does not refer to the question being asked. The question asks for the contents of Register2. Thus, the correct choice is option C.

38. Which of the following **MOST** accurately reflects an IPv6 address?

    A) 4098:4D7B::CA10:ABCD:3876::FEAD:12EA:CE54

    B) 4098:4D7B::12EA:CE54

    C) 4098:7B::2EX::/96

    D) 4098:00Fe::2aE::IX/64

    Answer: Options C and D have invalid hexa-decimal characters. Option A has 8 hextets but has the :: symbol twice, which is not allowed when all hextets are given. Option B is the **MOST** accurate.

39. In cryptography, what does the term "salting" **BEST** refer to?

A) Adding additional characters to create confusion

B) Removing random characters to create diffusion

C) Adding an additional string to create randomness

D) Removing the additional strings to generate a shorter string

Answer: Option C

40. A salesman trying to sell you a biometric scanner claims that the matching rate for his machine is 100% once all signatures are stored and will increase its accuracy to 120% as time passes. What is your **BEST** consideration to buy or reject the sales pitch?

A) It is a great machine since it will have 100% to 120% matches.

B) A 100% match for all biometric equipment is the industry standard; this is nothing new.

C) A 100% match for any biometric scanner is an indication of fraud.

D) Biometric scanners do not have any matching rate accuracies as a measurement.

Answer: Option C is correct.

41. A file is created for each user during their day-to-day transactions with a credit card company; the transactions must have which of the following characteristics?

A) Integrity and availability

B) Confidentiality and Integrity

C) Availability and confidentiality

D) Integrity and encryption

Answer: Option B. Option D looks close, but encryption alone cannot protect confidentiality.

42. A team trying to design a new phone service wants to conduct a test by meeting with all the stakeholders in a room but without any devices. The test can **BEST** be described as:

A) Predeployment test

B) Simulation exercise

C) Readiness test

D) Tabletop exercise

Answer: Option D

43. Which of the following biometric devices probably has the **LOWEST** crossover error rate (CER)?

A) Pupil scan system

B) Iris scan system

C) Voice recognition system

D) Fingerprint scan system

Answer: Option B

44. Guidelines issued by a company for longer and more complicated passwords are not being implemented by the staff. What is the **BEST** solution the company can resort to?

A) Delete accounts that do not follow the guidelines

B) Make password rules a company policy

C) Counsel the employees to implement guidelines

D) Disable accounts with shorter passwords

Answer: Option B. Guidelines work only as recommendations, but the staff may or may not follow them. Making the password rules a policy makes it mandatory for the staff to implement longer passwords.

45. Which of the following attacks at **BEST** can catch the network passwords?

    A) Network IP spoofing

    B) Network diddling

    C) Network data sniffing

    D) Network router smurfing

    Answer: Option C

46. Which Structure Query Language (SQL) is the **BEST** suited for creating tables and views and allotting roles to the users in a database environment?

    A) Data Modification Language (DML)

    B) Relational Data Modification Script (RDBMS)

    C) Data Definition Language (DDL)

    D) Relational Data Language (RDL)

    Answer: Option C

47. A company wants to implement secret key cryptography and prevent playback/replay attacks. It does not have resources to develop this software and is looking for a trusted third-party authentication protocol program to purchase. Which of the following is **BEST** suited for the company?

    A) Public Private Key Infrastructure (PPKI)

    B) Two-Factor Verification Authentication (TFVA)

    C) Kerberos Authentication Protocol (KAP)

    D) Secret Key Cryptography Authentication (SKCA)

    Answer: Option C. Kerberos is a third-party authentication protocol that uses secret key cryptography and prevents playback/replay.

48. Which of the following **MOST** closely reflects the rules of the Bell–LaPadula security model?

    A) Subjects have classifications, objects have clearances, and rules specify which object is accessible for which subject.

    B) Subjects and objects both have clearances, and if they match, a subject can access the corresponding matching object.

    C) Subjects have clearances, objects have classifications, and rules specify which subject can access which object.

    D) Subjects and objects have classifications, and any subject can access any object without rules or restrictions.

    Answer: Option C

49. Two users using a public-private key combination want to exchange email messages. For achieving the required privacy, what key **MUST** the sending user utilize to sign the email, and what key should the receiving user utilize to read the email?

    A) The sender utilizes his public key, and the receiver utilizes the sender's private key.

    B) The sender utilizes his private key, and the receiver utilizes the sender's public key.

    C) The sender utilizes the receiver's public key, and the receiver utilizes his private key.

    D) The sender utilizes the receiver's private key, and the receiver utilizes his public key.

    Answer: Option B. An email is always composed with a private key of the sender. It can only be unlocked with the sender's public key, which is published for all receivers on the global access list (GAL).

50. A biometric system used for authentication at the entrance of a building is granting access to users who should actually be rejected. What error, if any, can the system is the **BEST** description for the error the system is exhibiting?

    A) Type 1 error

    B) Type 3 or 100% error

    C) Type 2 error

    D) Type 4 or zero error

    Answer: Option C. The system with the given data is falsely accepting those who should be rejected. Or it is exhibiting a false acceptance rate (FAR), which is Type 2.

51. Which of the following authentication methods is the **MOST** reliable for a banking institution wanting to implement security for its customers when they access their accounts on the Internet?

    A) Public/Private Key Infrastructure

    B) One-time password in two-factor authentication

    C) Internet Protocol version 6 (IPv6)

    D) Nonrepudiation model

    Answer: Option B is the safest and best.

52. Which of the following models can be chosen as the **BEST** fit for rule-based access control (RuBAC) where users are employed in a lattice-based hierarchy system and given access by rules preset by the organization?

    A) Discretionary access control system (DACS)

    B) Mandatory access control system (MACS)

    C) Nondiscretionary access control system (NDACS)

    D) Lattice-based access control system (LBACS)

    Answer: Option C. The access system matters in how the employees are given access but **not** on what system they are employed. Option D is a clear distractor.

53. Which of the following **CORRECTLY** identifies the database property of isolation?

    A) The database is isolated and runs stand-alone from the executing program.

    B) When two operations are done on a database, each works in its own capacity.

    C) Each database object exhibits unique properties isolated from any other object.

    D) Database objects are ready for a read-only operation but not for overwriting.

    Answer: Option B. Note that any of the answers given may have a distracting word ("isolation" in this case in option C).

54. Which of the following detection systems is **MOST** invasive on the operating system on which it will be installed?

    A) Network intrusion detection system (NIDS)

    B) Host virus detection system (HVDS)

    C) Internet intrusion detection system (IIDS)

    D) Host intrusion detection system (HIDS)

    Answer: Option D. Note that the question says the detection system is installed on the operating system, which means the sitting computer (host).

55. Which of the following is the **MOST** accurate process in the order given for a user to gain secure access to a system?

    A) Authentication, identification, authorization, and credential validation

    B) Authorization, credential validation, authentication, and identification

C) Identification, credential validation, authentication, and authorization

D) Credential validation, identification, authorization, and authentication

Answer: Option C. Sometimes credential validation is described as a subprocess of identification. Authorization is the last step in giving access to a system.

56. Which network intrusion detection system works on the premise that that the intending attack was known to have already occurred somewhere on some other system and has a recorded/documented solution?

A) Host-attacking intrusion detection system

B) Signature-based intrusion detection system

C) Statistical anomaly intrusion detection system

D) Network-attacking intrusion detection system

Answer: Option B. Known attacks that already occurred and documented with a signature, which means the system would work on the known signature of the attack (usually a well known and documented virus).

57. Which of the following **BEST** describes the simple and star (*) properties of the Bell–LaPadula security model?

A) Star (*) property: no write up; Simple property: no read up

B) Simple property: no read down; Star (*) property: no write down

C) Star (*) property: no write down; Simple property: no read up

D) Simple property: no read down; Star (*) property: no write up

Answer: Option C

58. Which of the following is the **BEST** possible solution for a recently designed website that has frequently experienced Structure Query Language (SQL) injection attacks?

    A) Modify the database access rules on the back end of the program

    B) Validate input on the website before passing it to the database

    C) Store the username and password authentication data in a separate database

    D) Apply patches to the database and implement an antivirus program

    Answer: Option B. SQL injection is a user input validation problem, not a database problem.

59. An analyst was hired to conduct a penetration test on a network system, and he was provided with all the knowledge (both on paper and in person) of how the network was designed, where systems exist, and what systems are protecting the network. What test would be most appropriate for the analyst to conduct after he is provided with all the knowledge?

    A) Black-box penetration testing

    B) Blue-box penetration testing

    C) White-box penetration testing

    D) Gray-box penetration testing

    Answer: Option C. If the network details are known, it is a white-box test.

60. Which of the following **MOST** closely resembles a time-of-check, time-of-use attack?

    A) Masquerading attack

    B) Running condition attack

C) Race condition attack

D) Timing condition attack

Answer: Option C. A race condition is also known as a time-of-check, time-of-use attack (TOCTOU).

61. An organization using T1 lines for the communication of data between their two intranet websites finds the data transfer slow and wants to improvise with a better network. Which of the following **BEST** serves the organization for speeding up the communication?

A) Use a circuit-switched network

B) Use a packet-switched network

C) Replace the T1 lines with T10 lines

D) Use a booster network over T1 lines

Answer: Option B. T1 is the same as a circuit-switched network. Circuit-switched networks are dedicated and stay connected even if there is no data transfer. Packet-switched networks use unused bandwidth and speed up the data transfer.

62. Fill in the blanks: The address that is "burned" in the factory for a network interface card (NIC) or any such unit has a length of ___ bits and is known as _____.

A) 56 bits, MAC address

B) 52 bits, CAM address

C) 48 bits, MAC address

D) 48 bits, CAM address

Answer: Option C

63. If a host is accessing an IPv6 network via IPv4, the accessing method is **BEST** known as:

A) Bridging

B) Crossover

C) Tunneling

D) Broadband

Answer: Option C

64. Which protocol has no concept of ports but uses types and codes?

A) Transmission Control Protocol (TCP)

B) Internet Control Message Protocol (ICMP)

C) User Datagram Protocol (UDP)

D) Internet Information Server Protocol (IISP)

Answer: Option B

65. Which wireless standard offers **ONE** frequency of 5 GHz and has speeds faster than 1 gigabits per second (Gbps)?

A) 802.11ac

B) 802.11b

C) 802.11n

D) 802.11g

Answer: Option A. 802.11n offers both 1.4 GHz and 5 GHz frequencies, but 802.11ac offers only one frequency of 5 GHz and speeds in excess of 1 Gbps.

66. An organization currently using the Extensible Authentication Protocol (EAP) wants to improve its security and has no problem spending more money even if it is expensive. Which of the following frameworks is **BEST** suited for the organization?

A) Protected EAP (PEAP)

B) EAP and Transport Layer Security (EAP-TLS)

C) Lightweight EAP (LEAP)

D) EAP and Tunneled Transport Layer Security (EAP-TTLS)

Answer: Option B

67. Apple's iPhones have an application for face-to-face video chatting in real time called FaceTime. What type of communication **BEST** describes how FaceTime works?

    A) Simplex communication

    B) Half-duplex communication

    C) Full-duplex communication

    D) Double-duplex communication

    Answer: Option C. There is no double-duplex communication.

68. Which of the following networks is **BEST** suited for Bluetooth?

    A) Local area network

    B) Metropolitan area network

    C) Personal area network

    D) Wireless area network

    Answer: Option C

69. Which layer can **MOST** appropriately act as a bridge between the Internet and Application layers in a TCP/IP model?

    A)   Host-to-host Protocol layer

    B)   Host-to-host Transport layer

    C)   Host-to-host Internet layer

    D)   Host-to-host Presentation layer

    Answer: Option B

70. Which layer of the TCP/IP model can **BEST** handle access to LAN communication?

    A) Application layer

    B) Transport layer

    C) Network layer

    D) Internet layer

Answer: Option C. In fact, the Data Link layer in the OSI model handles the LAN communication, but the question is asking about the TCP/IP layer.

71. The term that is **MOST** appropriately used for a process that formally determines whether a person can be trusted with the given information is known as:

    A) Need to know

    B) Confidentiality

    C) Clearance

    D) Access approval

    Answer: Option C

72. Which of the following is the **MOST** appropriate definition of a dynamic password?

    A) A password dynamically generated by a website for one-time use only for each user

    B) Secure token generated every 60 seconds combined with a user's known PIN

    C) A complete full-length password created by the user once every 15 days

    D) A reusable password that is randomly created by a built-in program in the system

    Answer: Option B

73. During a review of a user's application, it was found that the user wants access that could defeat the purpose of need to know and least privileges. What is the **FIRST** step that should be taken while reviewing to grant ?

    A) Check the user's security clearance

    B) Revoke the user's current access

C) Elevate the user's access to a higher level

D) Check the user's existing entitlements

Answer: Option D

74. Garrison is using a program named PrintProfessional that uses a Kerberos client to access the printer. When Garrison sends a request to the authentication server (AS), tickets and keys are generated for exchange during the print process. What key does Garrison use during the printing process that is controlled by PrintProfessional?

A) Garrison's private key stored in the AS

B) Session key generated by the AS

C) Garrison's public key sent to the AS

D) Authentication server's unique key

Answer: Option B

75. RADIUS and DIAMETER are third-party authentication protocols that address the AAA system. What is the **MOST** appropriate definition of AAA?

A) Authorization, admission, automation

B) Authentication, access, authorization

C) Authorization, authentication, accounting

D) Access, authentication, accounting

Answer: Option C. Accounting is for auditing the user's authentication and authorization.

76. A company's technical support workers are allowed to access systems from 10 a.m. to 10 p.m. Pacific standard time, Monday through Thursday. On Friday, Saturday, and Sunday, the technical support desk is mandatorily closed. What access control can **BEST** implement these rules for successful operation of the technical support desk?

A) Content-based access control

B) Rule-based access control

C) Context-based access control

D) Mandatory access control

Answer: Option C. Times are set in context-based access controls.

77. Which protocol uses the Application layer and port 389 on either TCP or UDP?

A) Secure Data Access Protocol (SDAP)

B) Lightweight Directory Access Protocol (LDAP)

C) Multiple-Port Data Access Protocol (MDAP)

D) Application Data Access Protocol (ADAP)

Answer: Option B

78. George who lives in the United States wants to send money over the Internet to his brother who is in Brazil. The money transaction company has a website with two-factor authentication: one as a username and password combination and the second as a digital signature George uses. By supplying the digital signature, what does George guarantee to the money transaction company?

A) Authentication to send money

B) Authorization to deliver money

C) Nonrepudiation to pay the money

D) Confirmation to guarantee his identification

Answer: Option C. The question is asking what George guarantees to the website, not to his brother or his own self. Digital signatures are for nonrepudiation.

79. A factor that **MOST** likely determines the best accuracy of a fingerprint scanning system is known as

A) True rejection rate (TRR)

B) Crossover error rate (CER)

C) True acceptance rate (TAR)

D) Equal acceptance rate (EAR)

Answer: Option B. For any biometric system, CER determines the accuracy.

80. Which of the following **CLOSELY** describes a hash function?

    A) Reversible, one-way encryption, with no key used

    B) One-way encryption, valid known key, and reversible

    C) Valid known key, irreversible, and no encryption

    D) Algorithm to encrypt, no key used, and irreversible

    Answer: Option D

81. When files are stored on a disk, clusters of disk space are used to store a file or part of a file. The leftover space on a cluster that can be exploited by a hacker and to store hacking data is **BEST** known as:

    A) Bad blocks/cluster space

    B) Unallocated space

    C) Slack space

    D) Hacker allocated space

    Answer: Option C. A file can occupy more than one cluster of space. When a file occupies only a part of a cluster, the left over cluster space is known as slack space.

82. The study of data in motion with the main purpose of gathering evidence that can be used in a court of law is **MOST** likely referred to as

    A) Digital forensics

    B) Network forensics

    C) Broad data forensics

    D) Legal forensics

    Answer: Data in motion happens on a network. Thus, the correct answer is option B.

83. Which of the following devices has the **HARDEST** challenge to conduct device forensics?

    A) Magnetic tape drives

    B) CD/DVD/Blu-ray disks

    C) Solid-state devices

    D) Externally attached hard disks

    Answer: Option C. Solid-state devices are new, and forensics have no updated information on how to analyze or collect data from solid-state devices.

84. After suffering through a hacker attack as a major incident, an organization wants to find out all the vulnerabilities and weaknesses that made the incident possible to avoid future attacks. What is the **FIRST** step the organization must do?

    A) Conduct remedial measures

    B) Conduct a root-cause analysis

    C) Conduct a total asset evaluation

    D) Conduct existing policy analysis

    Answer: Option B. Note that the organization already had a hacker attack and now it wants to find out what weaknesses caused that attack.

85. An organization allows its programmers to use the Google website to search for solutions if the programmers have any doubts about programming in Microsoft's C# language. A programmer searching for a solution finds a viable solution on Microsoft website's discussion boards. But the network intrusion detection system (NIDS) sounds an alarm. What is the **BEST** description of this NIDS alarm?

    A) It is a false positive.

    B) It is a true positive.

C) It is a false negative.

D) It is a true negative.

Answer: Option A. Programmers are allowed to search through Google, and Microsoft is a reliable site for its own programming language, C#. NIDS sounded an alarm where it should not.

86. An organization allows users to run a list of programs that are already known and stored in a dictionary. Any programs that fall outside the dictionary list are blocked and cannot be run. The company's process of running only known programs can **BEST** be described as:

A) Application blacklisting

B) Application whitelisting

C) Application blocklisting

D) Application dictionary listing

Answer: Option B. What the company allows is from a known list that is called a whitelist. The question is asking what programs can be actually run.

87. Which of the following **MOST** likely makes up the task of configuration management?

A) Select hardware, select software, install systems, maintenance

B) Disable unnecessary services, enable security, configure audit logs

C) Install systems, install network detection, enable security

D) Create baseline image, enable audit, install and manage systems

Answer: Option B

88. If an organization decides to ignore a well known risk that there is a 2% chance an earthquake will occur, what is the organization **MOST** likely doing?

A) Risk transferring

B) Risk mitigation

C) Risk ignoring

D) Risk acceptance

Answer: Option D

89. During vulnerability management, the risk remediation and mitigation of vulnerabilities are **MOST** likely based on what factors?

A) Risk to the organization and ease of remedial measures

B) Costs of remedy and possibility of threat

C) Past statistics and a future possibility of risk materializing

D) Willingness and commitment of the chief executive officer

Answer: Option A. Option D looks tempting, but reading the question we find that we are asked about "during vulnerability management," which indirectly tells us that the CEO already approved the risk management program.

90. What is the **WORST** thing about zero-day vulnerabilities?

A) However best a company tries, they always exist.

B) They have no known patches.

C) They exist even after a patch was made.

D) They have zero solutions and cannot be resolved.

Answer: Option B. Option D is partially true because new vulnerabilities will soon have solutions and can be resolved.

91. What is the **LAST** step of the change management (CM) process?

A) Implementing the approved change

B) Reporting the results of the implementation

C) Approving the final implementation

D) Creating a lessons learned document

Answer: Option B. Option D looks tempting, but even after creating a lessons learned document, the change implemented must be reported as a final step.

92. A software contractor is required to have "errors and omissions" insurance while developing software for the State of Michigan. If the final deployed software causes a disruption, it is **MOST** likely categorized as:

A) Natural disaster

B) Manmade disaster

C) Software disaster

D) System environmental disaster

Answer: Option B. Software errors are made by humans.

93. Which of the following **MOST** likely defines the mean time between failures (MTBF)?

A) The time it takes for the installed software to fail

B) How long it takes for the outdated hardware to blow out

C) How successfully a new or repaired unit will run before failing

D) How quickly a newly designed hardware unit will stop working

Answer: Option C

94. Which factor does the maximum tolerable outage (MTO) consist of?

    A) Recovery time objective (RTO) and mean time between failures (MTBF)

    B) Mean time between failures (MTBF) and maximum recovery time (MRT)

    C) Work recovery time (WRT) and recovery time objective (RTO)

    D) Minimum recovery time (MRT) and work recovery metrics (WRM)

    Answer: Option C. Maximum tolerable downtime (MTD), or MTO = RTO + WRT.

95. Which of the following plans can be **BEST** utilized to protect human life and property damage in response to a valid threat and to protect the business process or an information technology functionality?

    A) Business salvage plan (BSP)

    B) Occupant emergency plan (OEP)

    C) Disaster recovery plan (DRP)

    D) Continuity support plan (CSP)

    Answer: Option B. Note the wording "protect human life and property damage" in the question, which clearly shows that option B is the best answer.

96. If a company wants to conduct walk-through testing before it conducts real-time testing of their disaster recovery plan, what testing is **MOST** suitable for the company?

    A) Simulation testing

    B) Tabletop exercise

    C) Read-through drill

    D) Partial interrupt test

    Answer: Walk-through testing is known as a tabletop exercise. The correct answer is option B.

97. Which of the following does the International Standards Organization (ISO) 27031 describe?

   A) The disaster recovery process framework for government organizations only

   B) The business continuity process framework for private, government, and nongovernment organizations

   C) The disaster recovery process framework for nonprofit organizations only

   D) The business continuity and disaster recovery framework for private organizations only

   Answer: Option B. ISO 27031 does **not** address the disaster recovery process.

98. What is the **MOST** important aim of a white-hat penetration tester?

   A) To protect the system's stability

   B) To find all the system's vulnerabilities

   C) To protect the system's data and integrity

   D) To accurately report all the materialized threats

   Answer: Option C

99. A technician found that there was a penetration test done internally in the middle of the night by someone who installed a backdoor to the system and erased the logs. The penetration test was **MOST** likely done by a

   A) Black-hat attacker

   B) Gray-hat tester

   C) White-hat attacker

   D) Red-hat tester

   Answer: Option A

100. Which of the following **CORRECTLY** describes the use of a
      requirements traceability matrix (RTM)?

      A) It traces the customer requirements to the software testing
          plan.

      B) It traces the software's ability to function well on the target
          system.

      C) It traces the customer requirements after the software is
          deployed.

      D) It traces the bugs found in the software during development.

      Answer: Option A

Index

© R. Sarma Danturthi 2020
R. S. Danturthi, *70 Tips and Tricks for Mastering the CISSP Exam*,
https://doi.org/10.1007/978-1-4842-6225-2

Printed in the United States
By Bookmasters